BUSINESS ISSUES, COMPETITION AND ENTREPRENEURSHIP

PATENT AND TRADEMARK ACTIVITY OF U.S. WOMEN ENTREPRENEURS

QUANTITATIVE AND QUALITATIVE ANALYSES

BUSINESS ISSUES, COMPETITION AND ENTREPRENEURSHIP

Additional books in this series can be found on Nova's website under the Series tab.

Additional e-books in this series can be found on Nova's website under the e-book tab.

BUSINESS ISSUES, COMPETITION AND ENTREPRENEURSHIP

PATENT AND TRADEMARK ACTIVITY OF U.S. WOMEN ENTREPRENEURS

QUANTITATIVE AND QUALITATIVE ANALYSES

DIANNA M. OGDEN
EDITOR

nova publishers
New York

For permission to use material from this book please contact us:
Telephone 631-231-7269; Fax 631-231-8175
Web Site: http://www.novapublishers.com

Library of Congress Cataloging-in-Publication Data

ISBN: 978-1-63117-740-8

Published by Nova Science Publishers, Inc. † New York

CONTENTS

PREFACE

The purpose of this book is to quantitatively define the number of women entrepreneurs applying for and receiving patents and trademarks, and analyze the differences in the number of women applying for and receiving patents and trademarks as compared to men.

Chapter 1 - This research focuses on the participation of U.S. based women entrepreneurs in Patents and Trademarks activity. Using data obtained from the United States Patents and Trademarks Office, the study probes, in-depth, the number of patents and trademarks obtained by women entrepreneurs as well as the concomitant gender gap for the period 1975-2010. Commercially available data on the most common names for men and women was used to net 94.11% of the patents granted in a given year. Particular attention was paid to include uncommon names of Chinese, Korean, Indian, Japanese and European origin to ensure that the contributions of immigrant U.S. based women were not overlooked. Both primary and non-primary patentees were examined. The contributions of women entrepreneurs in specific industries were segmented and analyzed. Differences in the rates at which patents and trademarks are assigned by men and women to companies were studied.

Several significant conclusions may be drawn from this research:

1. U.S. based women demonstrate increasing leadership in patent and trademark activities. It should be noted that this report summarizes results only for patentees and trademark holders and theses terms do not always connote entrepreneurship.

2. The number of patents granted to women is significantly higher than those reported in earlier studies. Importantly, the number of patents granted to women is increasing at an accelerating pace.
   The number of patents granted to women increased by approximately 34.72% from 2009 to 2010. In the same period (2009 to 2010), the number of primary patents granted to women increased by 28.57% and the number of non-primary patents granted to women increased by 38.23%. In this report, the first name on a patent disclosure is assumed to be the "primary" patent holder. Subsequent names are assumed to be "non-primary" patent holders. The USPTO does not classify "primary" and "non-primary" patentees this way. Sometimes, the names are just listed alphabetically.
3. The highest sustained rate of increase in the grant of U.S. patents to women was in the 1986-1993 period.
4. The slowest rate of increase in patents granted to women was in the 1999-2006 period.
5. The total number of patents obtained by women shows an accelerating rate of increase with time. Similarly, there is an accelerating rate at which women become primary inventors as judged by the first name on a patent disclosure. This suggests an increasing leadership by women entrepreneurs in R&D activities.
6. Of particular interest is the surge of innovation by women in some of the emerging high-tech industries. The field of optics and optical systems was selected to illustrate this observation. For instance, 11.55% of patents in Optical Waveguides had at least 1 woman inventor.
7. The participation of women in Trademark activity as measured by the percentage of Trademarks granted has more than doubled in the period between 1980 to 2010, from approximately 16.5% in 1980 to more than 33% in 2010.
8. Women have a significantly higher participation in Trademark activity as compared to Patent activity. For instance, whereas women received approximately 18% of all patents granted in the year 2010, the contribution of women to Trademark activity was more than 33%.
9. The ratio of successful women patent applicants to successful men patent applicants varies from a low of 73.36% in 1986 to a high of 93.57% in 2002.
10. There is no statistically measurable difference in the proportion of successful women Trademark applicants and successful men

Trademark applicants. The analysis shows no bias in the processing of trademark applications. The reasons for the apparent differences in IP protection activity between men and women must be sought in employment patterns, R &D opportunities, and perceptions of risk and reward.

Chapter 2 - In September 2011, the NWBC commissioned a broad study to analyze the relationship between women entrepreneurs and intellectual property. It consisted of two parts:

- Quantitative Research
- Qualitative Research

The quantitative research was completed in February 2012. A report, *Intellectual Property and Women Entrepreneurs, Quantitative Analysis,* was released by the NWBC on February 27, 2012 and presented at a featured meeting on March 1, 2012 in Washington, DC.

The current report covers the qualitative research whose stated goal was to conduct focus groups with women entrepreneurs, businesswomen and professionals, probe the questions that were raised in the quantitative study as well as additional ones of interest to the NWBC. Six focus groups were conducted in different parts of the US. Two of these focus groups were with women who had successfully obtained a patent or trademark, two were with women who had applied for but did not receive a patent or trademark and two were with women who had never applied for a patent or trademark. In addition to specific issues raised by the quantitative analysis, the following questions were also addressed by the focus groups:

- What are the perceived barriers facing women entrepreneurs surrounding protecting their IP?
- What are the actual barriers?
- How do we address these barriers?
- What are the long term effects on businesses that receive patents and successfully market their IP?

Accordingly, six focus groups were held, four in northern California and two in the Washington, DC metropolitan area. These locations were chosen based on the concentration of women patent and trademark holders in these regions. Data from the USPTO was used to recruit a random sample of women entrepreneurs. The assistance of the local chambers of commerce was also solicited in recruiting women who had never applied for a patent or trademark. Appropriate incentives were offered to the participants to cover costs.

The focus groups were conducted in accordance with OMB Regulations. The OMB control number was 3245-0380. The Paper Reductions Act of 1995 requires that Federal agency information collections employ effective methodologies appropriate to the purpose for which the information is to be collected (5 CFR 1320). This study meets the OMB requirements.

The study yielded significant insights into the IP processes as they affect women and women entrepreneurs. While major strides have been made in facilitating access to patent and trademark services, there remain significant opportunities for further improvement. The perceptions of the participants, the realities, the suggested fix as well as answers to questions raised in the quantitative study are summarized below.

In: Patent and Trademark Activity … ISBN: 978-1-63117-740-8
Editor: Dianna M. Ogden

Chapter 1

INTELLECTUAL PROPERTY AND WOMEN ENTREPRENEURS: QUANTITATIVE ANALYSIS*

National Women's Business Council

1.0. EXECUTIVE SUMMARY

This research focuses on the participation of U.S. based women entrepreneurs in Patents and Trademarks activity. Using data obtained from the United States Patents and Trademarks Office, the study probes, in-depth, the number of patents and trademarks obtained by women entrepreneurs as well as the concomitant gender gap for the period 1975-2010. Commercially available data on the most common names for men and women was used to net 94.11% of the patents granted in a given year. Particular attention was paid to include uncommon names of Chinese, Korean, Indian, Japanese and European origin to ensure that the contributions of immigrant U.S. based women were not overlooked. Both primary and non-primary patentees were examined. The contributions of women entrepreneurs in specific industries were segmented and analyzed. Differences in the rates at which patents and trademarks are assigned by men and women to companies were studied.

* This is an edited, reformatted and augmented version of a study conducted for the National Women's Business Council by Delixus, Inc., dated February 27, 2012.

Several significant conclusions may be drawn from this research:

1. U.S. based women demonstrate increasing leadership in patent and trademark activities. It should be noted that this report summarizes results only for patentees and trademark holders and theses terms do not always connote entrepreneurship.
2. The number of patents granted to women is significantly higher than those reported in earlier studies. Importantly, the number of patents granted to women is increasing at an accelerating pace.
   The number of patents granted to women increased by approximately 34.72% from 2009 to 2010. In the same period (2009 to 2010), the number of primary patents granted to women increased by 28.57% and the number of non-primary patents granted to women increased by 38.23%. In this report, the first name on a patent disclosure is assumed to be the "primary" patent holder. Subsequent names are assumed to be "non-primary" patent holders. The USPTO does not classify "primary" and "non-primary" patentees this way. Sometimes, the names are just listed alphabetically.
3. The highest sustained rate of increase in the grant of U.S. patents to women was in the 1986-1993 period.
4. The slowest rate of increase in patents granted to women was in the 1999-2006 period.
5. The total number of patents obtained by women shows an accelerating rate of increase with time. Similarly, there is an accelerating rate at which women become primary inventors as judged by the first name on a patent disclosure.
   This suggests an increasing leadership by women entrepreneurs in R&D activities.
6. Of particular interest is the surge of innovation by women in some of the emerging high-tech industries. The field of optics and optical systems was selected to illustrate this observation. For instance, 11.55% of patents in Optical Waveguides had at least 1 woman inventor.
7. The participation of women in Trademark activity as measured by the percentage of Trademarks granted has more than doubled in the period between 1980 to 2010, from approximately 16.5% in 1980 to more than 33% in 2010.
8. Women have a significantly higher participation in Trademark activity as compared to Patent activity.

For instance, whereas women received approximately 18% of all patents granted in the year 2010, the contribution of women to Trademark activity was more than 33%.

9. The ratio of successful women patent applicants to successful men patent applicants varies from a low of 73.36% in 1986 to a high of 93.57% in 2002.
10. There is no statistically measurable difference in the proportion of successful women Trademark applicants and successful men Trademark applicants. The analysis shows no bias in the processing of trademark applications. The reasons for the apparent differences in IP protection activity between men and women must be sought in employment patterns, R &D opportunities, and perceptions of risk and reward.

2.0. Technical Approach

2.1. Introduction

This study was conducted at the initiative of the National Women's Business Council.

The National Women's Business Council (NWBC), with its offices located in Washington, D.C., is a bi-partisan federal advisory council created to serve as an independent source of advice and counsel to the President, Congress and the U.S. Small Business Administration on economic issues of importance to women business owners. Members of the Council are prominent women business owners and leaders of women's business organizations.

The Council's mission is to promote bold initiatives, policies, and programs designed to support women's business enterprises at all stages of development in the public and private sector marketplace – from startups to significance.

One of NWBC's current priorities is to examine in-depth the relationship between intellectual property and women-owned businesses. There is some information on women and patents; but the NWBC would like to dive deeper and cast a wider net in this research project.

2.2. Objectives

The objectives of this study are:

1. Quantitatively define the number of women entrepreneurs applying for and receiving patents and trademarks.
2. Analyze the differences in the number of women applying for and receiving patents and trademarks as compared to men. Analyze sub-groups of women.

The quantitative study will be followed by a qualitative study whose objectives are:

1. Conduct focus groups with women who have received patents and trademarks; women who have applied for but have not received patents and trademarks; and women who do not even know they should or could apply for these.
2. Through the focus group probe questions such as
   - What are the long-term effects on businesses that receive patents or trademarks?
   - What are the perceived barriers facing women entrepreneurs surrounding protecting their IP?
   - What are the actual barriers?
   - How do we address these barriers (both perceived and actual)?

2.3. Scope

Only U.S. based women entrepreneurs were considered in this study. The data on patents and trademarks was purchased from the USPTO. Commercial sources based on data from the United States Bureau of Census and the United States Social Security Administration were used for men and women. A large number of lists were used to include not so common names of Korean, Indian, Chinese, Japanese, Hebrew, German and other European origin.

The scope of the study included the number of patents and trademarks granted to men and women for the period 1975-2010 as well as an analysis of the gender gap. Sub-groups of women in specific industries wherein the contribution of women entrepreneurs is the highest were identified. The gap between patents and trademarks filed versus granted was studied. Trends in the grant of patents and trademarks were examined and a regression analysis of patents granted was performed.

Future areas for research were identified. Results from the quantitative analysis will be used to conduct in-depth focus group studies of the issues facing women entrepreneurs in pursuing IP protection.

2.4. The Literature

The USPTO does not track patents and trademarks data by gender. Information about women entrepreneurs has to be deduced by interrogating the USPTO data using names that are commonly used for men and women. There is growing interest in the contribution of women to intellectual property; however, only a few studies have addressed this issue.

Lisa et al. [1] studied the commercialization gap between women patentees and the U.S. patentee population with a particular focus on the African American population. They found that there is a correlation between advanced degrees and the assignment of patents to businesses. The study also included a comprehensive bibliography of literature in this domain.

The United States Patents and Trademarks Office in its report, *Buttons to Biotech, 1996 Update Report, with supplement data through 1998, U.S. Patents by Women, 1977 to 1996*, examine the total grant of patents and the share of patents granted to women. The report also segments the data within major patent categories, namely, utility, design, plant and other categories.

The current study extends the USPTO research to 2010 and probes deeper into patents and trademarks granted to women.

2.5. Analysis of Patents

2.5.1. The Data

An optical disk containing data on patents granted between the years 1975 and 2010 was obtained from the United States Patents and Trademarks Office. Weekly USPTO database reports on patents were also downloaded.

2.5.2. Data for Names of Men and Women

This was a key step in the research, and a critical one. Multiple sources were used to gather names of men and women from all over the world. These lists were then used to allocate the inventors in the patent database to men and women:

The first iteration used the 10,000 most popular names for men and 10,000 most popular names for women available from a commercial source, Smashwords:

http://www.smashwords.com/books/view/61805
http://www.smashwords.com/books/view/61801

The Smashwords data is derived from data published by the U.S. Social Security Administration for the year 2010 and authored by Nancy Man. Other sources used for the analysis included:

- U.S. Census Bureau: http://www.census.gov/genealogy/names/dist.female.first
- U.S. Census Bureau: http://www.census.gov/genealogy/names/dist.male.first
- U.S. Social Security Administration: http://www.ssa.gov/OACT/babynames/limits.html

Data sources used to categorize and allocate uncommon names included:

- Japanese Names, Source: 20,000names.com
- Korean Names, Source: 20,000names.com
- Chinese Names, Source: 20,000names.com
- Hindi Names, Source: 20,000names.com
- French Names, Source; 20,000names.com
- German Names, Source: 20,000names.com
- Spanish Names, Source: 20,000names.com
- Polish Names, Source; 20,000names.com
- Persian Names, Source: 20,000names.com
- Russian Names, Source: 20,000names.com
- Yiddish Names, Source: 20,000names.com
- Greek Names, Source: 20,000names.com
- Canadian Names, Source: familyberry.com
- Brazilian Names, Source: familyberry.com
- African Names, Source: 20,000names.com
- Italian Names, Source: 20,000names.com

- United Kingdom Names, Source: 50 British women's names, BabyNames.co.uk
- Turkish Names, Source: 20,000names.com
- Arabic Names, Source: 20,000names.com
- Irish Names, Source: 20,000names.com
- Unisex Names: familyberry.com

2.5.3. Limitations of the Database of Names

1. The Social Security Data of births in the US suffers from the limitation of not including the changing demographics due to immigration.
2. There are limitations imposed by the USPTO data itself. Some of the patent disclosures do not show a first name. There are others with initials but no first name. As the sort is done by the first name, these patent disclosures cannot be sorted and allocated to men and women. In addition, the names as spelled in the patent award sometimes do not match the spelling that is used in the US Census data or the data from commercially available sources.
3. Some common names are used both for men and women. For instance, the name "John" appears both in the database of men and of women, although the frequency at which the name occurs in the database of men and women is different.
4. American names that have their apparent origin in China, Korea, Japan, India, France and Germany require highly specialized sorting to differentiate between the names of men and women. For instance, the name Suratha is usually used by men in India but can be easily misread as a woman's name.
5. The most common names change with time; the most common names used in 1977 were not necessarily the same as the ones used in 2010.
6. The patent applications filed data from 2003 to 2010 was as yet incomplete.

   Ideally, one would like to assign 100% of the patents deterministically to men and women. However, the limitations of the USPTO data as well as the changing demographics of the US population preclude a 100% capture rate.

   A concerted effort was made to reduce the number of names that are not deterministically male or female. Several passes were made using multiple databases of names to capture an acceptable number of patents for allocation to men and women. 94.11% of the names in patent disclosures were deterministically identified. The remainder, that is 5.89% of the names that could not be identified as male or female, were allocated based on the ratio of patents awarded to males and females for each year.

2.5.4. Data Preparation

A Data Warehouse was prepared using the ETL (extraction, transformation and loading) process. The structure of the Warehouse was prepared in accordance with the available data to facilitate loading and then querying the data for the desired results while maintaining data integrity.

The data was successfully loaded into the database following data Extraction, Transformation and Cleaning.

2.5.5. Data Sort

2.5.5.1. Gender Assignment

The first sort used only the names that were exclusively female or male. This assignment was based on two lists containing the 10,000 most common female names and 10,000 most common male names derived from the U.S. Social Security Administration data. The lists account for 90% of the male and female names in the United States.

2.5.5.2. Names Common to Both Men and Women

The two lists used for the first sort showed a substantial number of names that were common to men and women. The following procedure was used for gender assignment of unisex names:

1. After assigning a gender to the exclusively female and male names based on the 10,000 most common female names and 10,000 most common male names lists, the count of female and male patentees for every year from 1975 to 2010 was obtained. This is referred to as FemaleCountInDB and MaleCountInDB in the formulae below.
2. The two lists used for the base sort provided information on the occurrence of common names in 1 million females and 1 million males respectively. These values (referred to as FemaleName Occurence(Base1million) and MalesNameOccurence(Base1million) in the formulas below) were also taken into account.

   For a name 'XYZ' that occurred 'n' number of times in the database in a year and was used as a common name for men and women, the

following formulae were used to apportion male and female names to our database:
AllocatedFemaleShare =
[FemaleNameOccurance(Base1Million)]*
(FemaleCountInDB/(FemaleCountInDB + MaleCountInDB))
AllocatedMaleShare =
[MaleNameOccurance(Base1Million)]*
(MaleCountInDB/(FemaleCountInDB + MaleCountInDB))

Number of names 'XYZ' that were designated as females (nf) in that year=
(AllocatedFemaleShare * n)/(AllocatedFemaleShare + AllocatedMaleShare)

Number of names 'XYZ' that were designated as males (nm) in that year=
(AllocatedMaleShare * n)/(AllocatedFemaleShare + AllocatedMaleShare)

The first 'nf' names were marked as females and the subsequent 'nm' names were marked as males. This procedure was followed first for primary inventors and then for non-primary inventors. The procedure resulted in gender assignments to the bulk of the inventors in the US.

3. Multiple commercially available name lists were then used to assign gender to the remaining names. The bulk of these names were of Chinese, Japanese, Korean, Indian, Spanish, German and French origin. Names from all over the world were procured to assign gender to the names that appeared to be exclusively male or female. The names that appeared to be used by males and females were allocated based on the count of female and male names per year in the database at that point.
4. The number of unassigned records was further reduced by additional sorts using uncommon names from China, India, Korea, Germany and other countries.
5. These procedures resulted in the allocation of 94.11% of the names of patent holders to the male and female categories. However, of a total of 4,887,424 patent records from the USPTO database, about 287,980 (5.89%) records remained. These unassigned records were

apportioned to males and females based on the ratio of male to female patentees in the database. The allocation was done on a per year basis.

6. This procedure was followed first for primary inventors and then for non-primary inventors. This was done to ensure uniformity while assigning gender to the inventors.

2.5.5.3. Primary and Non-Primary Inventors

Separate sorts were used for the primary inventor and the non-primary inventors.

2.5.5.4. The Impact of Changing Demography

The commercially available lists of the names of men and women are drawn from the U.S. Census database which includes 90% of the U.S. population and stops when a name occurs less than 5 times. The changing demographics of the United States include immigrant groups from Japan, Korea, China, India and other countries that show a significant and growing participation in the patent process. Some of the names from these immigrant groups do not necessarily occur more than 5 times to be captured by the U.S. Census database which includes 90% of the U.S. population. This limitation was overcome by using commercially available names of men and women from these immigrant groups. Successive filters were applied to identify the names of men and women from the unassigned list of patent holders to ensure that the number of women patent holders was not undercounted.

2.5.5.5. Patent Disclosures from USPTO Database with No First Name or Initials Only

The USPTO Database has a large number of disclosures with no first name or only an initial. These were assigned to the male and female categories in proportion to the number of patents granted to men and women for that year.

2.5.5.6. Segmentation Analysis by Patent Class

A comprehensive and exhaustive segmentation analysis of all 464 Patent Classes contained in the USPTO database was conducted to determine the share of patents granted to women. The objective was to obtain quantitative information about the contribution of women to patent activity across all industries and then to interrogate the results further for insights into specific industries wherein the contribution of women entrepreneurs was the highest. A table is presented in Appendix 2.

2.5.5.7. Patents Granted in the Top 25 Classes – A Longitudinal Study

The USPTO database for the top 25 Classes as determined by the number of patents granted to women was interrogated for each of the years 1975-2010. The objective was to identify the trends in patent activity in specific industries.

The top 25 segments with the highest participation by women are shown in Table 1. The number as well as percentages of patents granted to women in the top 25 Classes are plotted for the years 1975-2010.

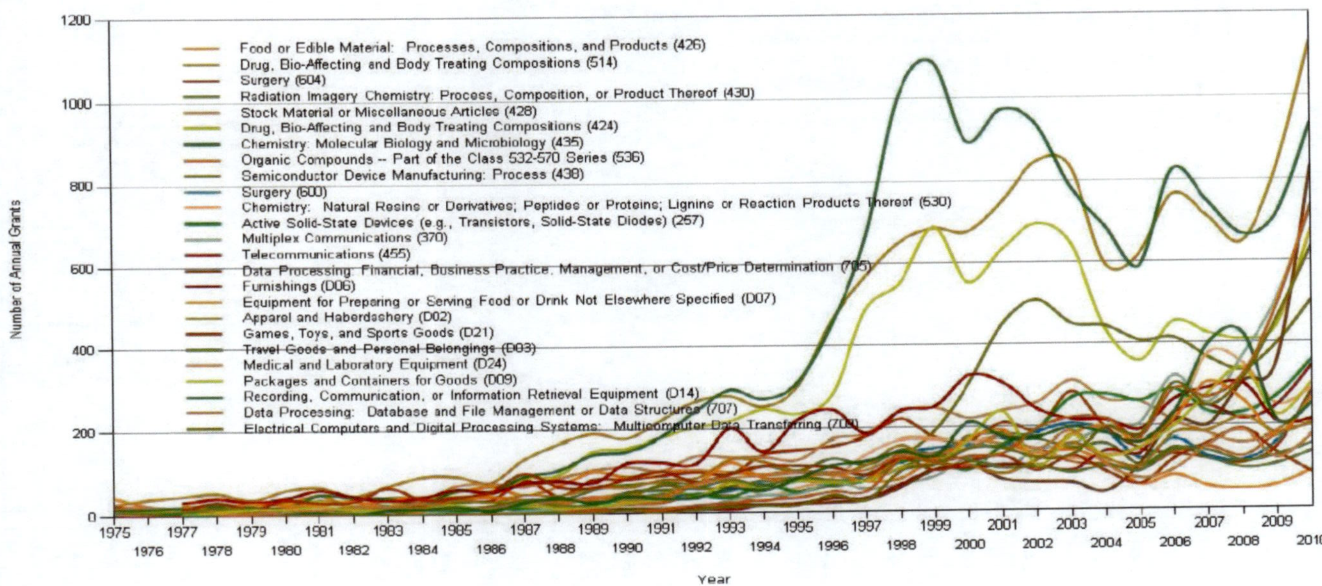

Patents Granted to Women (All)-Top 25 Patent Classes.

As a single chart for all 25 of the top Classes had too much information and was difficult to read, the same results were divided into five separate charts each containing 5 of the top Classes.

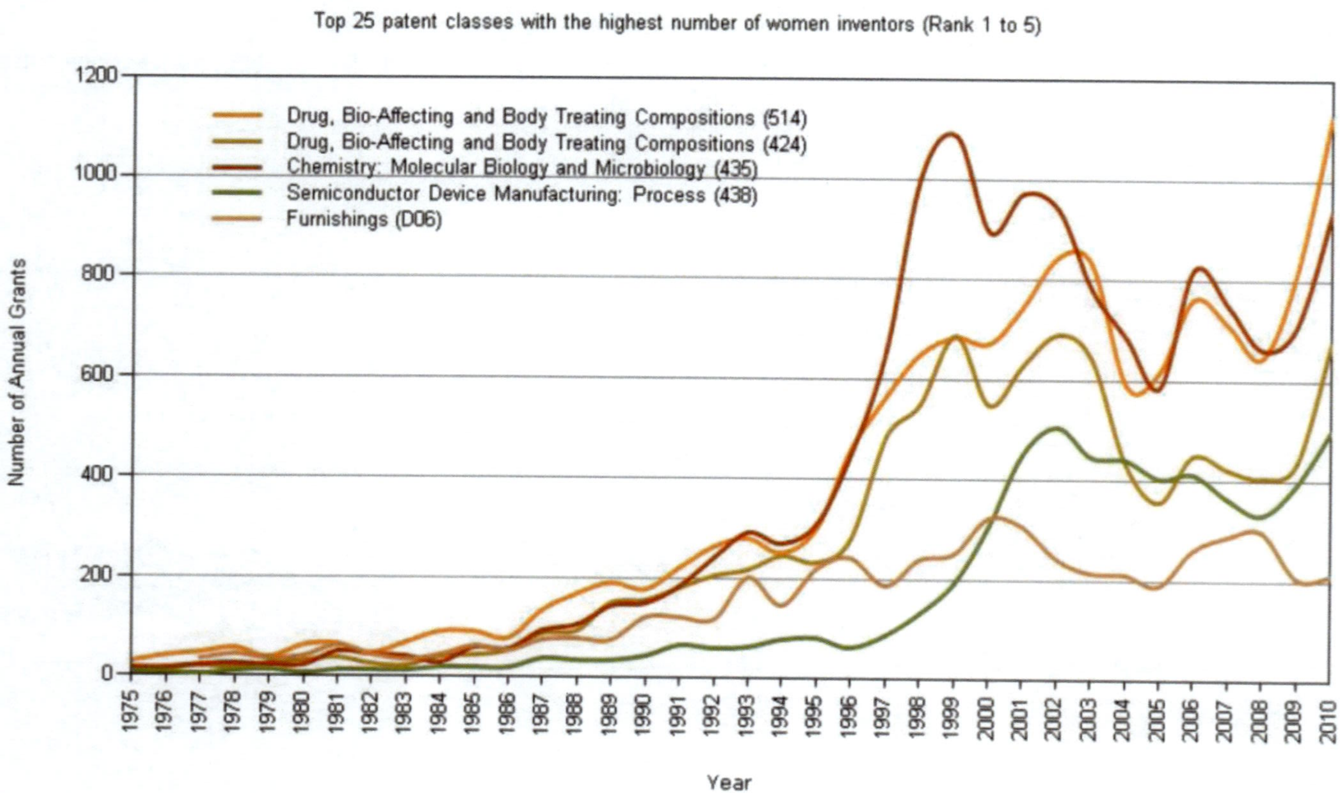

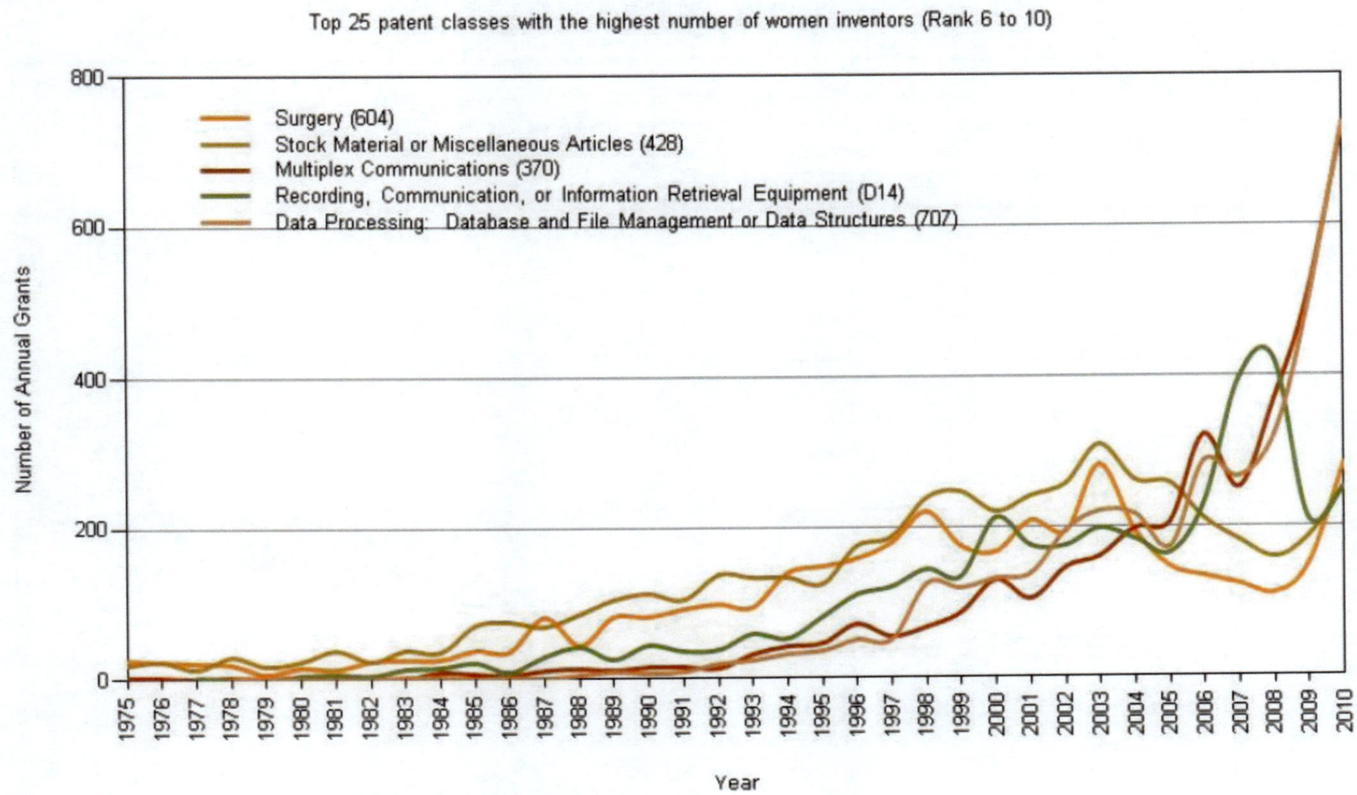
Top 25 patent classes with the highest number of women inventors (Rank 6 to 10)
Surgery (604)
Stock Material or Miscellaneous Articles (428)
Multiplex Communications (370)
Recording, Communication, or Information Retrieval Equipment (D14)
Data Processing: Database and File Management or Data Structures (707)
Number of Annual Grants
800
600
400
200
0
1975
1976
1977
1978
1979
1980
1981
1982
1983
1984
1985
1986
1987
1988
1989
1990
1991
1992
1993
1994
1995
1996
1997
1998
1999
2000
2001
2002
2003
2004
2005
2006
2007
2008
2009
2010
Year

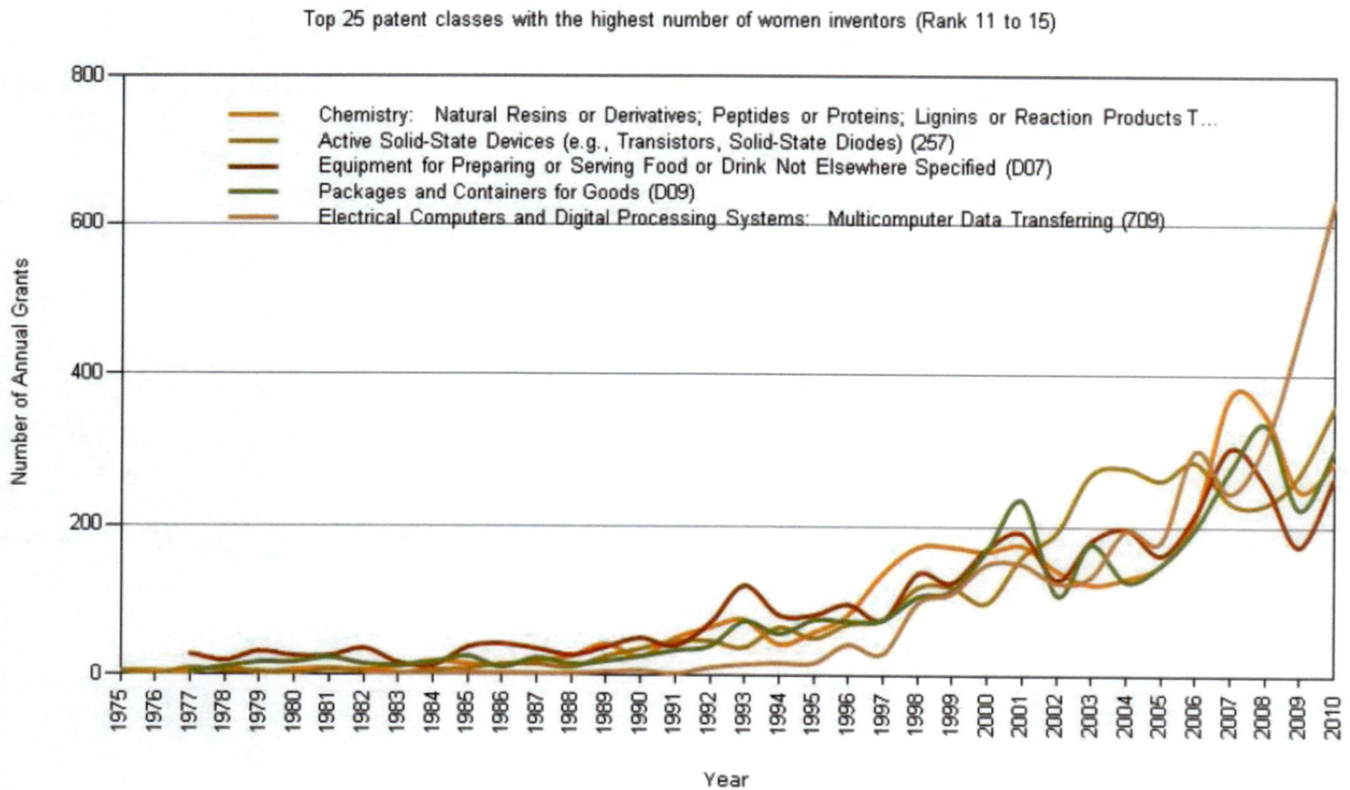

Top 25 patent classes with the highest number of women inventors (Rank 11 to 15)
Chemistry: Natural Resins or Derivatives; Peptides or Proteins; Lignins or Reaction Products T...
Active Solid-State Devices (e.g., Transistors, Solid-State Diodes) (257)
Equipment for Preparing or Serving Food or Drink Not Elsewhere Specified (D07)
Packages and Containers for Goods (D09)
Electrical Computers and Digital Processing Systems: Multicomputer Data Transferring (709)
Number of Annual Grants
800
600
400
200
0
1975
1976
1977
1978
1979
1980
1981
1982
1983
1984
1985
1986
1987
1988
1989
1990
1991
1992
1993
1994
1995
1996
1997
1998
1999
2000
2001
2002
2003
2004
2005
2006
2007
2008
2009
2010
Year

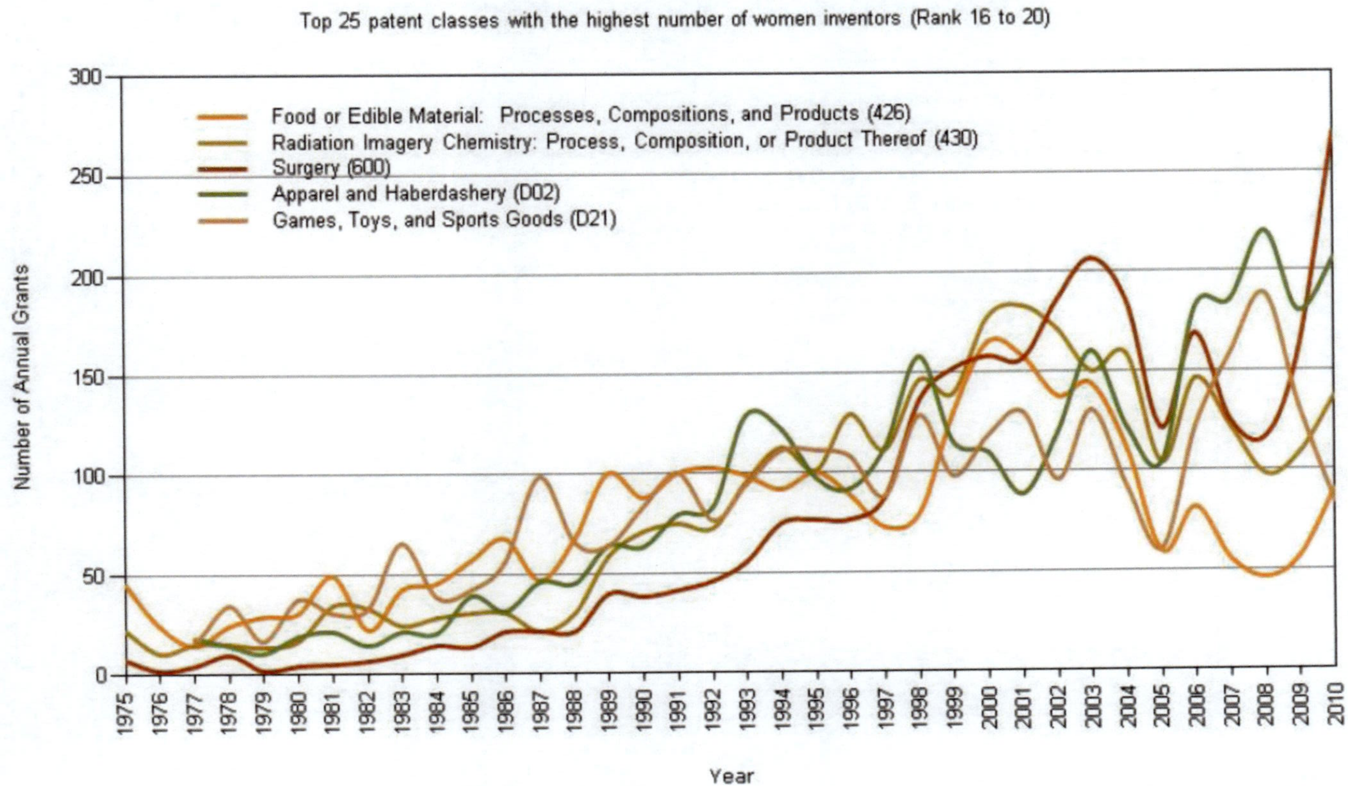
Top 25 patent classes with the highest number of women inventors (Rank 16 to 20)
Food or Edible Material: Processes, Compositions, and Products (426)
Radiation Imagery Chemistry: Process, Composition, or Product Thereof (430)
Surgery (600)
Apparel and Haberdashery (D02)
Games, Toys, and Sports Goods (D21)
Number of Annual Grants
0
50
100
150
200
250
300
1975
1976
1977
1978
1979
1980
1981
1982
1983
1984
1985
1986
1987
1988
1989
1990
1991
1992
1993
1994
1995
1996
1997
1998
1999
2000
2001
2002
2003
2004
2005
2006
2007
2008
2009
2010
Year

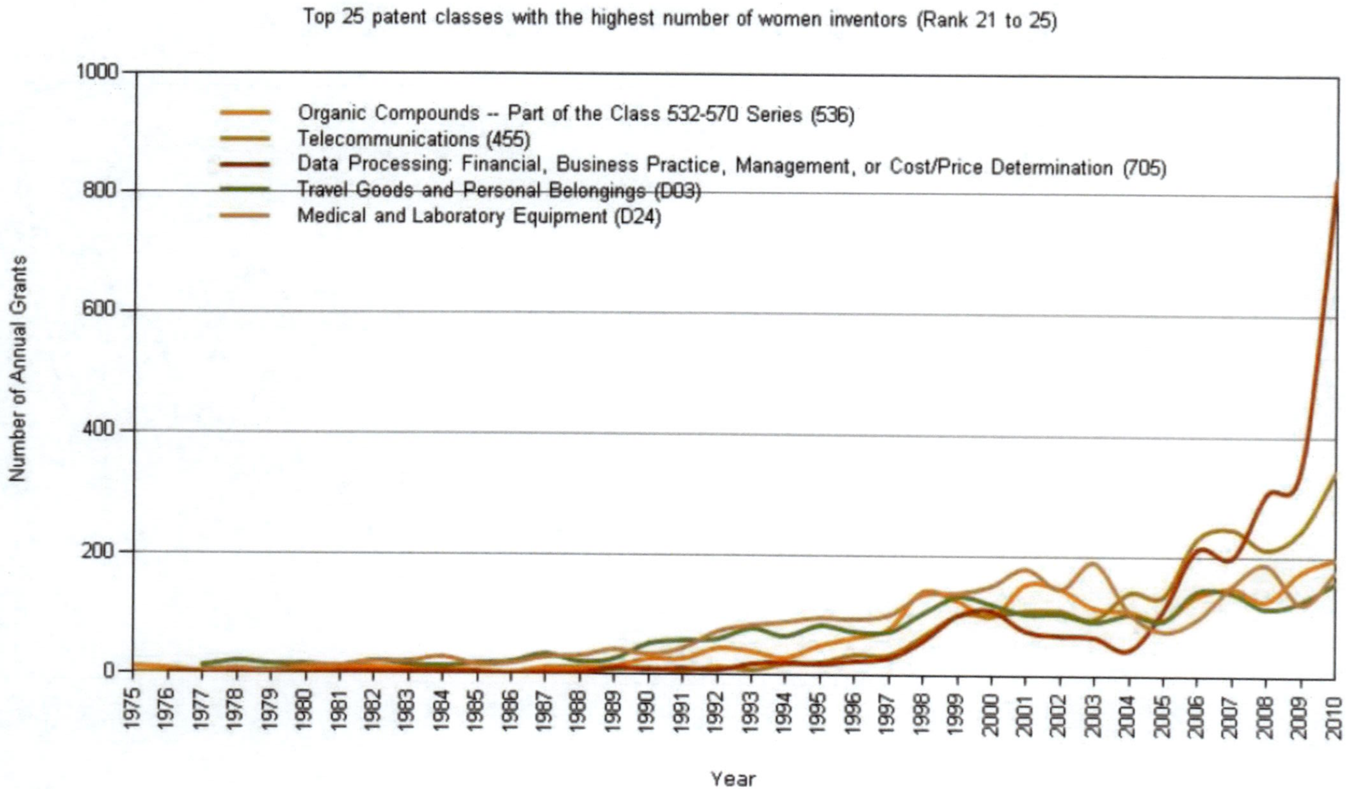

The USPFO database was probed further to Identify the number of patents wherein a woman was the primary inventor. The results for the top 25 of the Classes are presented in the following charts.

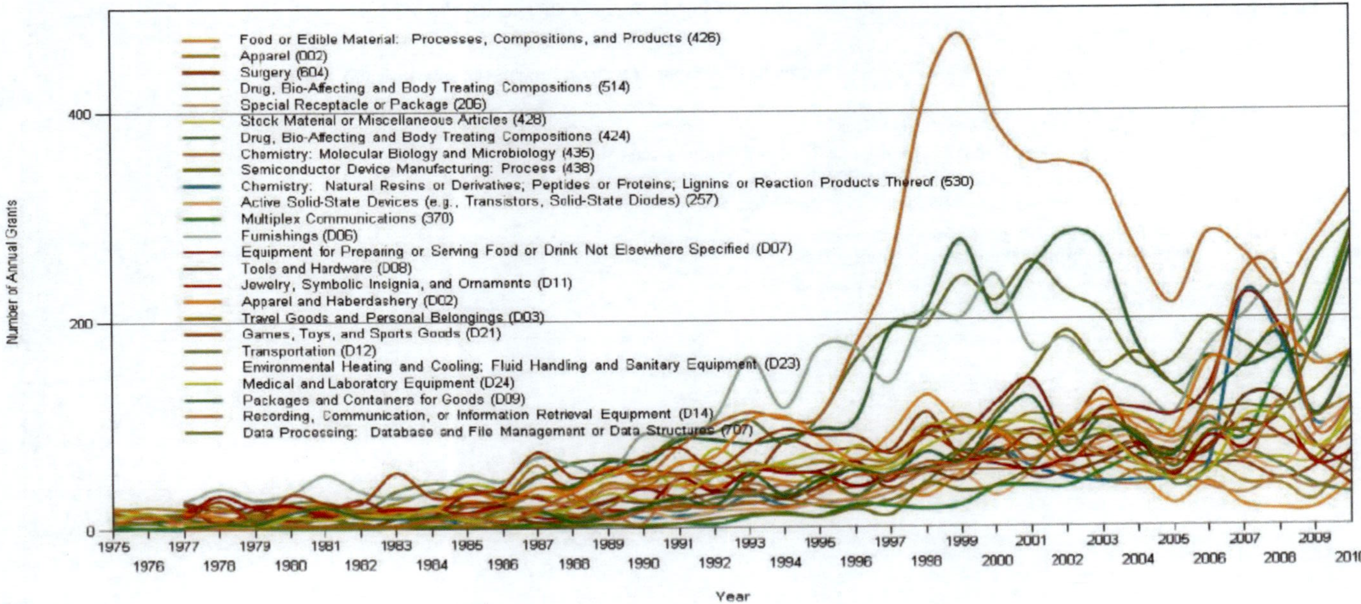

Patents Granted to Women (Prinary Inventor) – Breakdown by Patent Class.

The results were divided into five separate charts each containing 5 of the top Classes.

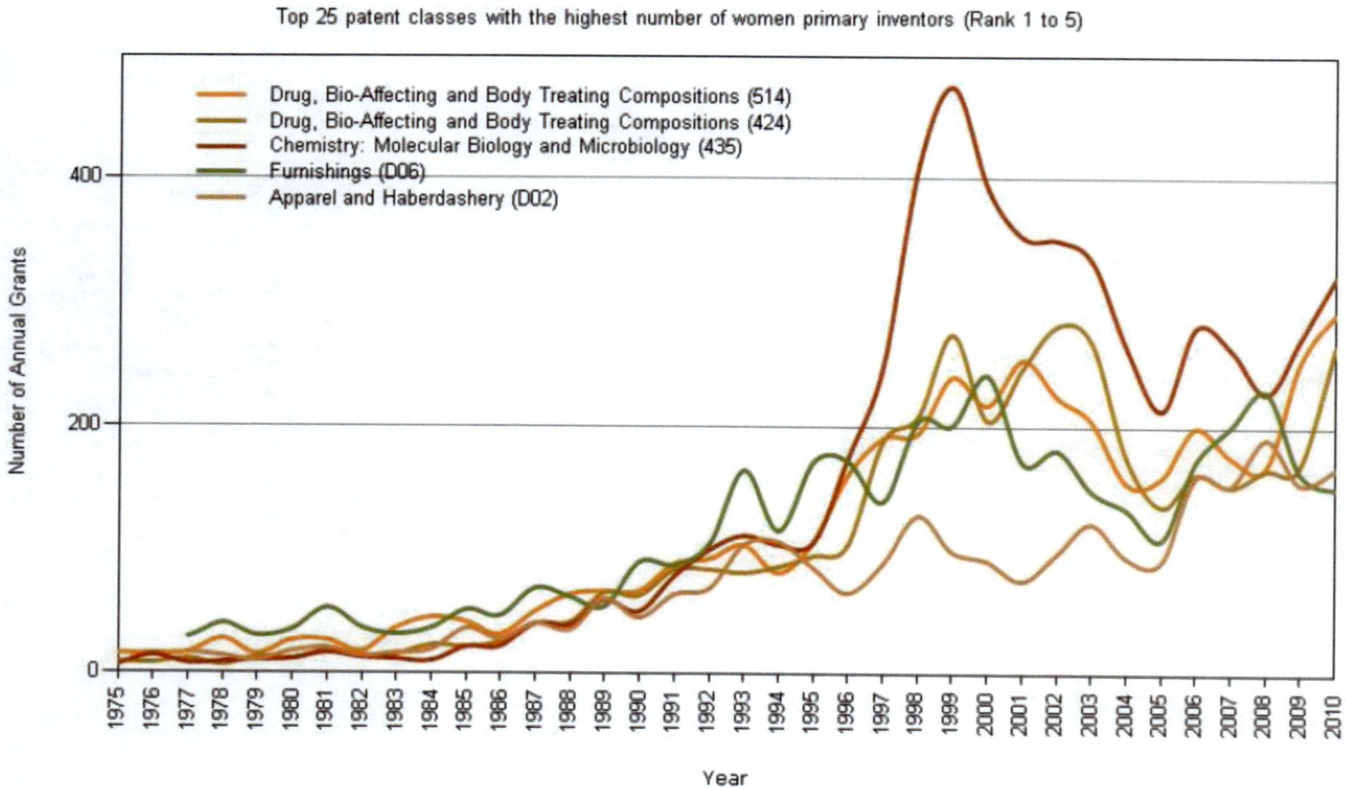

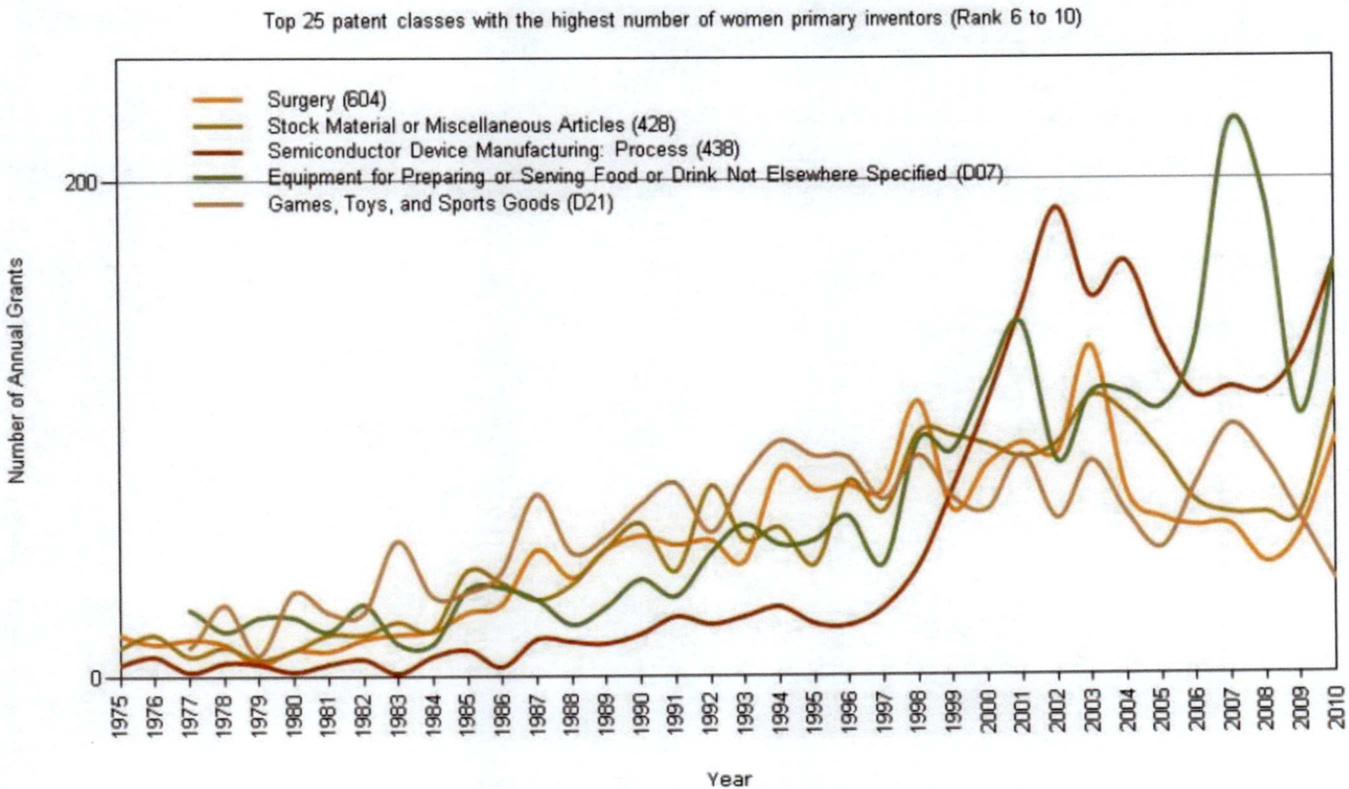
Top 25 patent classes with the highest number of women primary inventors (Rank 6 to 10)
Surgery (604)
Stock Material or Miscellaneous Articles (428)
Semiconductor Device Manufacturing: Process (438)
Equipment for Preparing or Serving Food or Drink Not Elsewhere Specified (D07)
Games, Toys, and Sports Goods (D21)
Number of Annual Grants
200
0
1975
1976
1977
1978
1979
1980
1981
1982
1983
1984
1985
1986
1987
1988
1989
1990
1991
1992
1993
1994
1995
1996
1997
1998
1999
2000
2001
2002
2003
2004
2005
2006
2007
2008
2009
2010
Year

Top 25 patent classes with the highest number of women primary inventors (Rank 11 to 15)

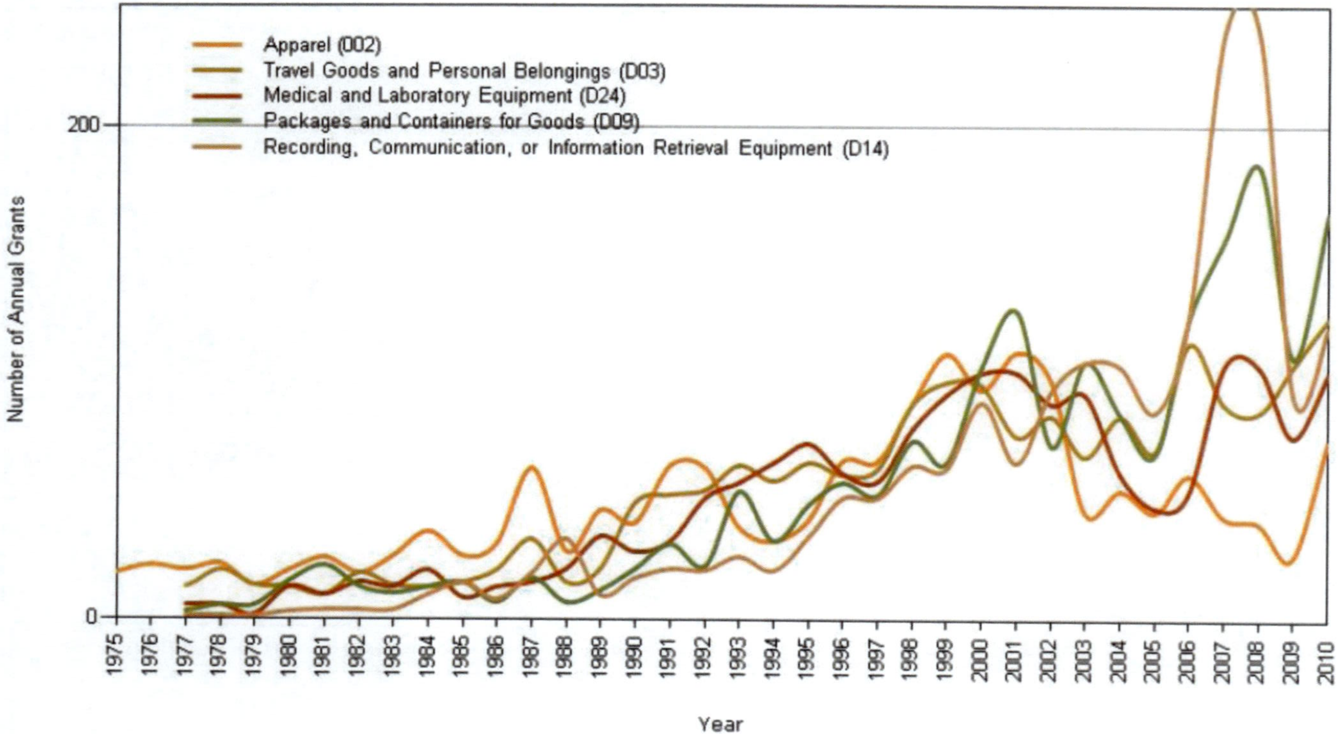

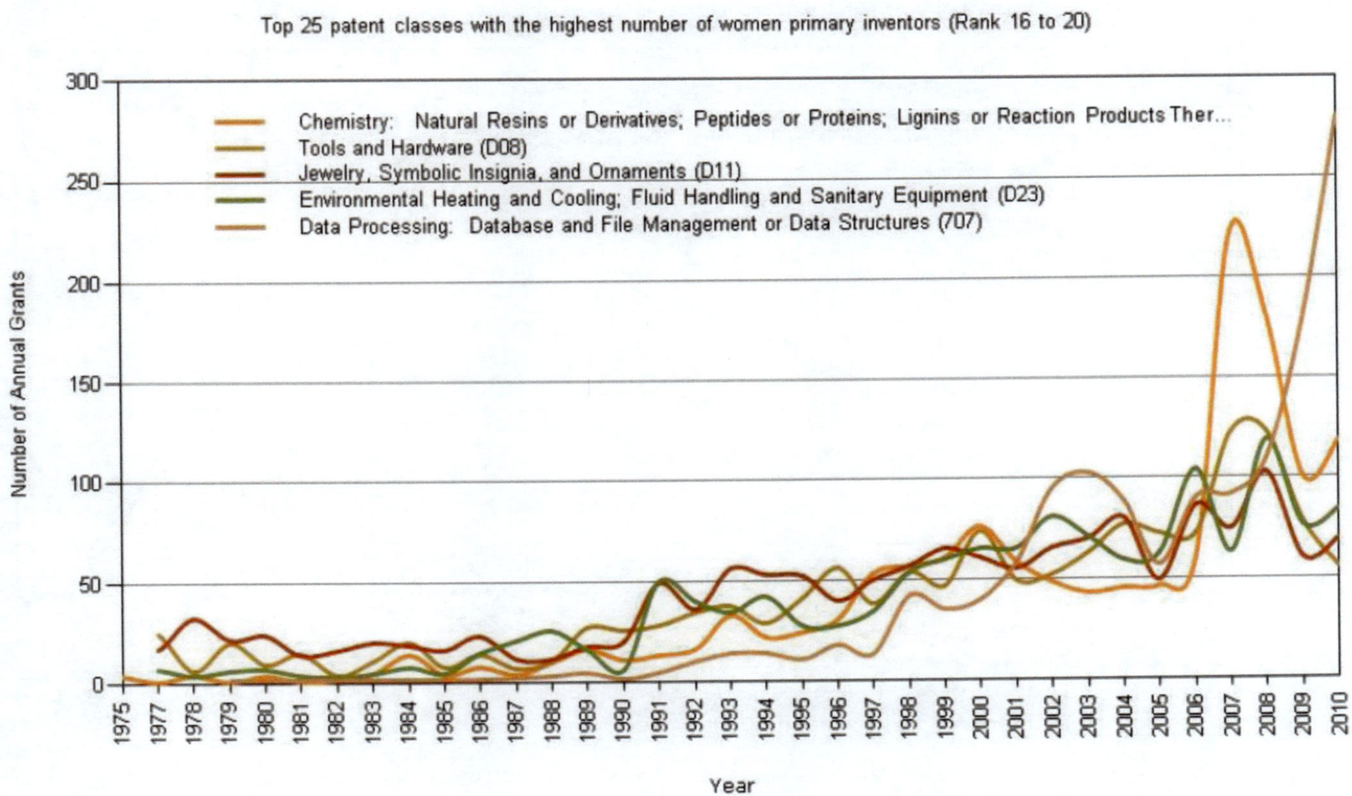

Top 25 patent classes with the highest number of women primary inventors (Rank 16 to 20)
Chemistry: Natural Resins or Derivatives; Peptides or Proteins; Lignins or Reaction Products Ther...
Tools and Hardware (D08)
Jewelry, Symbolic Insignia, and Ornaments (D11)
Environmental Heating and Cooling; Fluid Handling and Sanitary Equipment (D23)
Data Processing: Database and File Management or Data Structures (707)
Number of Annual Grants
300
250
200
150
100
50
0
1975
1977
1978
1979
1980
1981
1982
1983
1984
1985
1986
1987
1988
1989
1990
1991
1992
1993
1994
1995
1996
1997
1998
1999
2000
2001
2002
2003
2004
2005
2006
2007
2008
2009
2010
Year

Top 25 patent classes with the highest number of women primary inventors (Rank 21 to 25)

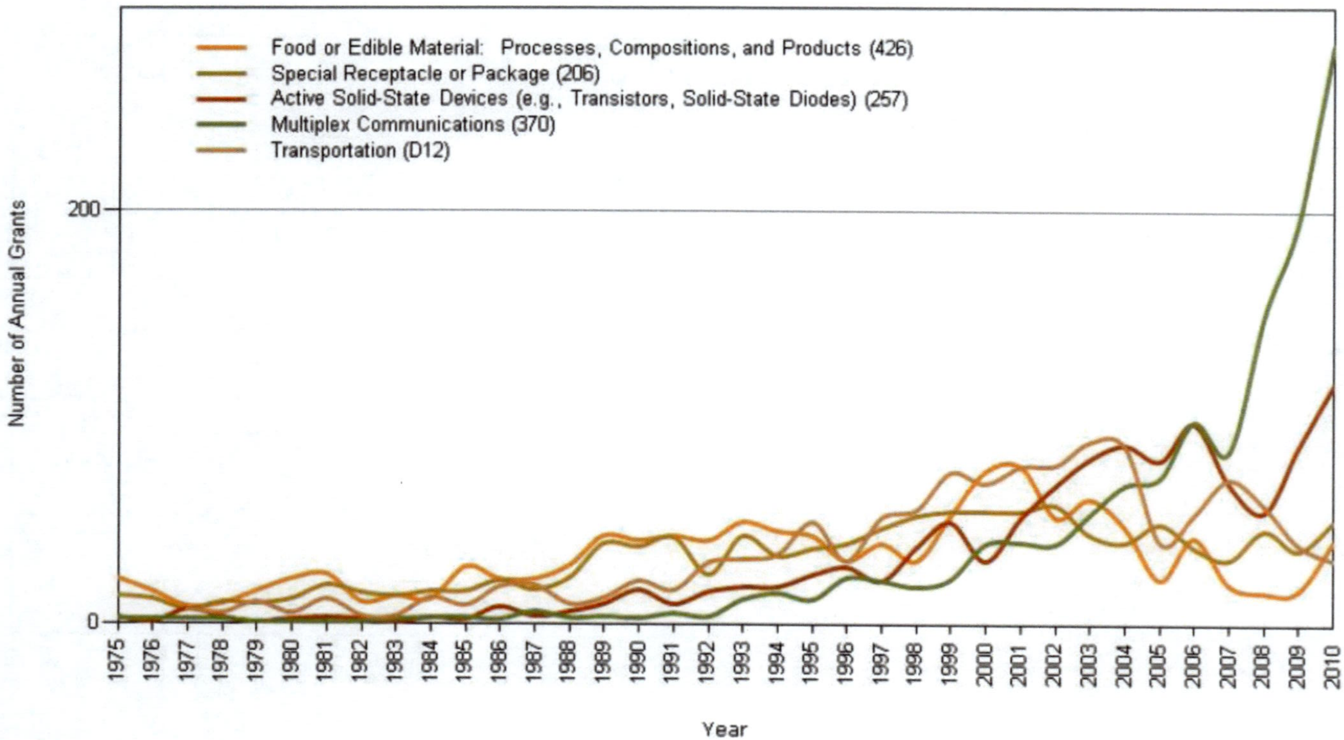

Similarly, the results for patents wherein a woman was a non-primary inventor are presented in the following chart.

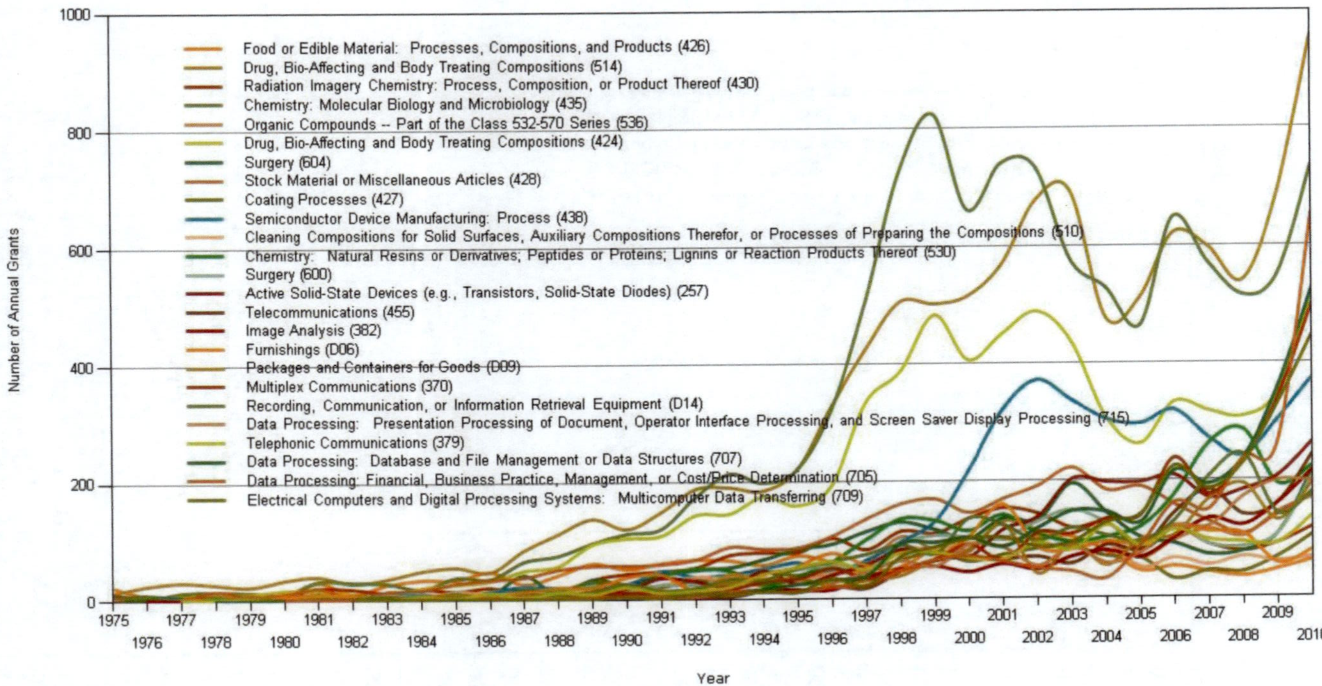

Patents Granted to Women (Non-Primary Inventor) – Breakdown by Patents Class.

For clarity, the results were divided into five separate charts each containing 5 of the top Classes.

Top 25 patent classes with the highest number of women non-primary inventors (Rank 1 to 5)

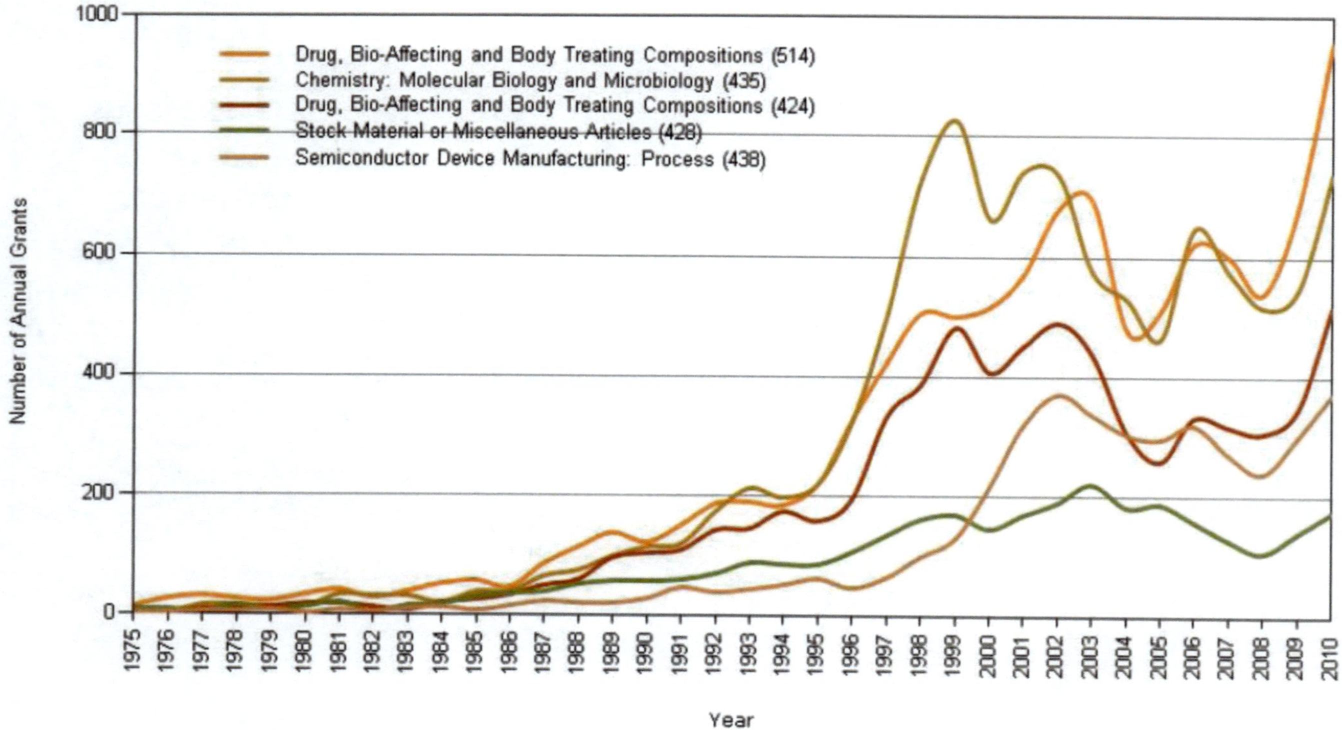

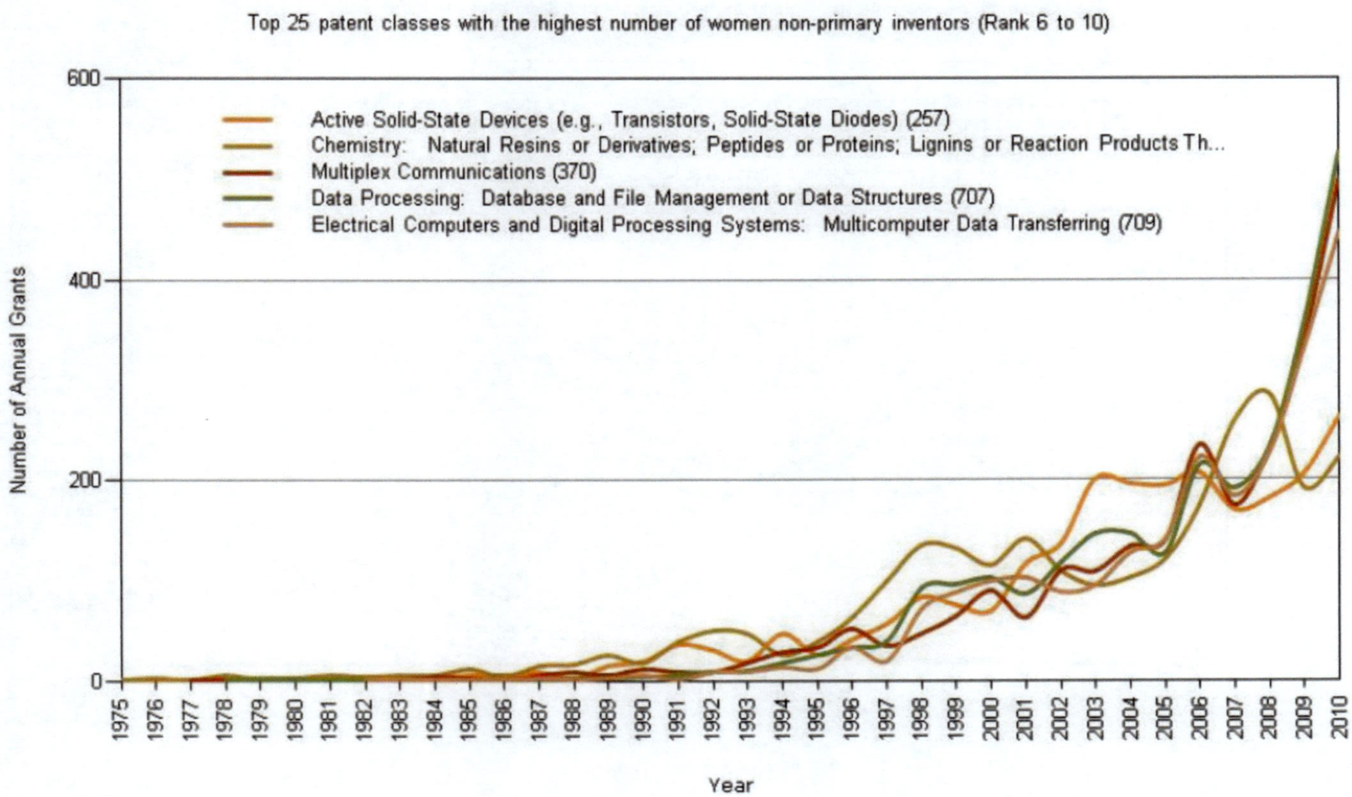

Top 25 patent classes with the highest number of women non-primary inventors (Rank 6 to 10)
Active Solid-State Devices (e.g., Transistors, Solid-State Diodes) (257)
Chemistry: Natural Resins or Derivatives; Peptides or Proteins; Lignins or Reaction Products Th...
Multiplex Communications (370)
Data Processing: Database and File Management or Data Structures (707)
Electrical Computers and Digital Processing Systems: Multicomputer Data Transferring (709)
Number of Annual Grants
600
400
200
0
1975
1976
1977
1978
1979
1980
1981
1982
1983
1984
1985
1986
1987
1988
1989
1990
1991
1992
1993
1994
1995
1996
1997
1998
1999
2000
2001
2002
2003
2004
2005
2006
2007
2008
2009
2010
Year

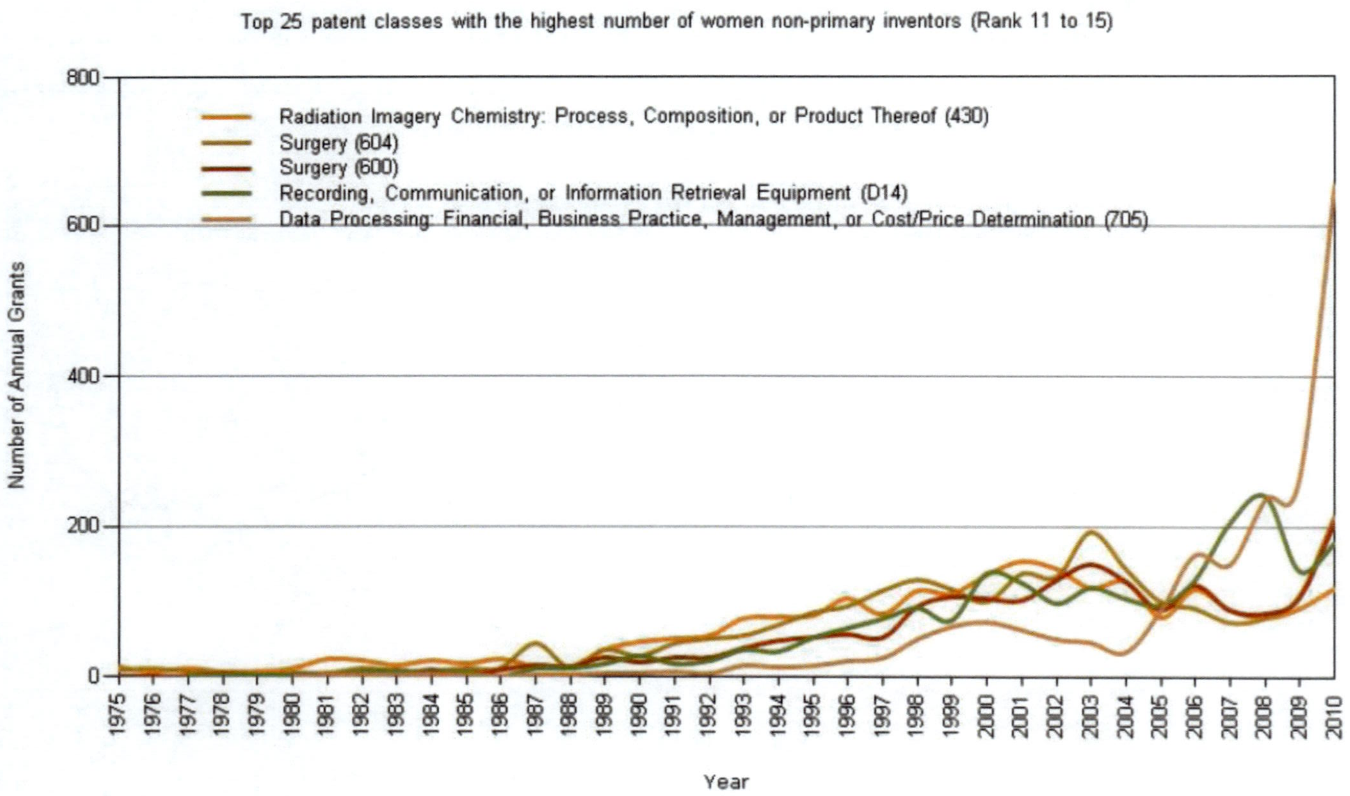
Top 25 patent classes with the highest number of women non-primary inventors (Rank 11 to 15)
Radiation Imagery Chemistry: Process, Composition, or Product Thereof (430)
Surgery (604)
Surgery (600)
Recording, Communication, or Information Retrieval Equipment (D14)
Data Processing: Financial, Business Practice, Management, or Cost/Price Determination (705)
Number of Annual Grants
800
600
400
200
0
1975
1976
1977
1978
1979
1980
1981
1982
1983
1984
1985
1986
1987
1988
1989
1990
1991
1992
1993
1994
1995
1996
1997
1998
1999
2000
2001
2002
2003
2004
2005
2006
2007
2008
2009
2010
Year

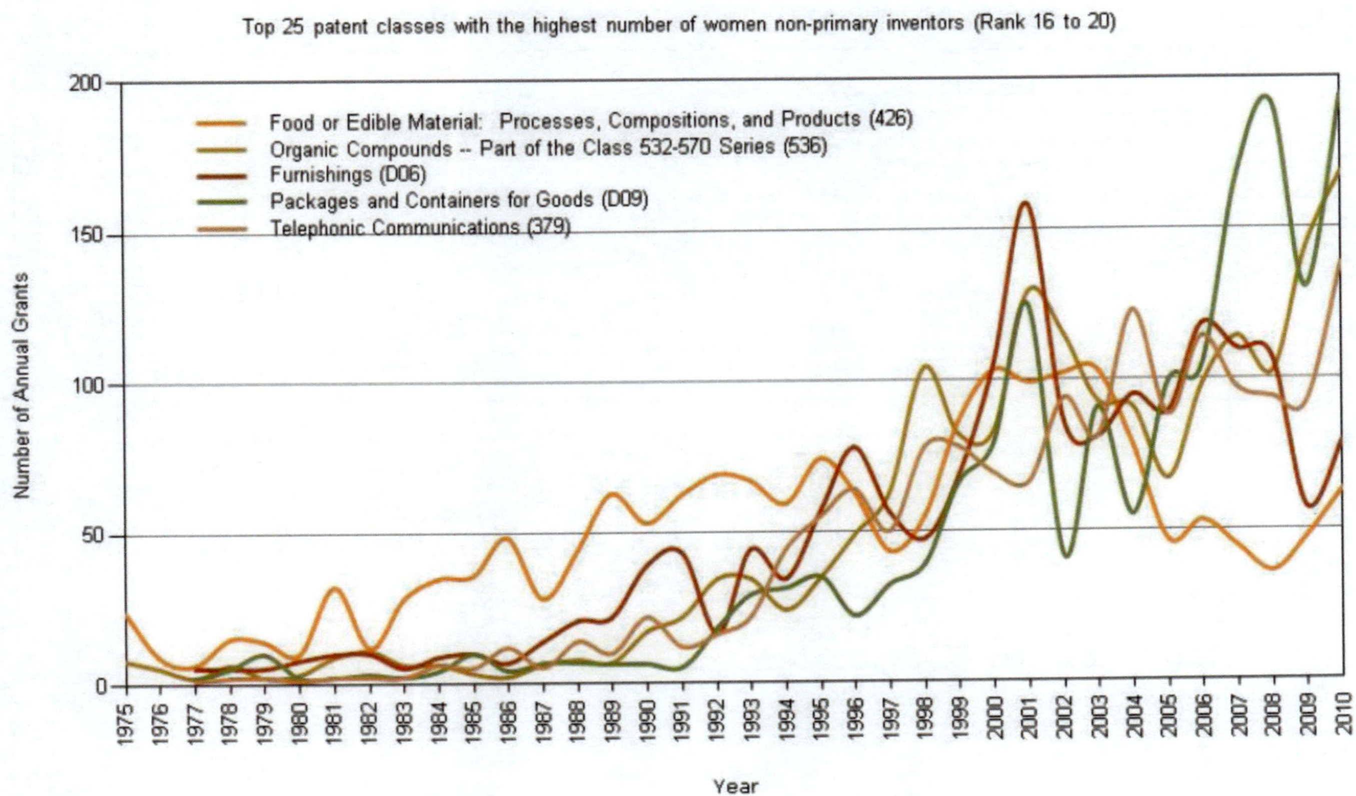
Top 25 patent classes with the highest number of women non-primary inventors (Rank 16 to 20)
Food or Edible Material: Processes, Compositions, and Products (426)
Organic Compounds -- Part of the Class 532-570 Series (536)
Furnishings (D06)
Packages and Containers for Goods (D09)
Telephonic Communications (379)
Number of Annual Grants
0
50
100
150
200
1975
1976
1977
1978
1979
1980
1981
1982
1983
1984
1985
1986
1987
1988
1989
1990
1991
1992
1993
1994
1995
1996
1997
1998
1999
2000
2001
2002
2003
2004
2005
2006
2007
2008
2009
2010
Year

Top 25 patent classes with the highest number of women non-primary inventors (Rank 21 to 25)

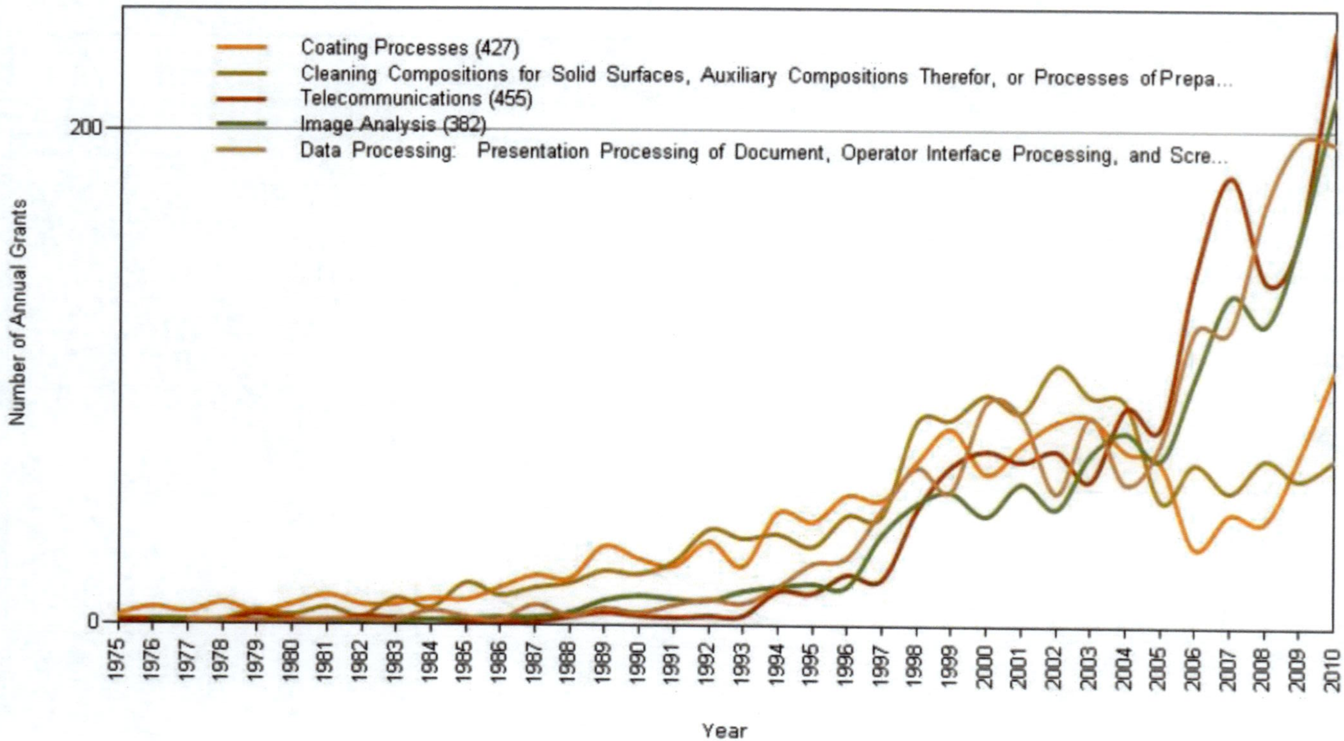

Table 1. The top 25 of the segments with the highest participation by women

Patent Class Code	Patent Class Title (according to the United States Patents and Trademarks Office (USPTO))	Total no. of Patents	No. of Patents with at least 1 Woman Inventor	% Women Patents
435	Chemistry: Molecular Biology and Microbiology	40,314	14,129	35.05
514	Drug, Bio-Affecting and Body Treating Compositions	49,801	13,434	26.98
424	Drug, Bio-Affecting and Body Treating Compositions	32,515	9,625	29.60
438	Semiconductor Device Manufacturing: Process	34,848	5,677	16.29
D06	Furnishings	26,707	5,297	19.83
428	Stock Material or Miscellaneous Articles	32,518	4,780	14.70
604	Surgery	22,666	3,838	16.93
707	Data Processing: Database and File Management or Data Structures	17,901	3,664	20.47
370	Multiplex Communications	28,613	3,615	12.63
D14	Recording, Communication, or Information Retrieval Equipment	17,071	3,602	21.10
D07	Equipment for Preparing or Serving Food or Drink Not Elsewhere Specified	14,138	3,496	24.73
530	Chemistry: Natural Resins or Derivatives; Peptides or Proteins; Lignins or Reaction Products Thereof	9,356	3,413	36.48
257	Active Solid-State Devices (e.g., Transistors, Solid-State Diodes)	26,534	3,412	12.86
709	Electrical Computers and Digital Processing Systems: Multicomputer Data Transferring	19,922	3,239	16.26
D09	Packages and Containers for Goods	13,414	3,174	23.66
D02	Apparel and Haberdashery	10,807	3,087	28.56
430	Radiation Imagery Chemistry: Process, Composition, or Product Thereof	14,736	2,987	20.27
D21	Games, Toys, and Sports Goods	15,817	2,905	18.37
600	Surgery	23,491	2,812	11.97
426	Food or Edible Material: Processes, Compositions, and Products	12,503	2,719	21.75
D24	Medical and Laboratory Equipment	11,088	2,719	24.52
705	Data Processing: Financial, Business Practice, Management, or Cost/Price Determination	13,276	2,692	20.28

Table 1. (Continued)

Patent Class Code	Patent Class Title (according to the United States Patents and Trademarks Office (USPTO))	Total no. of Patents	No. of Patents with at least 1 Woman Inventor	% Women Patents
D03	Travel Goods and Personal Belongings	8,571	2,330	27.18
455	Telecommunications	20,520	2,322	11.32
536	Organic Compounds, Part of the Class 532-570 Series	6,964	2,239	32.15

2.5.5.8. Categories with the Sharpest Increase in the Number of Patents

The top 5 categories that show the sharpest increase in the number of patents with at least 1 woman inventor are shown in Table 2a. Data processing as applied to Financial, Business Practice, Management, or Cost/Price Determination (705) shows a whopping 172.13% increase from 2008 to 2010. Surgery (604) is in the second place with an increase of 156.36%. Surgery (600) is in the third place with an increase of 129.91%. Data processing as applied to Database and File Management or Data Structures (707) is in the fourth place with an increase of 127.95%. Electrical Computers and Digital Processing Systems as applied to Multicomputer Data Transferring (709) is in the fifth place with an increase of 101.92%.

Table 2a. Industries with the Highest Recent Surge in Patent Activity - The top 5 Patent Categories with the largest percentage increase in patents with at least 1 woman inventor in the two year period 2008-2010

Patent Class Code	Patent Class Title	2008	2009	2010	2 year % increase 2008- 2010
705	Data Processing: Financial, Business Practice, Management, or Cost/Price Determination	305	354	830	172.13
604	Surgery	110	148	282	156.36
600	Surgery	117	160	269	129.91
707	Data Processing: Database and File Management or Data Structures	322	489	734	127.95
709	Electrical Computers and Digital Processing Systems: Multicomputer Data Transferring	313	456	632	101.92

Table 2b. The above 5 patent categories showing all the patents awarded in the two year period 2008-2010

Patent Class Code	Patent Class Title	2008	2009	2010	2 year % increase 2008-2010
705	Data Processing: Financial, Business Practice, Management, or Cost/Price Determination	1,324	1,621	3,419	158.23
604	Surgery	496	642	1,249	151.81
600	Surgery	729	881	1,401	92.18
707	Data Processing: Database and File Management or Data Structures	1,458	2,153	3,301	126.4
709	Electrical Computers and Digital Processing Systems: Multicomputer Data Transferring	1,986	2,421	3,330	67.67

Table 3. Highlighting Women's Contributions to Optical Technologies, an Emerging High-tech Sector

Patent Class Code	Patent Class	Total no. of Patents	Patents with at least 1 woman inventor	Percent
D16	Photography and Optical Equipment	2,995	388	12.95
385	Optical Waveguides	15,112	1,746	11.55
351	Optics: Eye Examining, Vision Testing and Correcting	3,859	421	10.91
398	Optical Communications	4,084	441	10.80
720	Dynamic Optical Information Storage or Retrieval	348	35	10.06
359	Optical: Systems and Elements	16,434	1,402	8.53
356	Optics: Measuring and Testing	14,657	1,200	8.19
353	Optics: Image Projectors	1,783	116	6.51
352	Optics: Motion Pictures	614	16	2.61

2.5.5.9. Contributions in Emerging High-Tech Sectors

Of particular interest is the surge of innovation by women in some of the emerging high-tech industries. The field of optics and optical systems was selected to illustrate this observation. Optics and optical communications have a broad range of applications in both civilian and defense sectors and constitute an important differentiator in the strength of an economy. Table 3 shows that 12.95% of the patents in Photography and Optical Equipment had at least 1 U.S. woman inventor. For Optical Waveguides, 11.55% of the patents had at least 1 woman inventor. Optics, Eye Examining, Vision Testing and Correcting came in third at 10.91%. Specific data on the employment of women in these industries is required to correlate this data with employment patterns.

This is an issue to investigate in future studies as it would throw more light on the growing presence of and contribution of women in high-tech segments.

Table 4 represents the results obtained by querying the database for primary patent holders only. This data is a measure of leadership provided by women since the primary patent holder tends to be the idea generator or the team lead in an R&D project.

While it is premature to draw long term conclusions from these statistics, if this trend continues, it would be a significant finding of this study. Of particular interest is the increase in patent activity by women in specialized fields such as surgery and high tech sectors like multiplex communications which have broad technological implications for macro-economics. As to why these Categories lead the way in innovation by women would be a worthwhile project for future research.

Questions of interest would include: What structural, environmental, motivational and business factors influence innovation by women? What factors discourage innovation? How can the U.S. unleash and harness the creative potential of women? Is there a correlation between innovation and employment? Is there a correlation (after subtracting out a time lag) between innovation and SAT scores by graduating women in science and mathematics? Is there a marginal difference in the inventiveness of men and women given a certain investment in education, employment and supporting R&D infrastructure?

2.5.5.10. Patents by Ownership Category

The USPTO database was interrogated to determine the number of assigned and unassigned patents.

The results for different US and foreign categories are shown in Table 5 below.

Table 4. Highlighting Women's Contributions as Primary Inventors to Optical Technologies, an Emerging High-tech Sector

Patent Class Code	Patent Class	Total no. of Patents	Patents with at least 1 woman primary inventor	Percent
D16	Photography and Optical Equipment	2,960	225	7.60
351	Optics: Eye Examining, Vision Testing and Correcting	3,793	241	6.35
398	Optical Communications	3,975	168	4.23
385	Optical Waveguides	14,823	619	4.18
720	Dynamic Optical Information Storage or Retrieval	344	14	4.07
359	Optical: Systems and Elements	16,073	587	3.65
356	Optics: Measuring and Testing	14,407	432	3.00
353	Optics: Image Projectors	1,749	45	2.57
352	Optics: Motion Pictures	610	9	1.48

Table 5. Shows the number of patents assigned to private and government organizations

Ownership Category	Total no. of Patents	% of Total no. of Patents (1975-2010)	Patents with at least 1 woman inventor	% of Total no. of Patents with at least 1 woman inventor
Assigned to a U.S. non-government organization	1,809,666	74.118	220,060	75.839
Unassigned	489,495	20.048	52,975	18.257
Assigned to a foreign non-government organization	77,889	3.190	10,290	3.546
Assigned to the U.S. (Federal) Government	38,643	1.583	4,124	1.421
Assigned to a U.S. individual	25,372	1.039	2,667	0.919
Assigned to a foreign individual	436	0.018	46	0.016
Assigned to a foreign government	100	0.004	7	0.002
Total no. of Patents (1975-2010)	2,441,601		290,169	

Table 6. Shows the number of patents by U.S. based men and women assigned to private and government organizations. This table includes the primary inventors only

Ownership Category	Total no. of Patents	% of Total no. of Patents (1975-2010)	Patents with a woman primary inventor	% of Total no. of Patents with a woman primary inventor	Patents with a man primary inventor	% of Total no. of Patents with a man primary inventor
Assigned to a U.S. non- government organization	1,787,695	74.423	87,181	64.975	1,700,514	74.982
Unassigned	487,902	20.312	39,463	29.411	448,439	19.773
Assigned to a foreign non-government organization	62,426	2.599	4,045	3.015	58,381	2.574
Assigned to the U.S. (Federal) Government	38,413	1.599	1,630	1.215	36,783	1.622
Assigned to a U.S. individual	25,302	1.053	1,835	1.368	23,467	1.035
Assigned to a foreign individual	292	0.012	20	0.015	272	0.012
Assigned to a foreign government	54	0.002	2	0.001	52	0.002
Total no. of Patents (1975-2010)	2,402,084		134,176		2,267,908	

Table 6 represents the results obtained by querying the database for primary inventors only.

The analysis shows a slightly lower percentage of patents by women that were assigned to private companies. 64.97% of all patents with women primary inventors in the period 1976-2010 were assigned to a U.S. non-governmental organization. This is a lower percentage than that for men who assigned 74.98% of patents to private companies. 19.77% of all patents by men were unassigned as compared to 29.41% for women. Together, these results suggest a slight difference between men and women in independent entrepreneurship: women are more likely to be independent entrepreneurs and keep their patents unassigned while men are more likely to be leading the research in businesses and corporations.

It must be cautioned that assignment must not be confused with commercial success as has been done in some earlier studies. Only a small number of patents, perhaps as few as 10%, are brought to the marketplace and become commercially viable. The commercialization of Patents and Trademarks and its impact on the economy is an issue that needs to be studied in future research. The assignment or non-assignment of a patent merely confirms a decision on the part of the inventor or his/her employer to seek IP protection for an innovation and keep the concomitant technology "in-house". A patentable technology may not be marketable on a "stand-alone" basis, but it may have a print-through on the development of subsequent systems or technologies that do become economically viable.

2.5.6. Regression Analysis: Patents Granted to Women

A regression analysis was performed on the data to identify longitudinal trends as well as identify benchmarks. Since it currently takes an average of 3.6 years to obtain a patent, consideration was given to using a 4 year moving average for the regression analysis. This option was discarded as the moving average would smooth out the data and might conceal significant "bends" in the longitudinal trends. It was therefore decided to use a piecewise linear analysis. The table below summarizes the results for Patents Granted to Women, Share of all Patents.

Women's Share of Patents Granted 1975-2010

Data Source: USPTO

Piecewise Linear Analysis

Percentage of patents granted to women = (a + b(t1-t2))*100, where, a and b are constants, t2-t1 is the time lapse, measured in years, for each segment.

Date analysis performed: November 27, 2011

Period (Segment)	a	b	Yearly percentage rate of increase
1975-1986	0.028	0.0029	0.29%
1986-1993	0.06	0.007	0.70%
1993-1999	0.109	0.0051	0.51%
1999-2004	0.14	0.002	0.20%
2004-2010	0.152	0.0050	0.50%

The following inferences may be drawn from the regression analysis:

1. The number of patents granted to women increased by approximately 34.72% from 2009 to 2010.
2. In the same period, the number of primary patents granted to women (where a woman is the first inventor) increased by 28.57% and the number of non-primary patents (where a woman is the second, third or fourth inventor) granted increased by 38.23%.
3. If a single formula is desired, a non-linear regression such as

x= a+ b (t2-t1) + c (t2-t1)2 +d ((t2-t1) 3

where a, b, c and d are constants, would be more appropriate to capture the accelerating pace at which patents are granted to women. This is a non-linear equation with one unknown "x"; multiple solutions are possible with different values for the coefficients a, b, c and d.

2.5.7. Patents Filed versus Patents Granted

The patents filed data obtained from the USPTO was plotted for men and women. As seen from the charts in Figures 2 and 6, Appendix 1, the USPTO data for patents filed drops off after the year 2002. Apparently, the USPTO data, as reflected in the disc supplied to Delixus, is as yet incomplete.

Alternate sources for patents filed data were investigated: http://www.uspto.gov/web/offices/ac/ido/oeip/taf/us_stat.htm

This source has more complete information about the number of patents filed and the number of patents granted up to the year 2010. However, it has no information about names; hence, it is of no help in determining the gender of the patent applicants.

It was therefore decided to analyze the USPTO data for patents filed and patents granted for men and women only up to the year 2002. The results are plotted in several charts presented in Figures 1-14, Appendix 1.

The ratio of successful women patent applicants (patents granted/ patents filed by women) to successful men patent applicants (patents granted/ patents filed by men) varies from a low of 73.36% in 1986 to a high of 93.57% in 2002. The factors that influence this slow but steady progress in closing the gender gap in the processing of patent applications will be probed further in focus groups.

1. Patents Filed versus Patents Granted to Women - 1975-2010

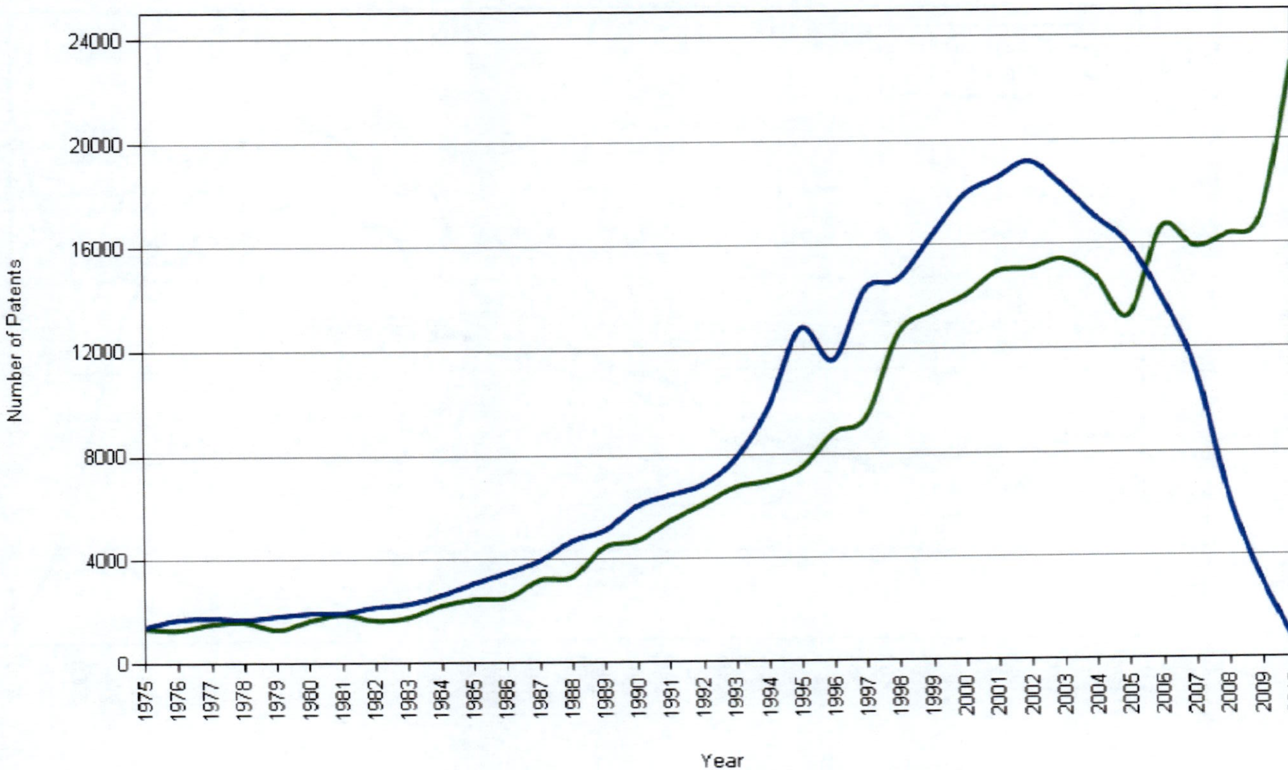

Patents filed vs patents granted to women.

2. Patents Filed versus Patents Granted to Men – 1975-2010

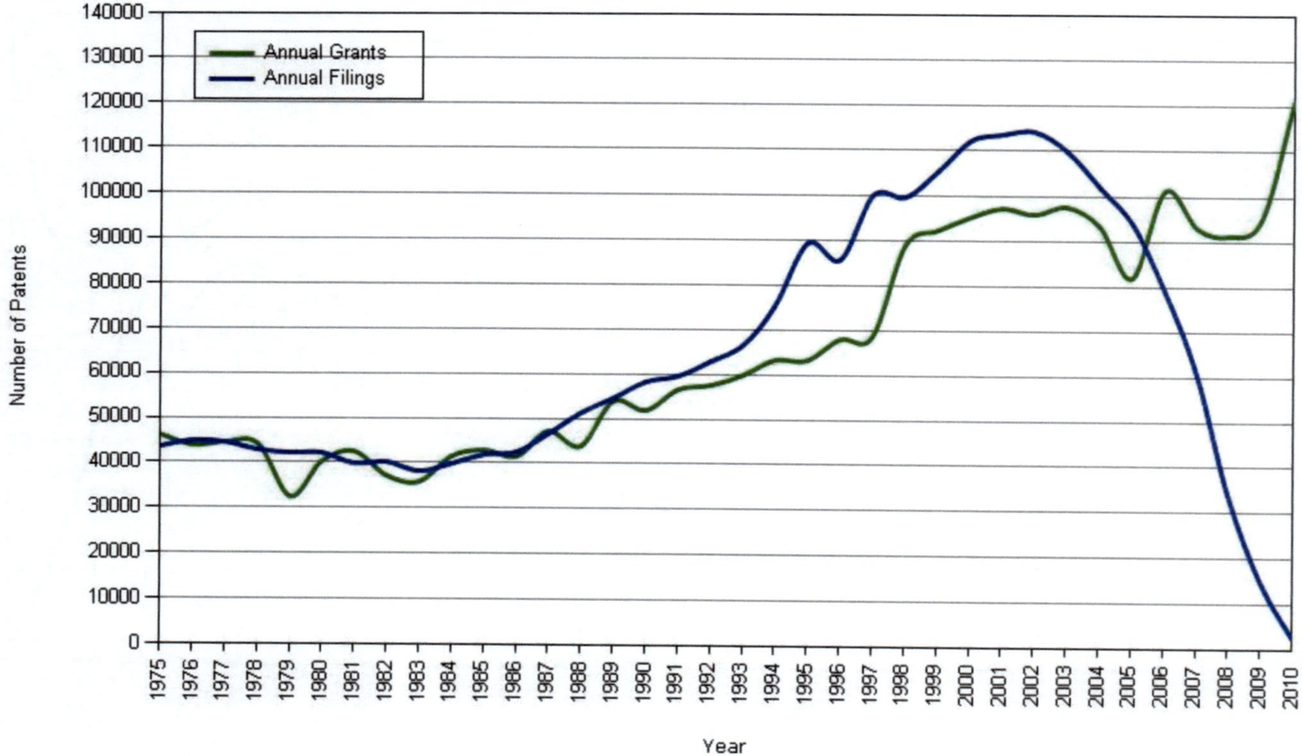

Patents filed vs patents granted to men.

3. % Successful Women Patent Applicants/% Successful Men Patent Applicants, 1975-2002

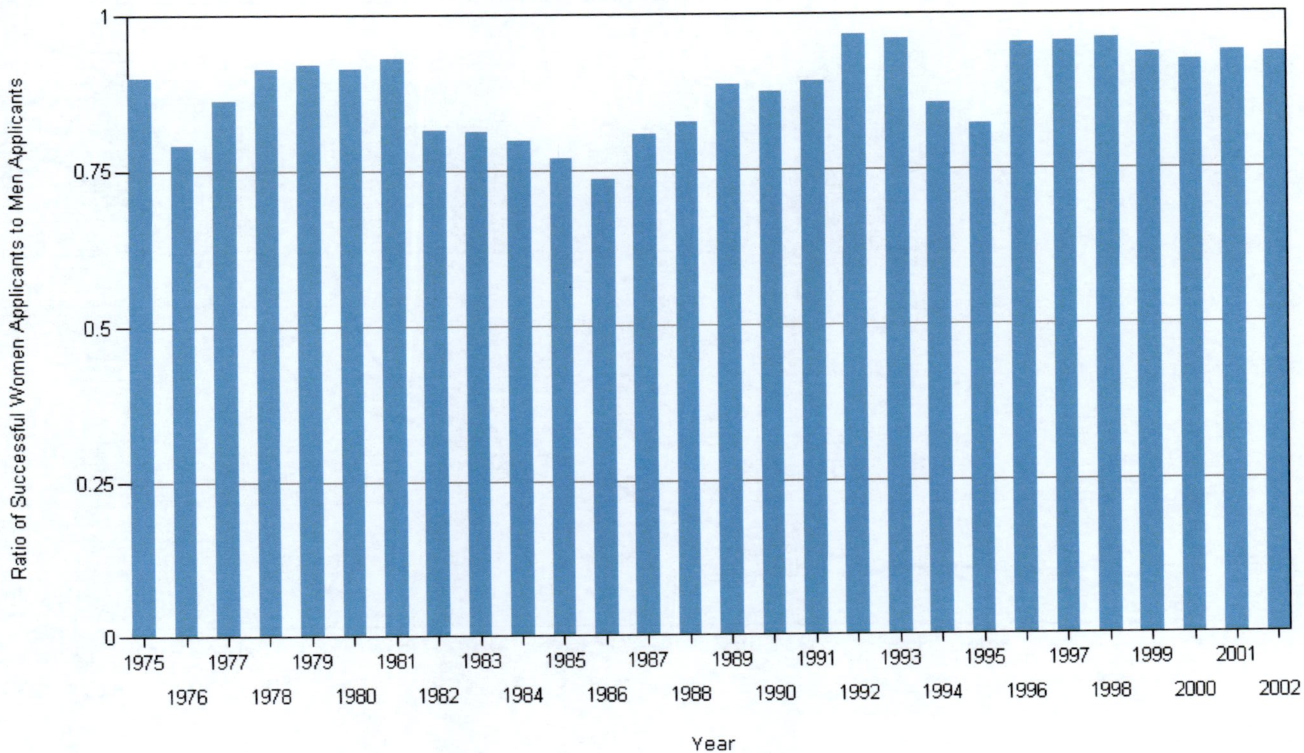

% Successful Women Patent Applicants/% Successful Men Patent Applicants.

4. Patents Filed versus Patents Granted to Women - 1975-2002

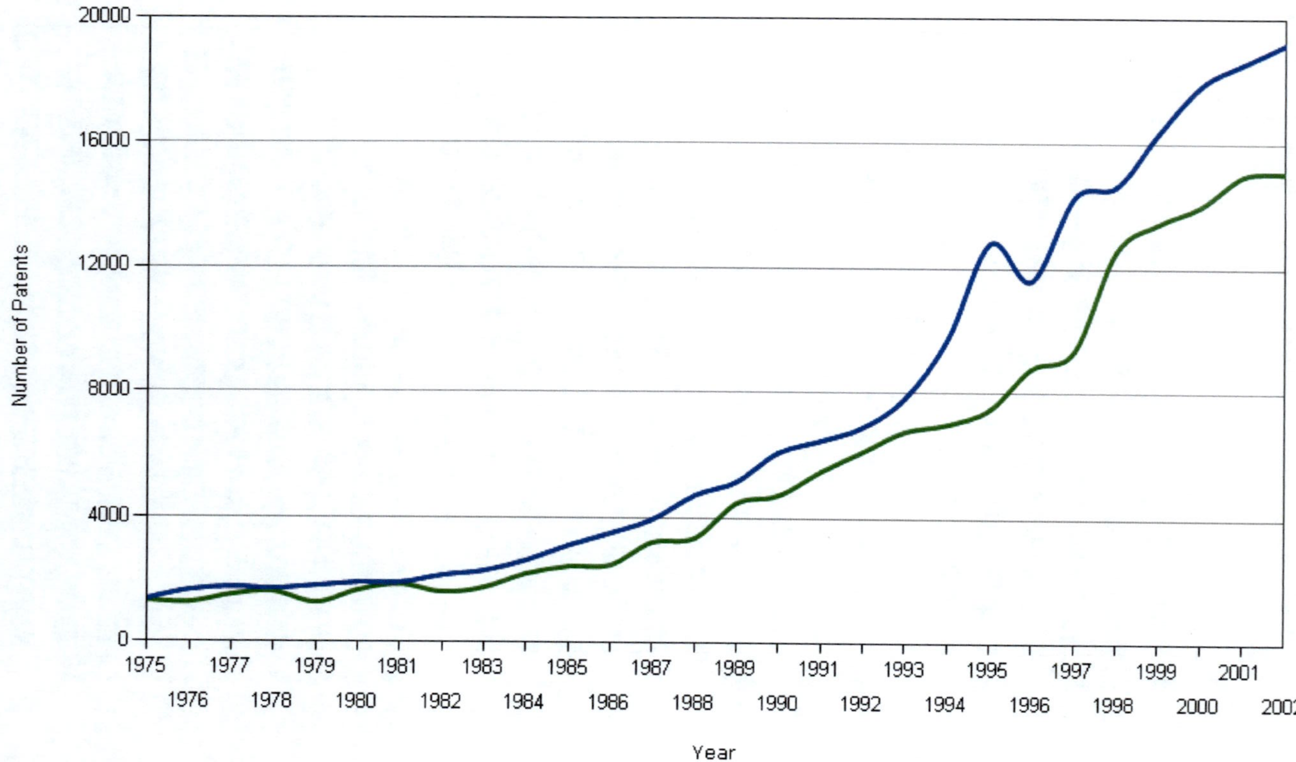

Patents filed vs patents granted to women.

5. Patents Filed versus Patents Granted to Men - 1975-2002

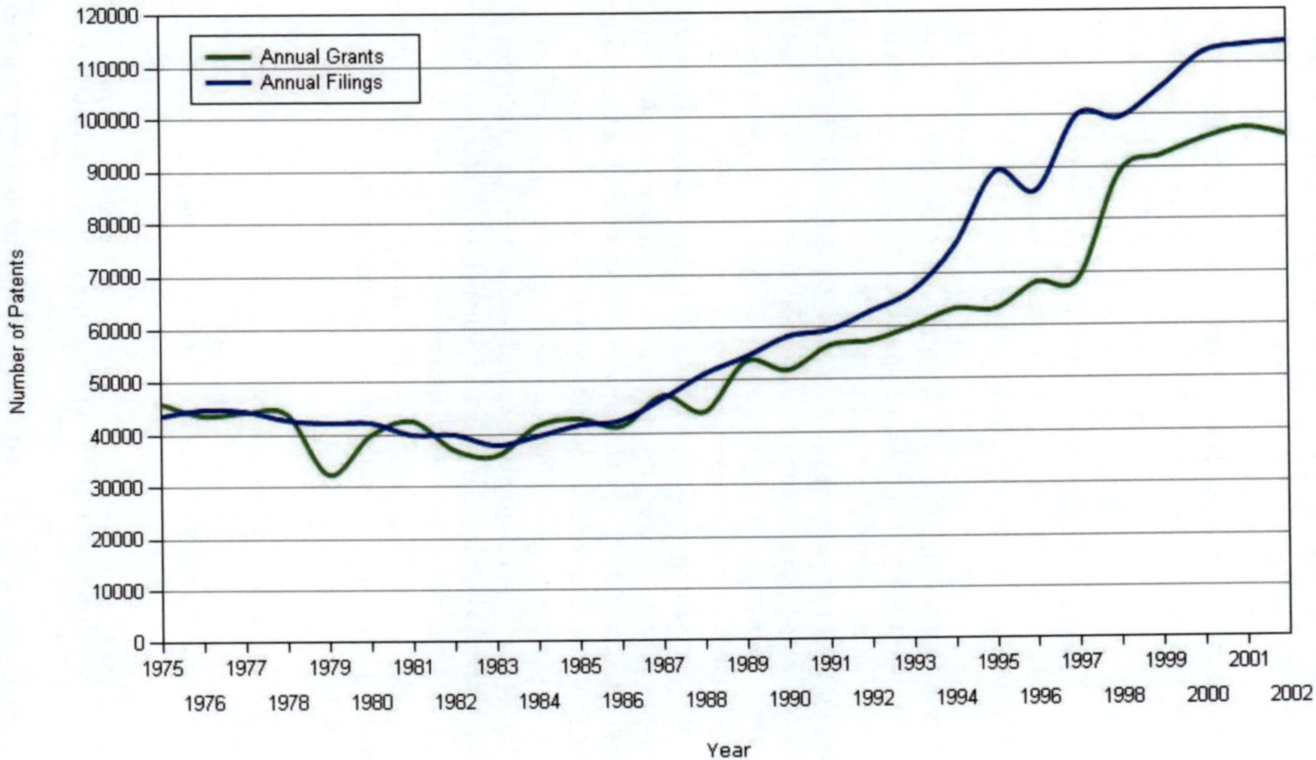

Patents filed vs patents granted to men.

2.6. Conclusions-Patents Data Analysis

Several significant conclusions may be drawn from the quantitative study on patents:

1. The number of patents granted to women are significantly higher than those reported in earlier studies [1, 2].
2. The number of patents granted to women is increasing at an accelerating pace.
3. There was a noticeable jump in the number of patents granted in the year 2010. The number of patents granted to women increased by approximately 34.72% from 2009 to 2010.
   It is too early to draw a definite conclusion from the recent yearly jump in the grant of patents. Some of these patents might have been filed years earlier. The results may also reflect the USPTO's focus on increasing efficiency and productivity in order to reduce the backlog of applications. Notwithstanding these reservations, there is a definite increase in the participation of women in U.S. patent activity in recent years. Several questions present themselves: Why is there a noticeable jump in patent activity in the midst of a continuing, prolonged recession? Is it a reflection of more women becoming entrepreneurs? Does it reflect increasing investment by U.S. companies in R&D (which is not supported by macro-economic data)? Does it reflect an increasing awareness by women of the benefits of patent protection? Does it show increasing participation in patent activity by recent immigrants? Are the standards for granting of patents more lenient now as compared to those thirty years ago? These are issues worth investigating.
4. In the same period (2009 to 2010), the number of primary patents granted to women increased by 28.57% and the number of non-primary patents granted to women increased by 38.23%.
5. The highest sustained rate of increase in the grant of U.S. patents to women was in the 1986-1993 period.
6. The slowest rate of increase in patents granted to women was in the 1999-2006 period. A relevant question here would be: Does a reduction in IP activity presage an economic downturn, and if so, what is the degree of correlation between the two? Similarly, does resurgence in IP activity presage economic expansion, and if so, what is the correlation between the two? The technology sector is only one

element in the macro-economic picture. So, there would be secondary and tertiary effects involved.

7. The total number of patents obtained by women shows an accelerating rate of increase with time. Similarly, there is an accelerating rate at which women become primary inventors as judged by the first name on a patent disclosure. This shows increasing leadership of women in R&D activity.
8. 19.77% of all patents by men were unassigned as compared to 29.41% for women.

   Together, these results suggest a slight difference between men and women in independent entrepreneurship: women are more likely to be independent entrepreneurs and keep their patents unassigned while men are more likely to be leading the research in businesses and corporations.

3.0. Analysis of Trademarks

3.1. The Data

Trademark data files were obtained from http://www.google.com/googlebooks/uspto- trademarks.html

3.2. Data Preparation

The USPTO data was approximately 151.3 GB in size, and it required a substantial amount of programming. The processing was optimized 3 times, each time using a different XML parsing technology:

- The first processing used a DOM parser as we needed to read forward and backward in the XML file.
- In the second processing, we used a SAX parser.
- In the third processing, we used a modified SAX parser.

The modified SAX parser had a substantial performance benefit whereby we were able to process each 1GB of raw data in approx. 30 seconds. Additionally, huge performance gains were obtained by switching to a single pass, read forward only approach. As we also required the ability to read backwards, we updated our parsing application to maintain state in the application layer. This provided the best of both worlds in terms of performance and state.

1. 30 seconds of CPU time per 1 GB of XML data
2. Approx. 151.3 GB of raw XML from the USPTO was reduced to 7 GB of data which was imported into the database.

Importantly, we changed some data types as this optimized the file size. As a simple example, Boolean values were changed from True/False to 1/0, which reduced the data size.

Once the data was processed, it had to be loaded into the database. Here too we optimized significantly. Initially, we connected directly to the database within the parsing application. This provided the benefit of eliminating an intermediate step and eliminating the need for an intermediate file format. However, we eventually settled on using an export of the data to an import ready file format (which added the intermediate step back into our process), but provided the following benefits: (1) reducing data loads to a matter of seconds for each gigabyte of data, and (2) providing atomic commits at a batch level. The batch level atomic commits are critical as they enabled us to ensure data quality at a higher level, and we were able to use this assurance to add new data quality checks.

Data quality was an important driver in this work.

1. We created a "self-destruct" mechanism in the parser whereby an error in the input file (raw XML) would cause the parser to exit without saving its work. This is important as it ensures that each data load file is accurate.
2. Next, we added a file origin marker within the data load file, and within the database. This "origin" marker allows us to track each data point back to its original file.
3. Next, we added data quality checks using the origin markers. Essentially, the parser is able to provide frequencies within the XML file which can be compared against frequencies in the database.
    a. These frequency checks allow us to verify that the data in the raw USPTO XML files was loaded perfectly into the relational database. (i.e., we can verify data input quality).

b. Importantly, the vast improvements in performance as listed above made this possible within reasonable time frames.

3.3. Data Processing

The XML files were processed to extract the Trademarks data and loaded into a data warehouse. There were many duplicates in the USPTO database as the entries for the same trademarks had been made multiple times.

- First, the data was filtered to consider only trademark applicants in the US.
- Next, filters were applied to exclude all data other than data pertaining to trademarks filed by individuals and sole proprietorship businesses (LegalEntityTypeCodes 1 and 19).
- Multiple passes were made through the records in order to extract the first name from the trademark applicant's name. This required complex and repetitive querying as the names in the USPTO database have not been saved in any well defined format.

3.4. Gender Assignment

The applicants were marked as men or women following the same procedure as in the case of patents, outlined in Section 2.5.5. First the lists for the 10,000 most common names for boys and the 10,000 most common names for girls were used to assign gender to exclusive male and female names. A formula (the same as in the case of patents) was used to allocate gender for the common names. Various name lists were used to assign gender to the remaining names followed by allocating the yet unassigned names based on the male female ratio in the database.

3.5. Analysis

The data was then used to generate the attached reports. The period 1980-2010 was used as the base period as the data for the years 1976-1979 was meager and the data for the year 2011 was as yet incomplete.

1. Trademark Applications Filed by Year

Trademark applications show a spike just prior to Y2K; however, trademark applications have fallen from a high of 49,256 in 2007 to 42,950 in 2009, a drop of 12.8% reflecting the onset of a recession.

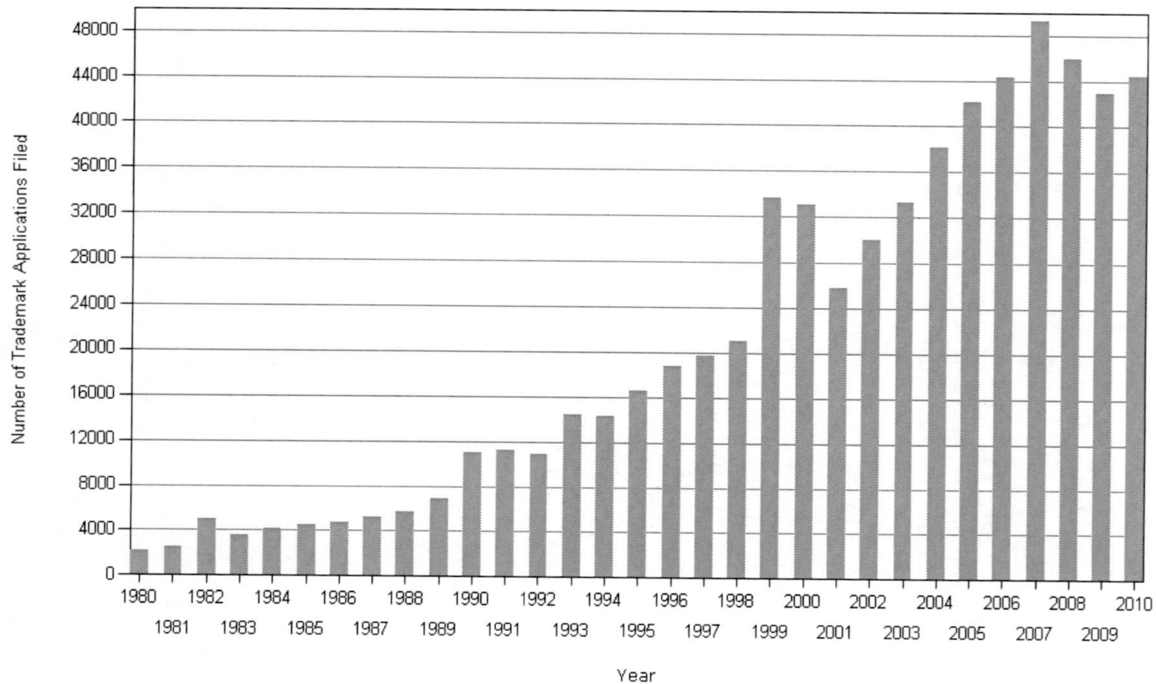

Trademark applications filed by year.

2. Trademark Applications Filed by Women by Year

Trademark applications filed by women show a cadence similar to the total number of trademarks filed. There is a spike just prior to Y2K. At the onset of the recession, they drop off, from a high of 14,353 in 2007 to a low of 12,604 in 2009, a drop of 12.19%.

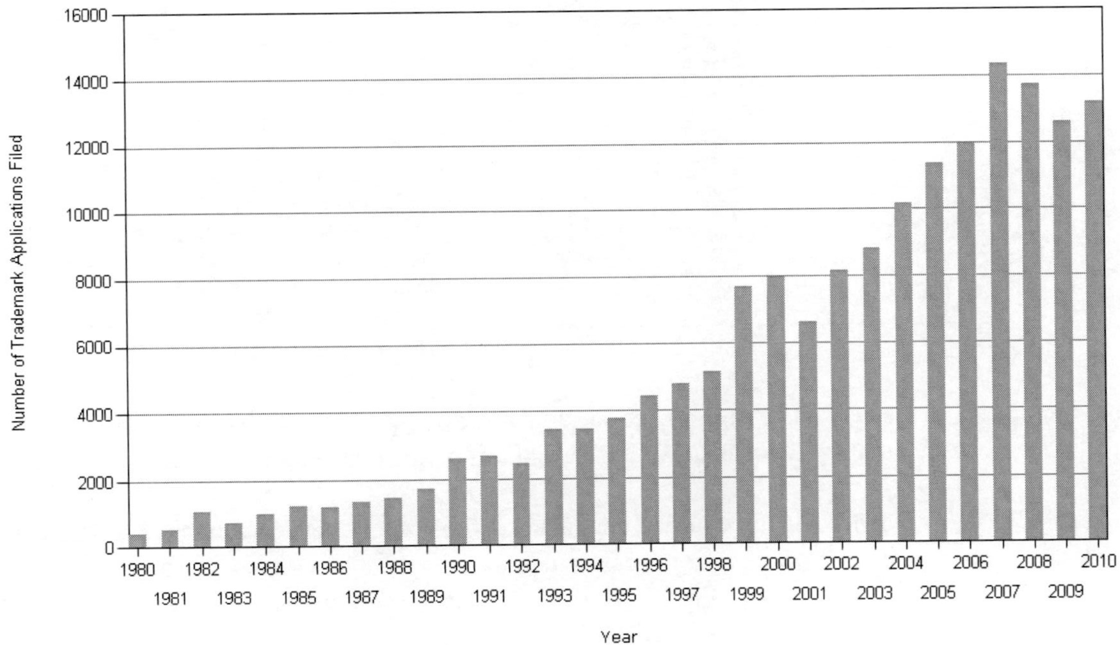

Trademark applications filed by women by year.

3. *Trademark Applications Filed by Men by Year*

Trademark applications by men show a cadence similar to those for the total trademarks and those for women. The number of trademark applications by men shows a drop from a high of 34,063 in 2007 to a low of 29,807 in 2009, a drop of 12.5%.

The sum of the numbers for the trademarks filed for men and for women shows a slight variance from the total number of trademarks filed due to processing errors; the interrogation for each of these categories was carried out independent of the other.

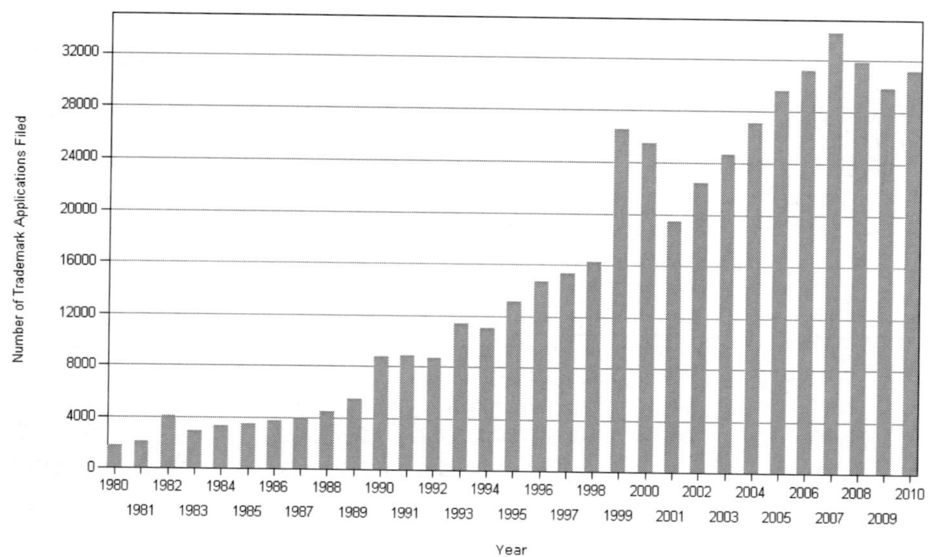

Trademark applications filed by men by year.

4. Total Trademarks Granted by Year

The total number of trademarks granted shows a steady, albeit uneven climb over the last three decades. Taking the year 1985 as a baseline, the number of trademarks granted has increased from 4,268 in 1985 to 23,709 in 2007. There is a recent drop to a low of 20,547 in 2010 due perhaps to the recession. No attempt has been made to correlate the number of trademarks granted to the periods of economic expansion and contraction. This would be a worthwhile subject for future research.

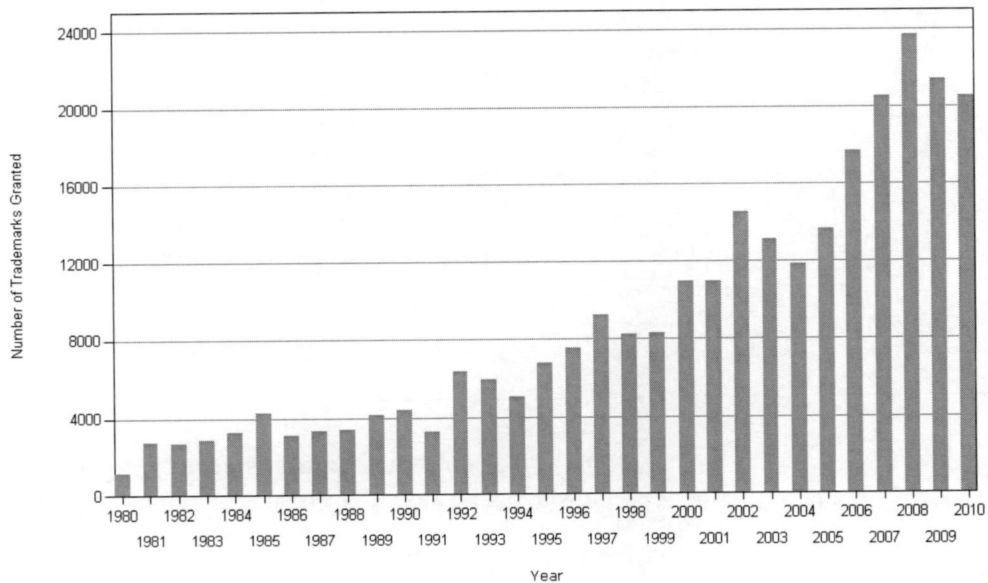

Total trademarks granted by year.

5. Trademarks Granted to Women by Year

Trademarks granted to women entrepreneurs follow a pattern similar to those of total trademarks. They increase from 1,077 in 1985 to a high of 7,274 in 2008. There is a drop off to 6,533 in 2010.

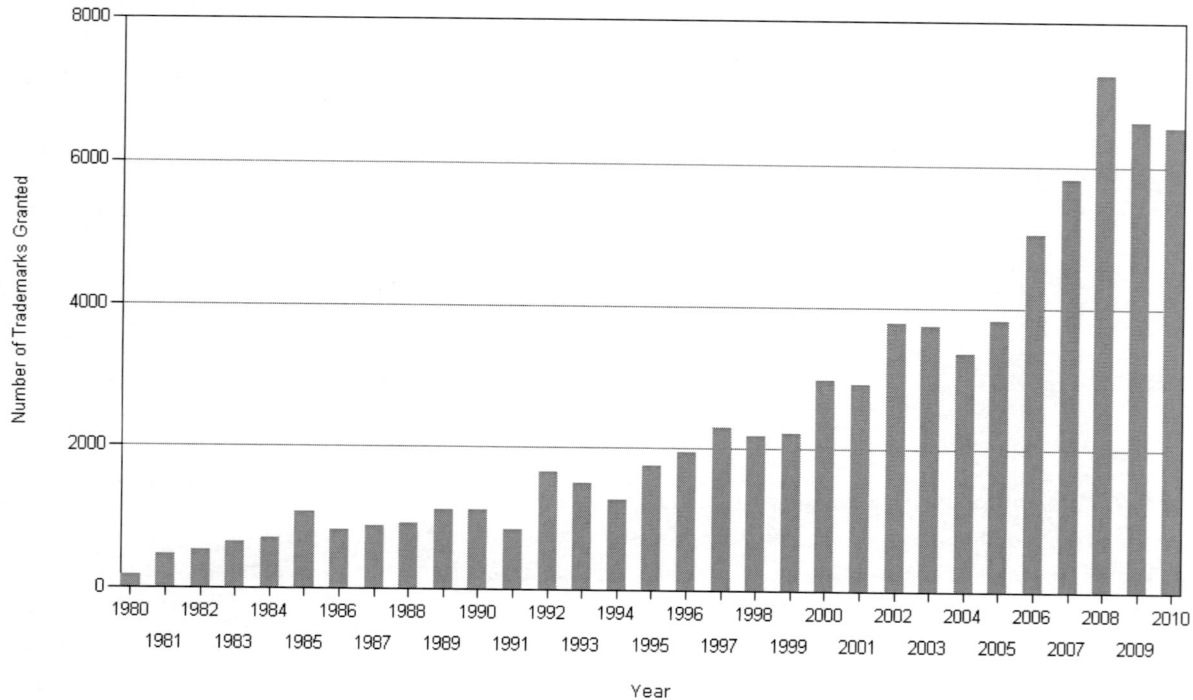

Trademarks granted to women by year.

6. Trademarks Granted to Men by Year

Trademarks granted to men follow a similar pattern. They increase from 3,328 to a high of 16,074 in 2008. There is a drop off to 13,881 in 2010.

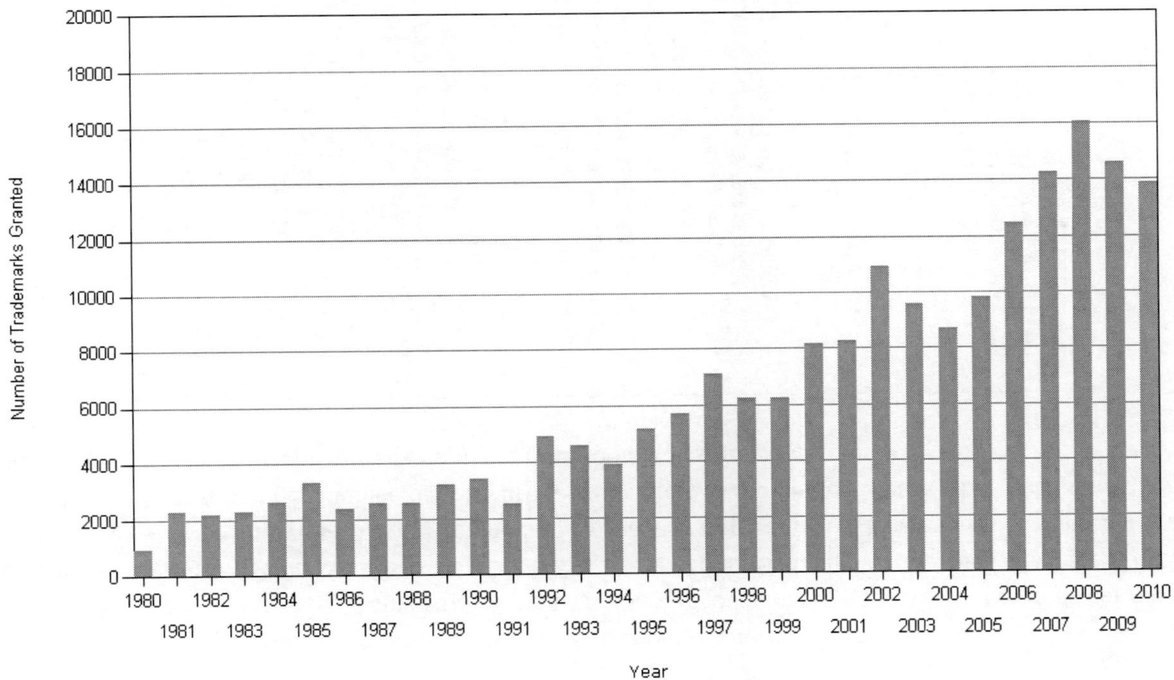

Trademarks granted to men by year.

7. Trademarks Granted to Women – Share of Total Trademarks Granted to Individuals

One of the most significant results of this study is that the share of trademarks granted to women has climbed steadily over the last three decades. In 1985, 25.25% of all trademarks granted to individuals were granted to women. In 2010, fully a third of all trademarks to individuals were granted to women entrepreneurs. Clearly, women entrepreneurs are an increasingly important constituent of intellectual property development in the United States. The educational, demographic and institutional factors that influence this development need to be investigated in future research.

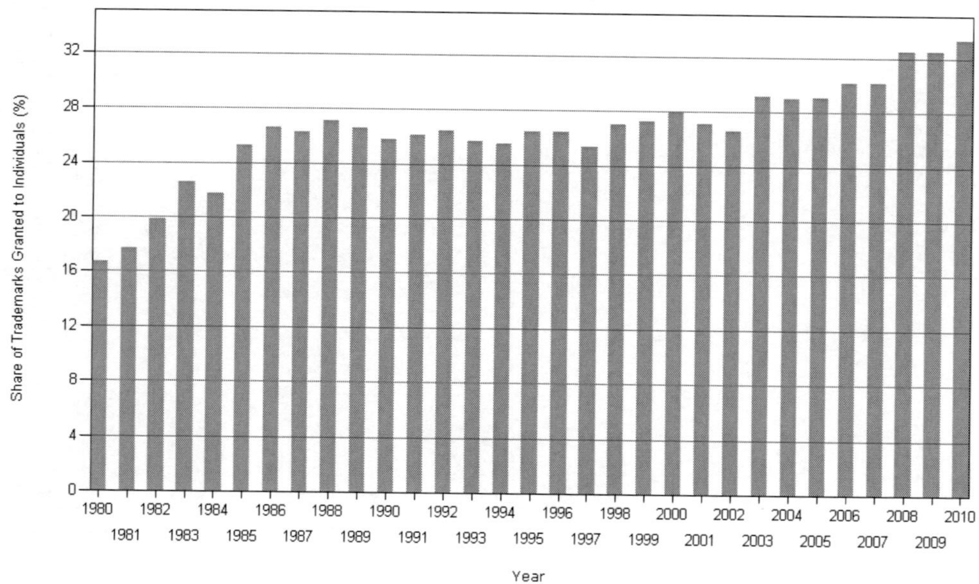

Trademarks granted to women – Share of total trademarks granted to individuals.

8. Trademarks Granted to Men – Share of Total Trademarks Granted to Individuals

Corresponding with an increase in the share of trademarks granted to women, there has been a decrease in the share of trademarks granted to men. In 1985, men entrepreneurs accounted for 78.03% of all trademarks granted to individuals. In 2010, this dropped to 70.78%.

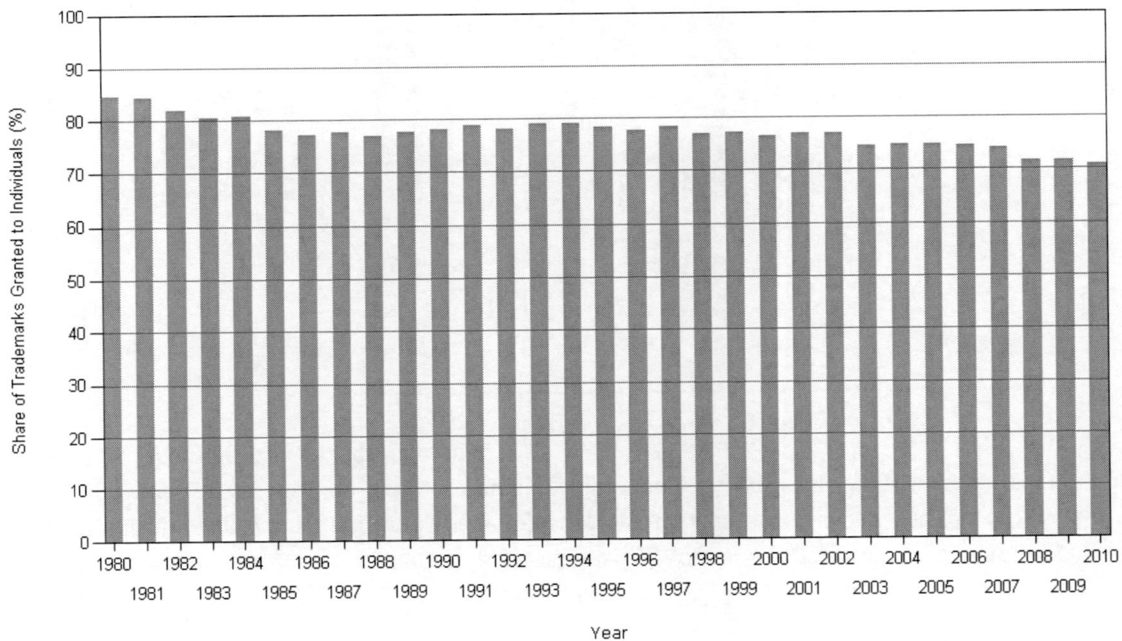

Trademarks granted to men – Share of total trademarks granted to individuals.

9. Successful Women Trademark Applications %/Successful Men Trademark Applications %

An analysis of the ratio of successful trademark applications by women to successful trademark applications by men shows no consistent bias in the processing of trademark applications. This ratio consistently hovers around 1.0, although for a period of about 12 years, from 1988 to 2000, women entrepreneurs showed greater resilience in pursuing trademark protection than men and the ratio was greater than 1.0.

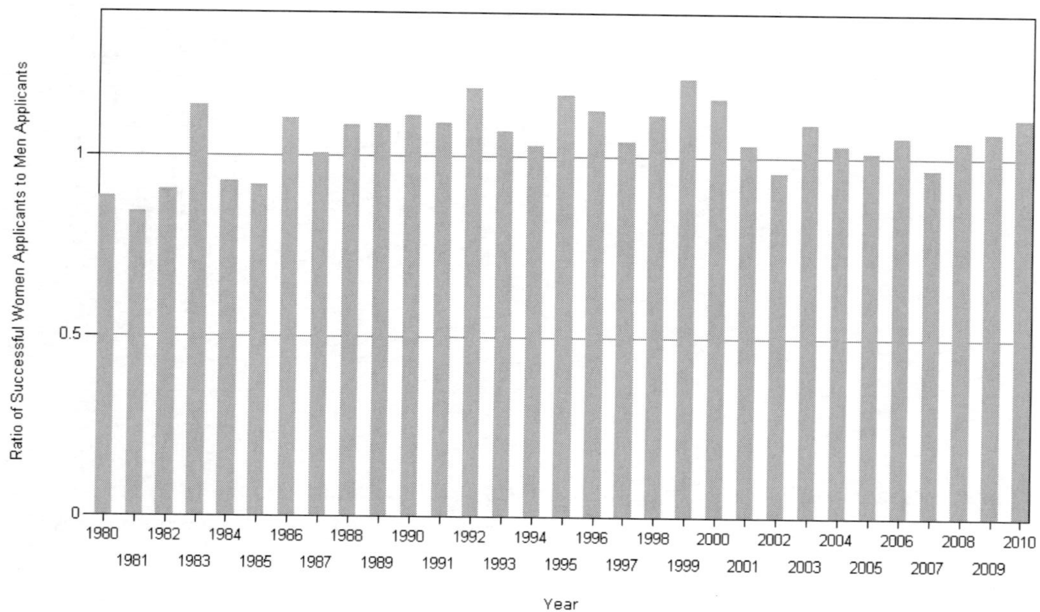

Successful women trademark applications %/Successful men trademark applications %.

10. Trademarks Granted to Women – Share of Applications Filed by Women

An analysis of the ratio of trademarks granted to trademark applications filed shows that it is increasingly more difficult to obtain a trademark from the USPTO. In 1985, 88.28% of all women applicants were successful in obtaining trademark protection. In 2010 it dropped to 49.6%.

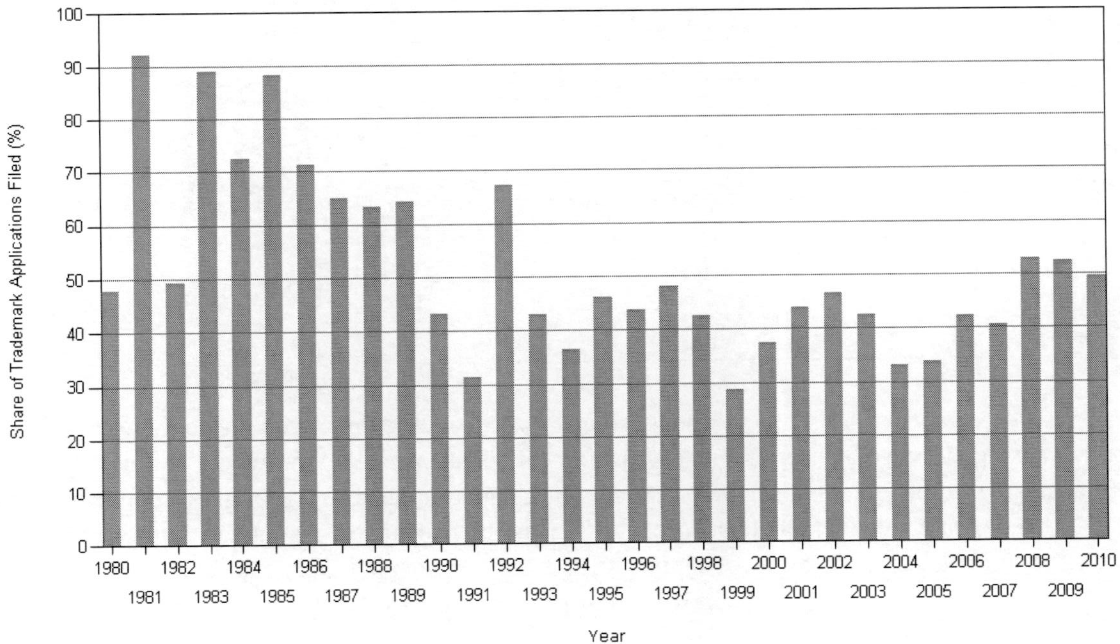

Trademarks granted to women – Share of applications filed by women.

11. Trademarks Granted to Men – Share of Applications Filed by Men

The pattern of success in obtaining a trademark for men is similar to those for women. In 1985, 96.18% of men applicants were successful in obtaining a trademark. The success rate dropped to 44.63 percent in 2010.

The drop in the success rate of both men and women in obtaining trademark protection may indicate the effect of a change in rules governing the award of a trademark, or it may be a sign of increased willingness on the part of entrepreneurs to file for trademark protection despite the risk of rejection.

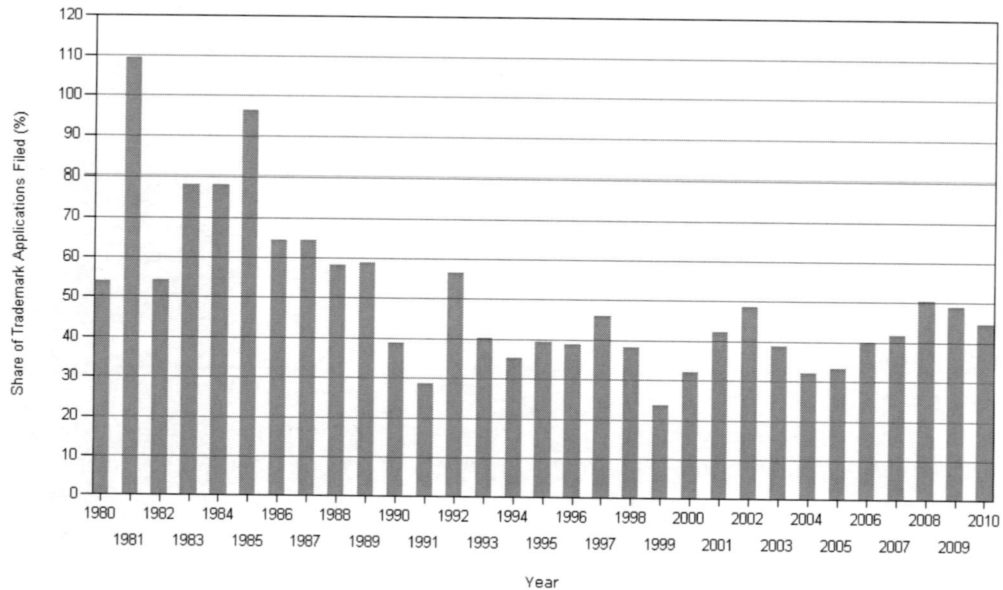

Trademarks granted to men – Share of applications filed by men.

12. Trademarks Granted to Women – Share of Trademarks Granted to Men

The ratio of trademarks granted to women entrepreneurs as measured by a percentage of trademarks granted to men is very revealing. In 1985 this ratio was 32.36%. This ratio has steadily climbed to 47.06% in 2010. Women entrepreneurs account for fully a third of all trademarks currently granted in the United States showing the resilience and dynamism of this section of the work force.

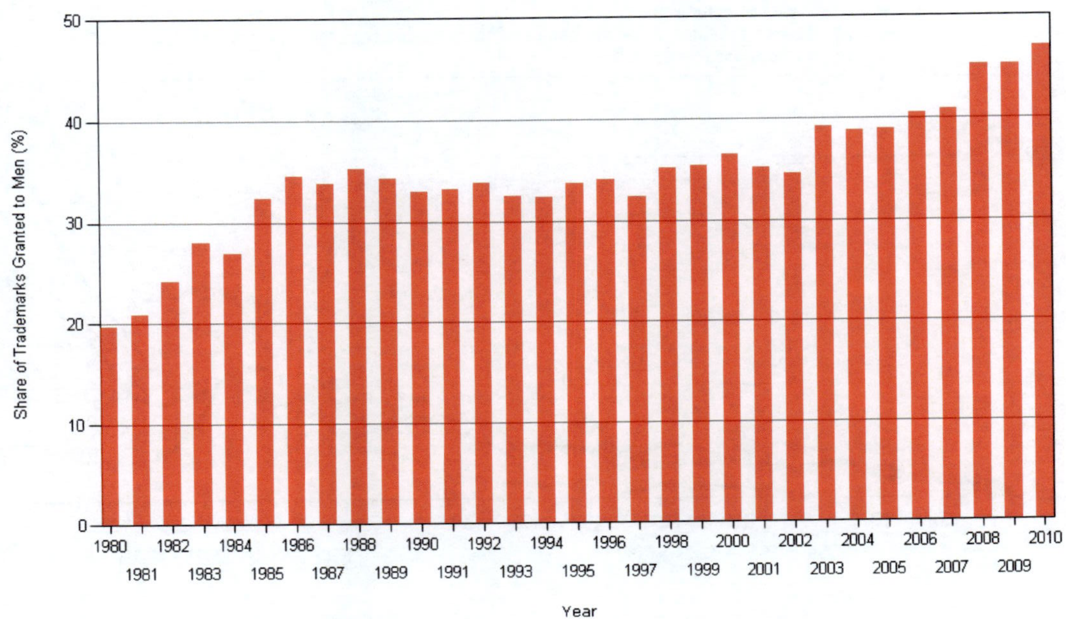

Trademarks granted to women – Share of trademarks granted to men.

13. Trademarks Granted to Women by Industry (Top 5 Industries)

The Trademarks data was probed to determine the industries with the highest participation by women entrepreneurs. The top five industries with the highest participation in trademark activity by women were:

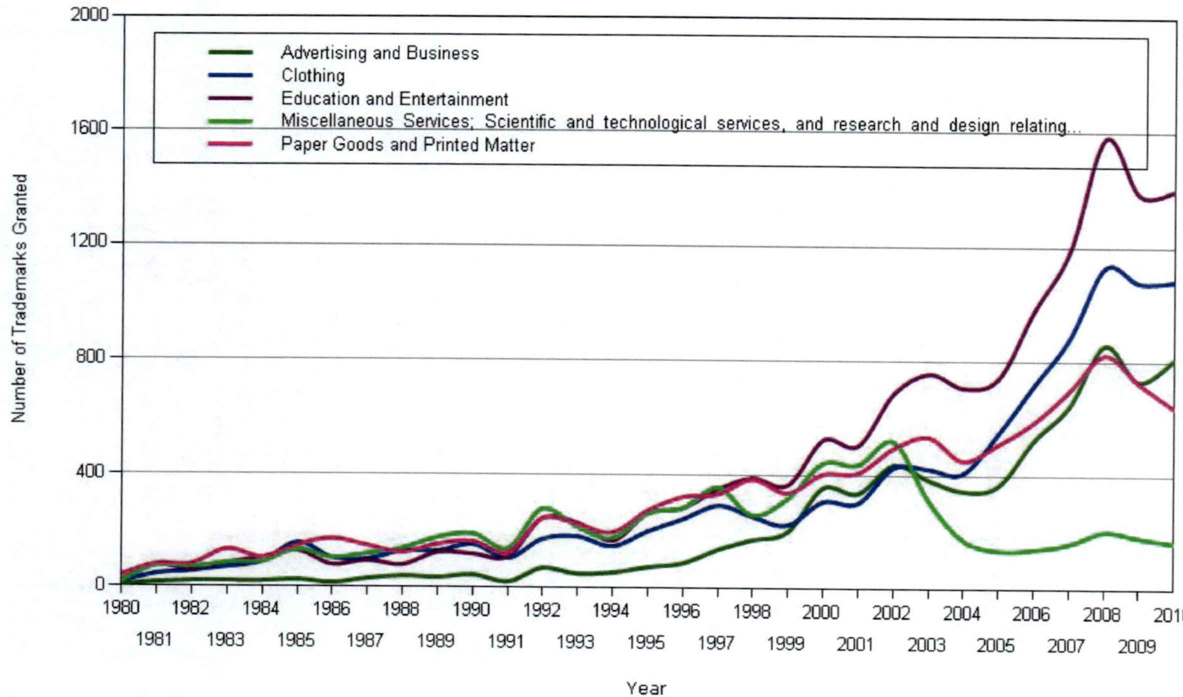

Trademarks granted to women by industry (top 5 industries).

- Advertising and Business
- Clothing
- Education and Entertainment
- Miscellaneous Services- Scientific and Technological Services and Design
- Paper Goods and Printed Matter

The emergence of Scientific and Technological Services among the top 5 contributors to trademark activity by women is of particular significance as it shows the increasing penetration of women entrepreneurs in this field.

Further research is required to probe whether this concentration is due to demographic reasons, employment or other factors.

14. Trademarks Granted Annually – Individuals vs. Businesses

The data was probed to determine how entrepreneurship influences the pursuit of trademark protection. The number of trademarks granted to individuals was separated from those granted to sole proprietorship businesses. The analysis showed an overwhelming number of trademarks were granted to individuals as determined by their filing. In 2010, only 4.8% of trademarks were awarded to sole proprietorship businesses.

As to why this is so is also a possible area for further research.

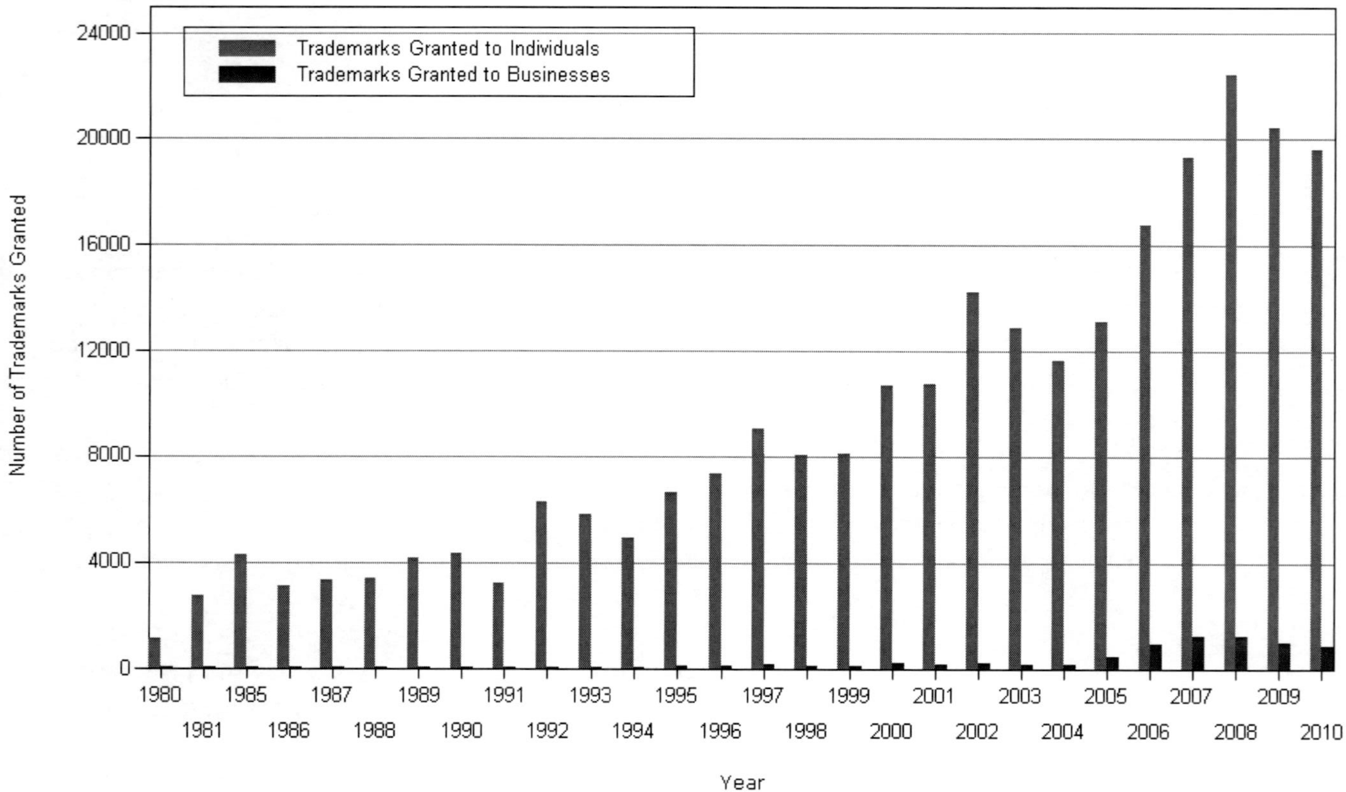

Trademarks granted annually – individuals vs. businesses.

3.6. Conclusions-Trademarks Data Analysis

1. The participation of women in Trademarks activity as measured by the percentage of Trademarks granted has more than doubled from 1980 to 2010, from approximately 16.5% in 1980 to more than 33% in 2010. Whether this increase is due to demographic reasons such as employment patterns, education, or a greater inclination on the part of women entrepreneurs to file for IP protection is a possible subject for further research.
2. Women have a significantly higher participation in Trademark activity as compared to Patent activity. For instance, whereas women received approximately 18% of all patents granted in the year 2010, the contribution of women to Trademark activity was more than 33%.
3. There is no statistically measurable difference in the proportion of successful women Trademark applications and successful men Trademark applications; there is no measurable bias in the processing of applications by women.
   Further research is required to probe whether gender differences in Trademark activity are more a reflection of employment patterns, demographics, risk and reward perception.
4. The results in this report reflect only the trademarks for U.S. based individuals and proprietorships wherein the first name is identified. Caution must be exercised in applying the results to the entire USPTO database on trademarks.

4.0. References

[1] *The Idea Commercialization Gap and Pink and Black*, Lisa D. Cook and Chaleampong Kongcharoen, November 14, 2009, Michigan State University.

[2] *Buttons to Biotech, 1996 Update Report, with supplement data through 1998*, U.S. Patents by Women, 1977 to 1996, United States Patents and Trademarks Office

APPENDIX 1

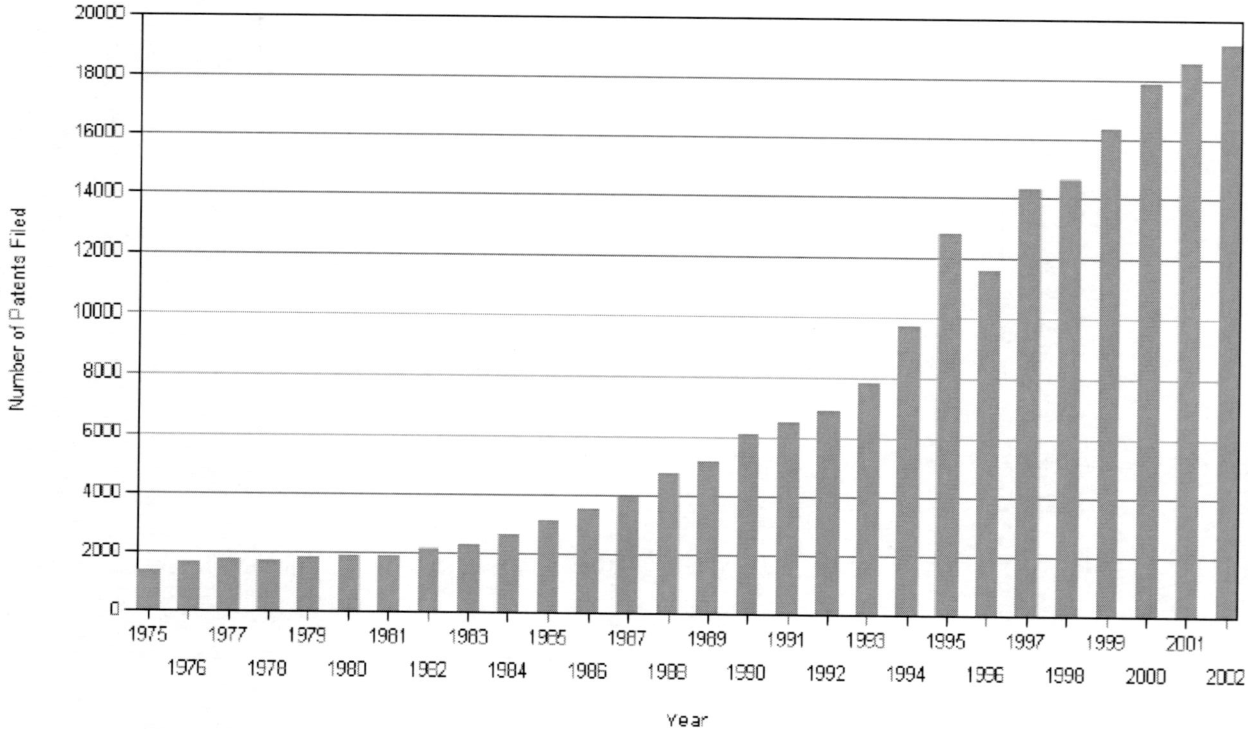

Annual U.S. Origin Patents Filed by Women, 1975-2002.

Figure 1. Patents Filed by Women – Annually (1975-2002).

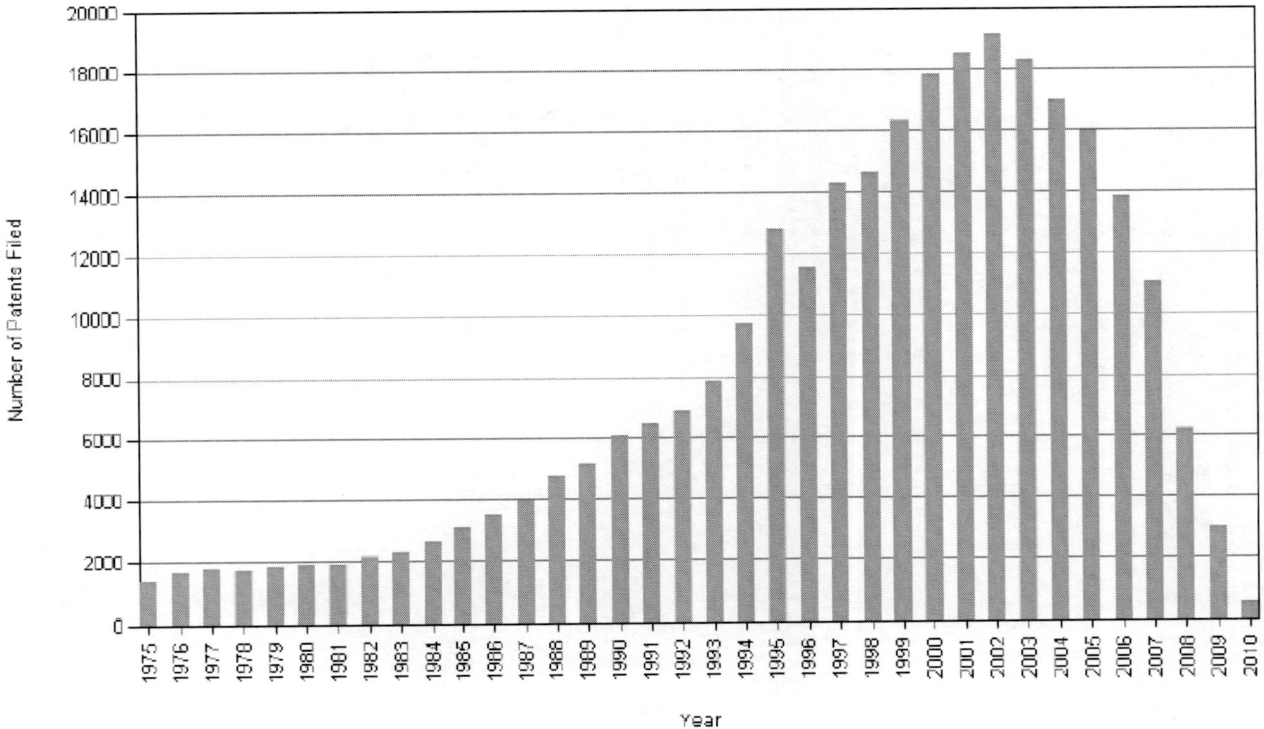

Annual U.S. Origin Patents Filed by Women, 1975-2010.

Note: The USPTO data for patents filed drops off after the year 2002. Apparently, the USPTO data, as reflected in the disc supplied to Delixus, is as yet incomplete.

Figure 2. Patents Filed by Women – Annually (1975-2010).

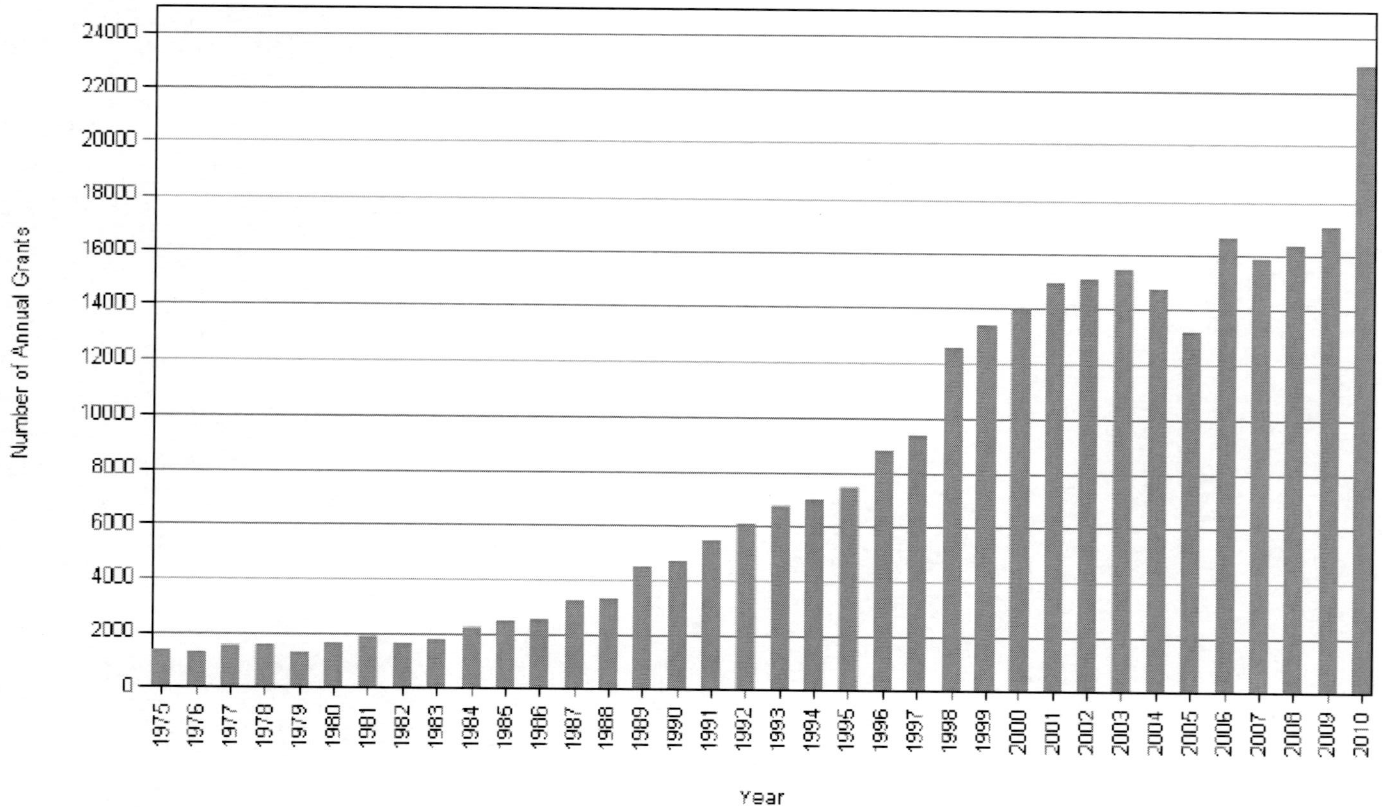

Annual Grants of U.S. Origin Woman-Inventor Patents, 1975-2010.

Figure 3. Patents Granted to Women – Annually.

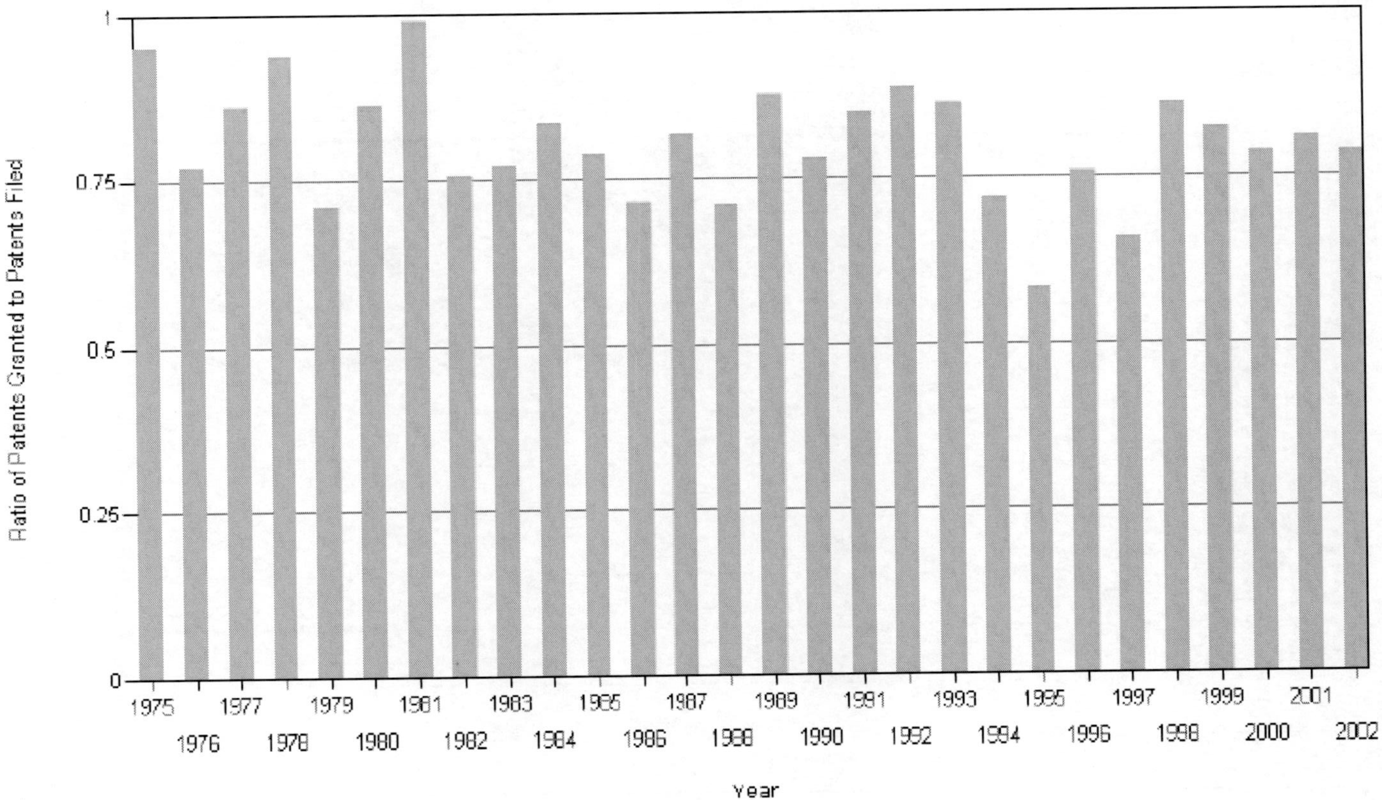

Ratio of Patents Granted to Women to Patents Filed by Women, 1975-2002.

Figure 4. Ratio of Patents Granted to Patents Filed by Women – Annually.

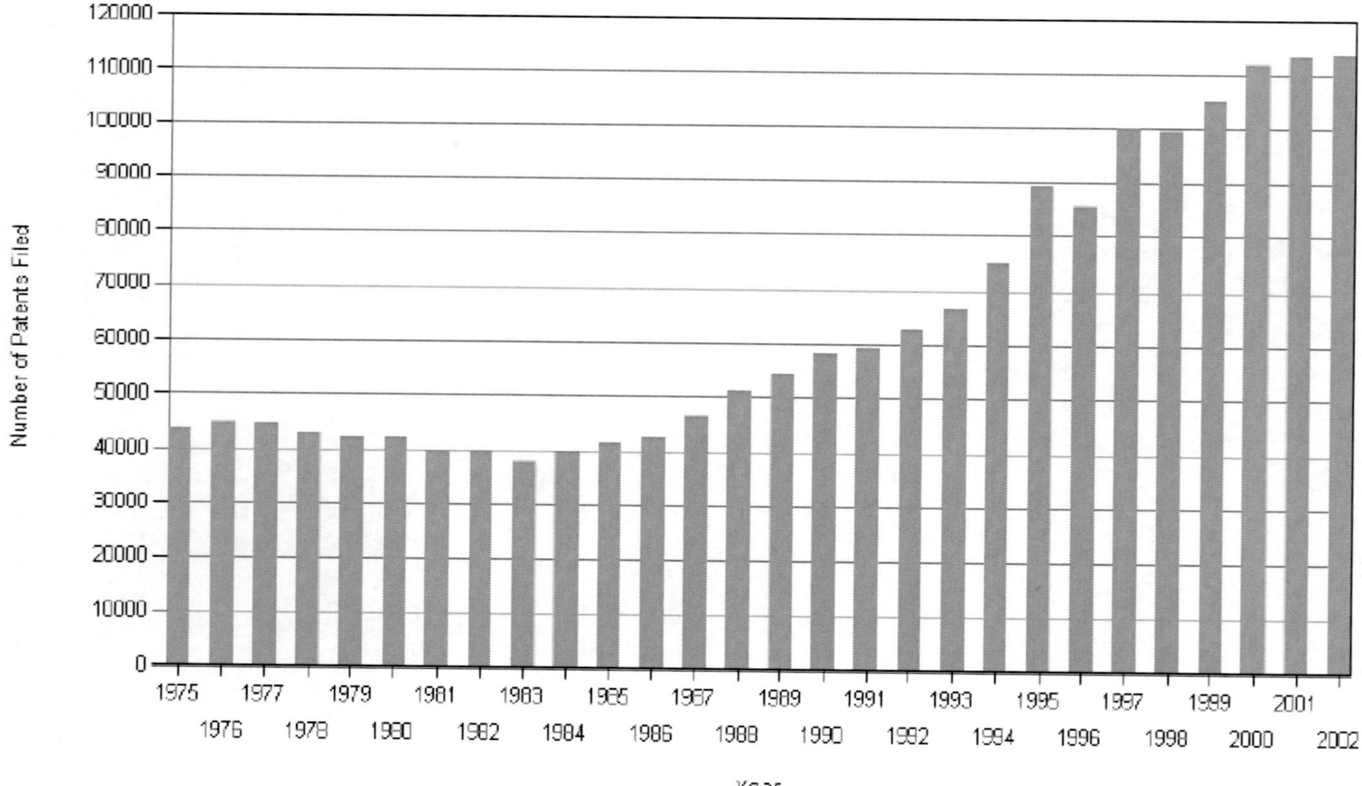

Annual U.S. Origin Patents Filed by Men, 1975-2002.

Figure 5. Patents Filed by Men – Annually (1975-2002).

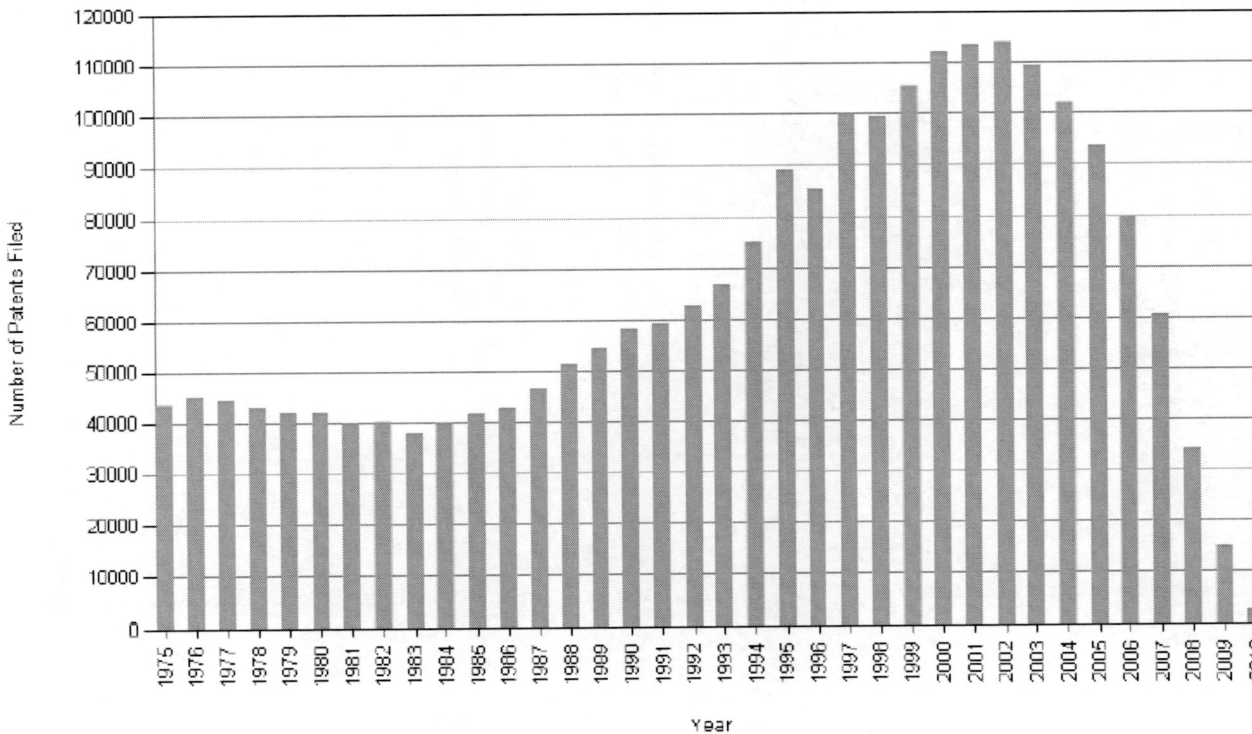

Annual U.S. Origin Patents Filed by Men, 1975-2010.

Note: The USPTO data for patents filed drops off after the year 2002. Apparently, the USPTO data, as reflected in the disc supplied to Delixus, is as yet incomplete.

Figure 6. Patents Filed by Men – Annually (1975-2010).

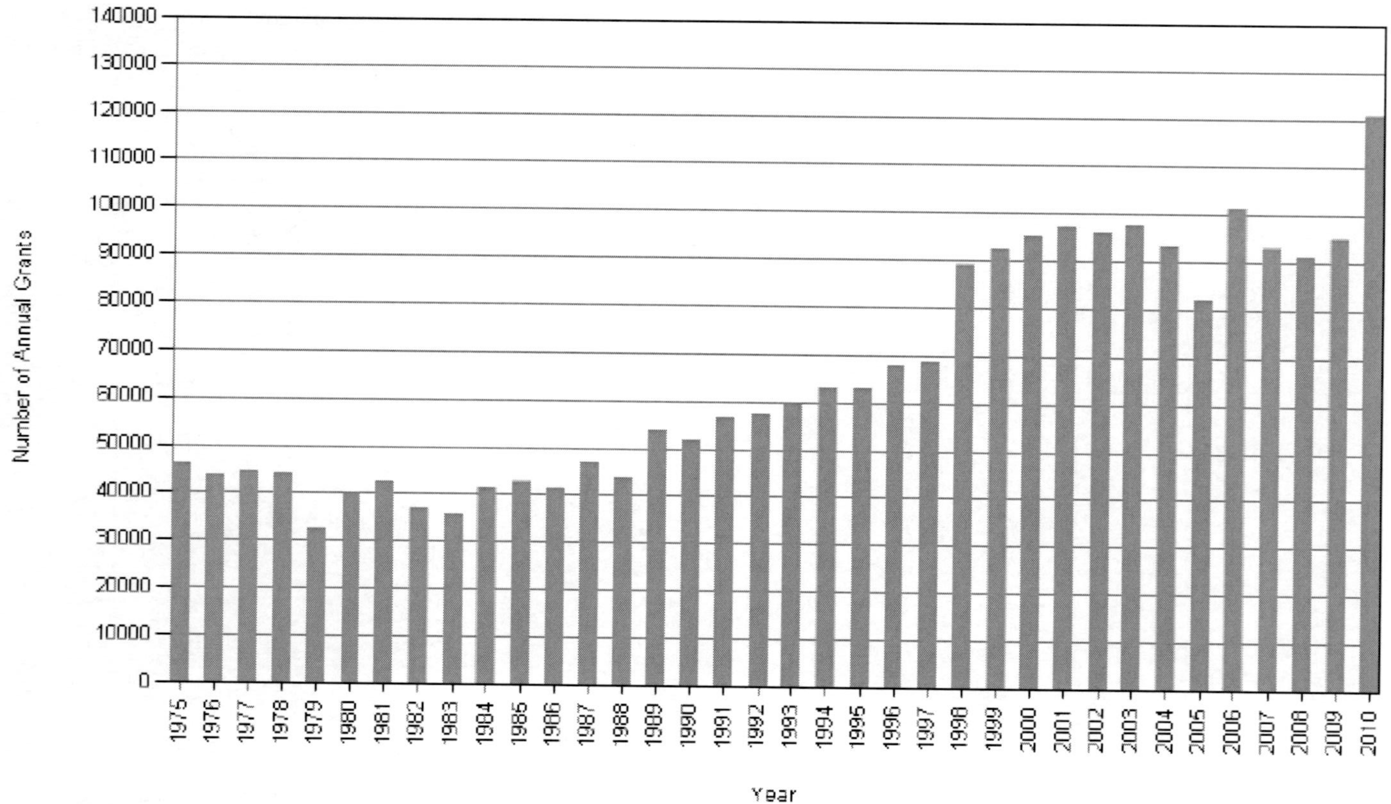

Annual Grants of U.S. Origin Man-Inventor Patents, 1975-2010.

Figure 7. Patents Granted to Men – Annually.

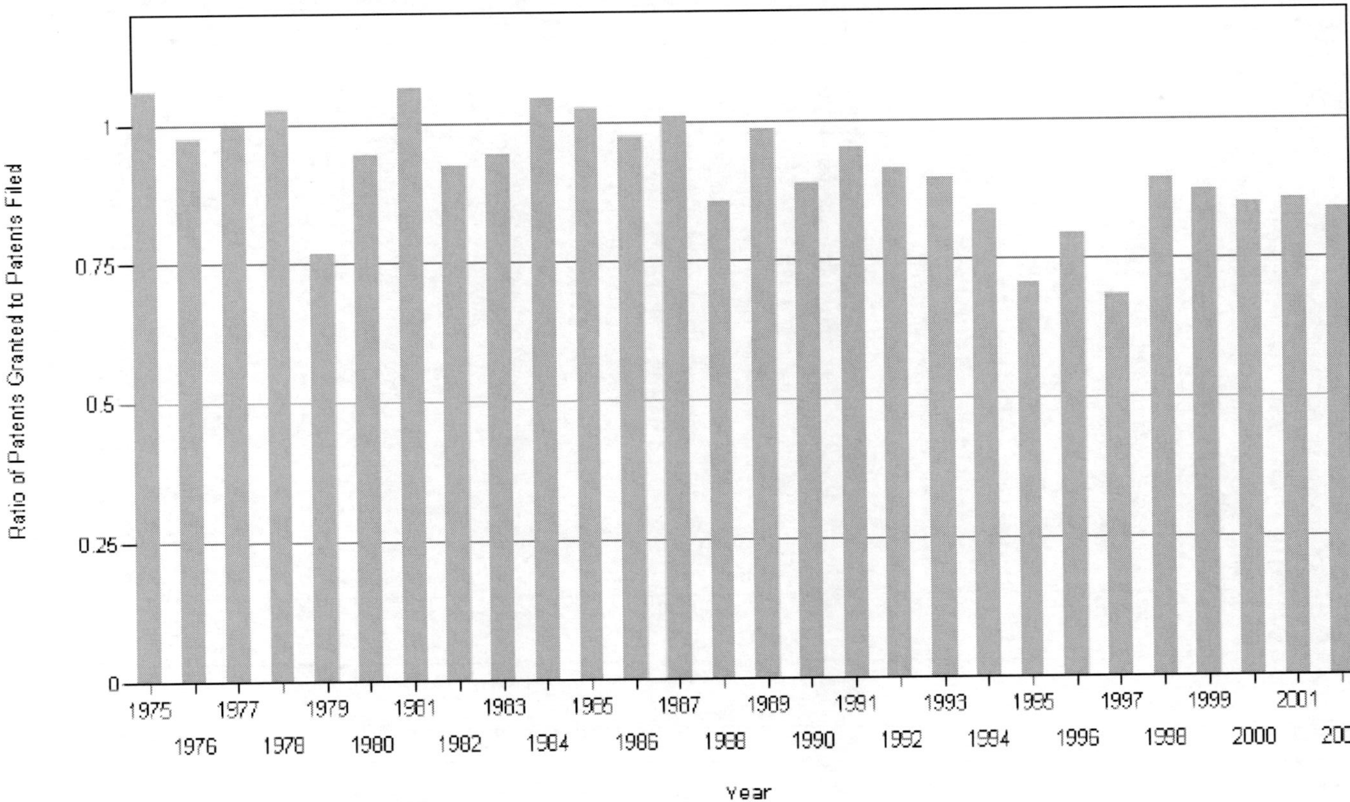

Ratio of Patents Granted to Men to Patents Filed by Men, 1975-2002.

Figure 8. Ratio of Patents Granted to Patents Filed by Men – Annually.

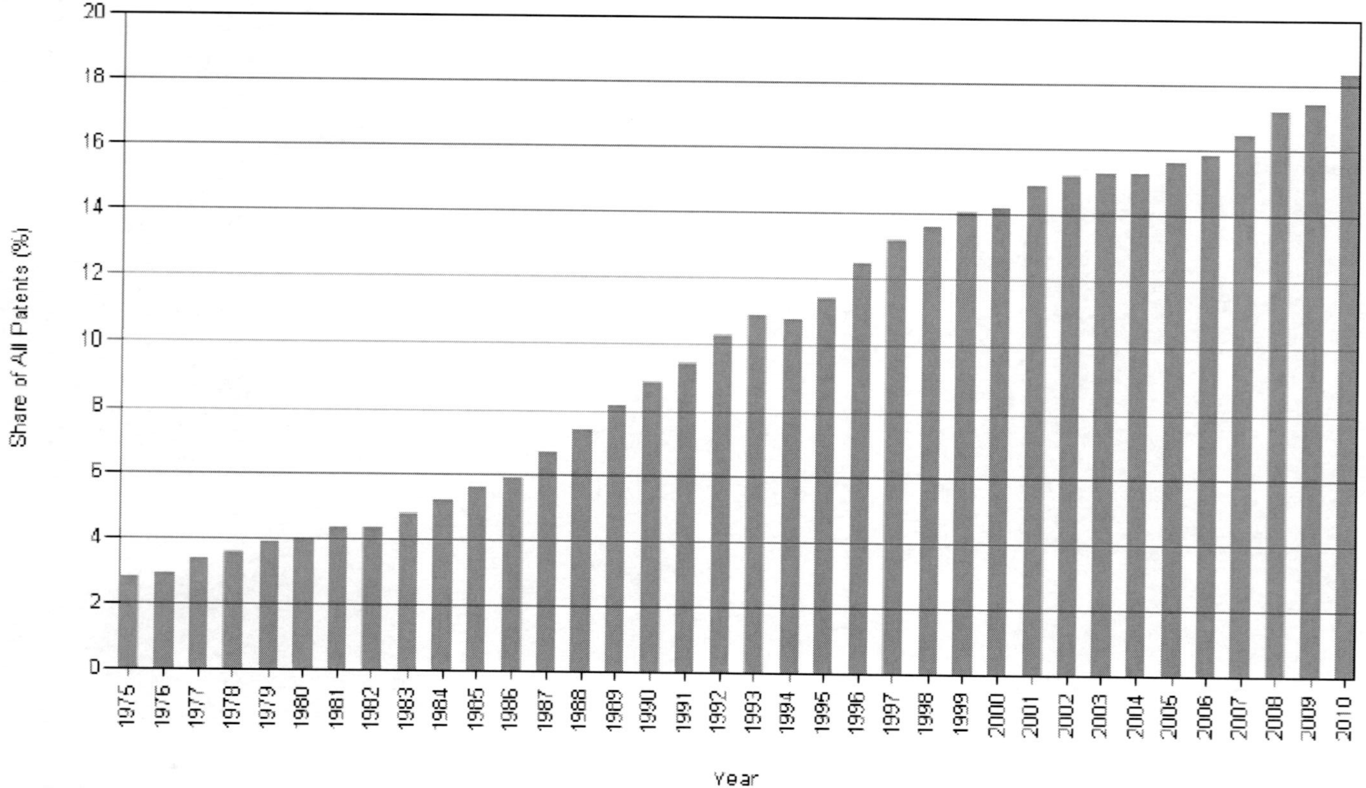

Share of U.S. Origin Patents which have a Woman Inventor, 1975-2010.

Figure 9. Patents Granted to Women – Share of All Patents.

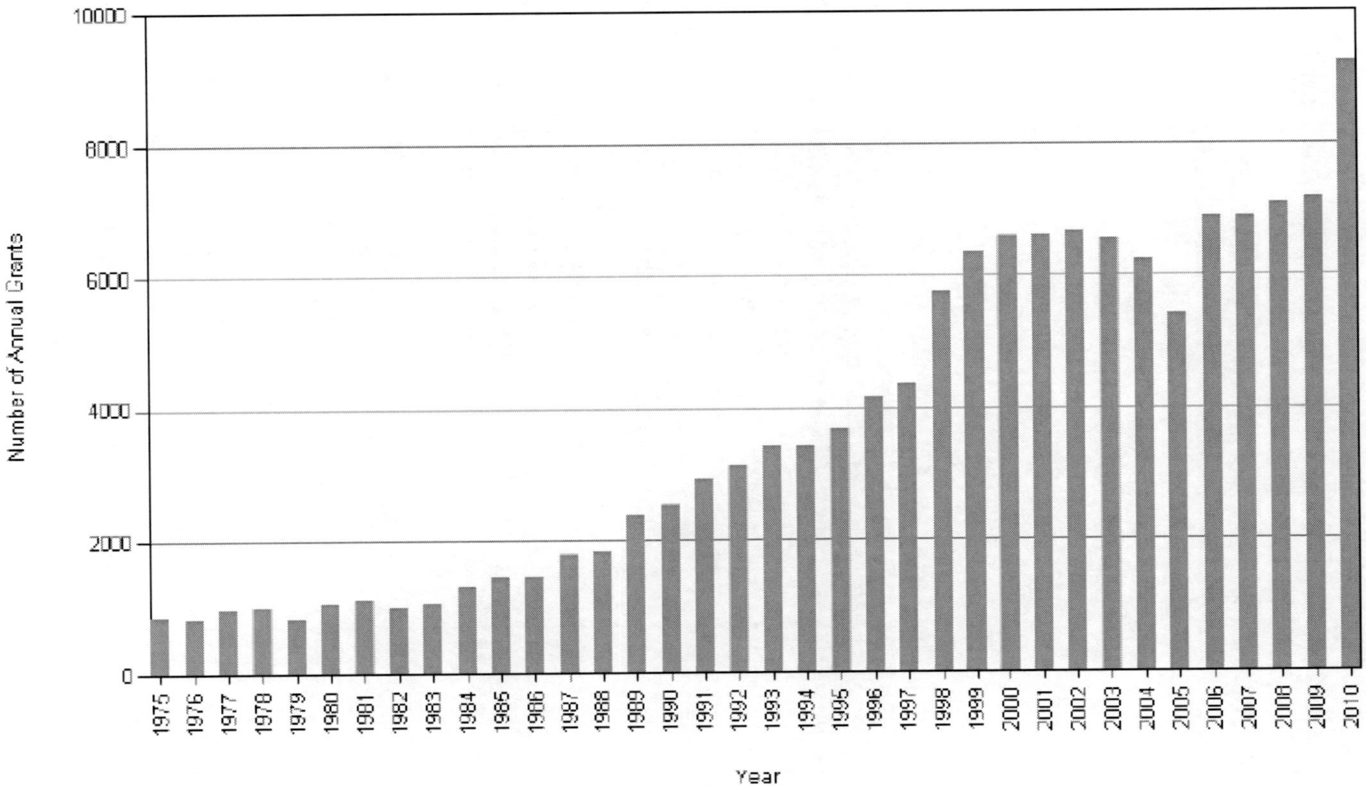

Annual Grants of U.S. Origin Woman-Inventor (Primary) Patents, 1975-2010.

Figure 10. Patents Granted to Women (Primary Inventor) – Annually.

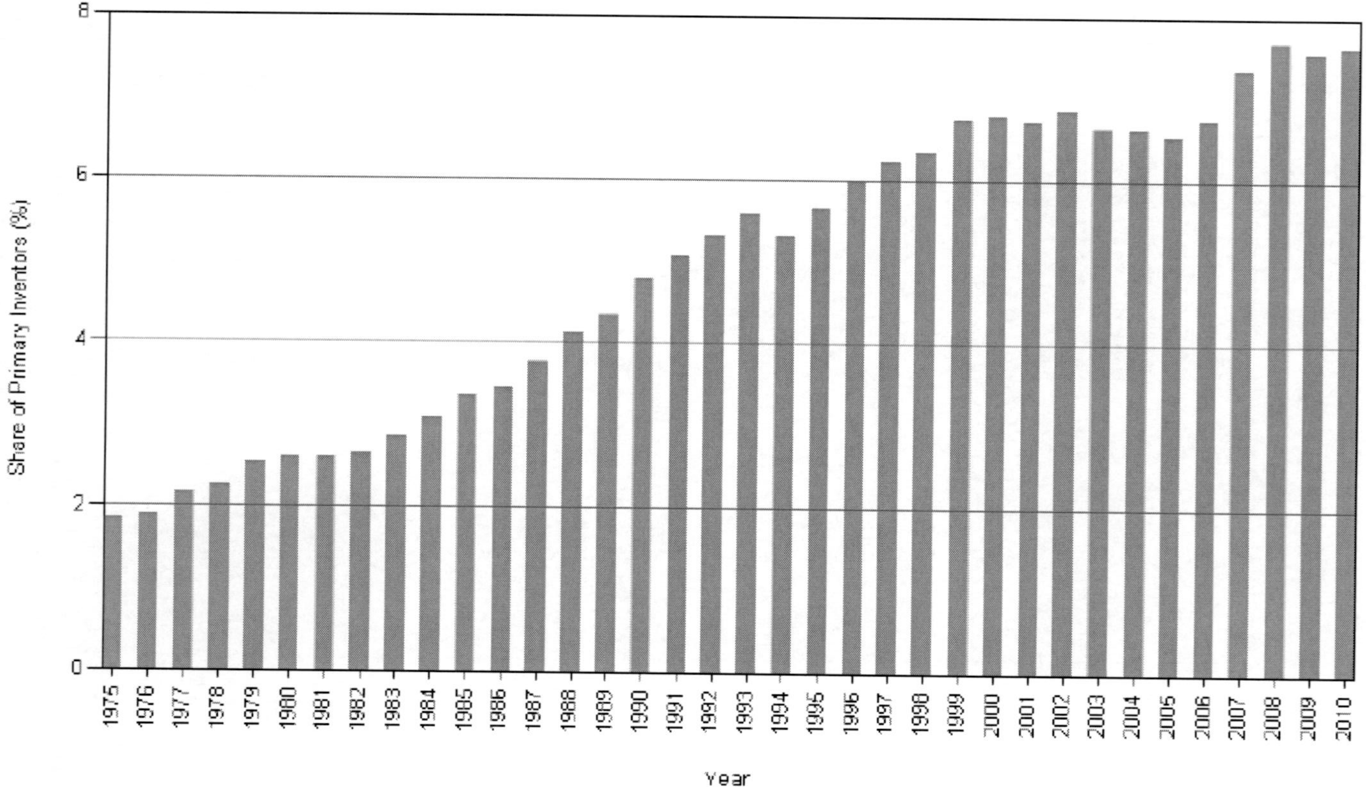

Share of U.S. Origin Patents which have a Woman as the Primary Inventor, 1975-2010.

Figure 11. Patents Granted to Women – Share of Primary Inventors.

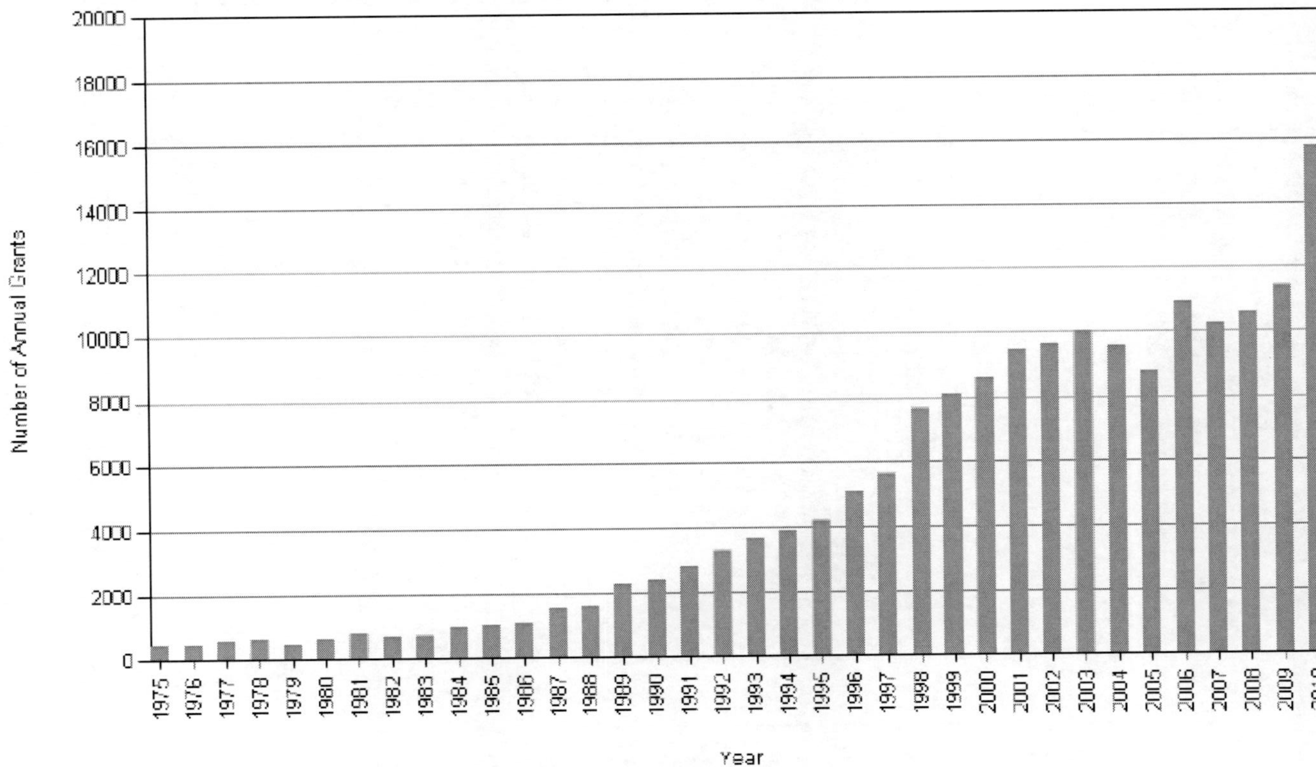

Annual Grants of U.S. Origin Woman-Inventor (Non-Primary) Patents, 1975-2010.

Figure 12. Patents Granted to Women (Non-Primary Inventor) –Annually.

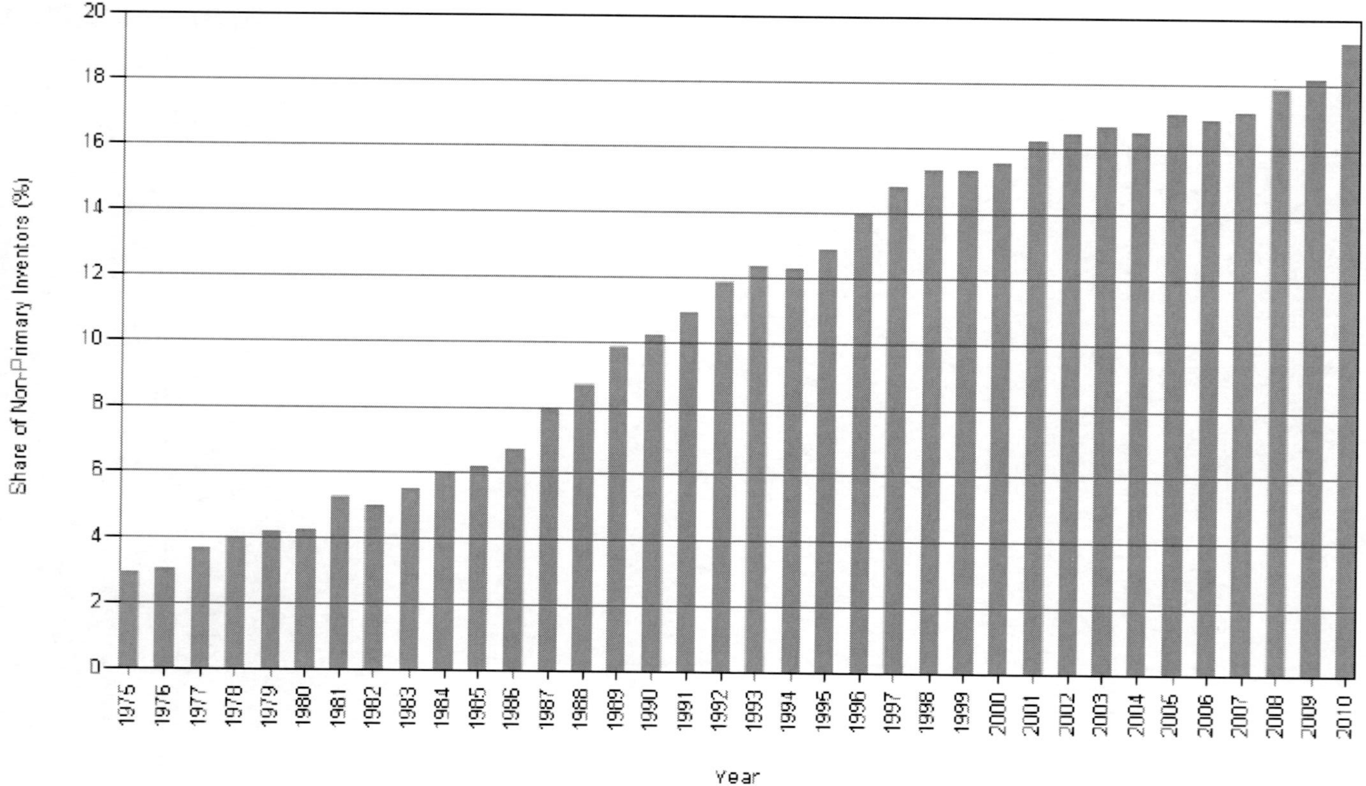

Share of U.S. Origin Patents which have a Woman as a Non-Primary Inventor, 1975-2010.

Figure 13. Patents Granted to Women - Share of Non-Primary Inventors.

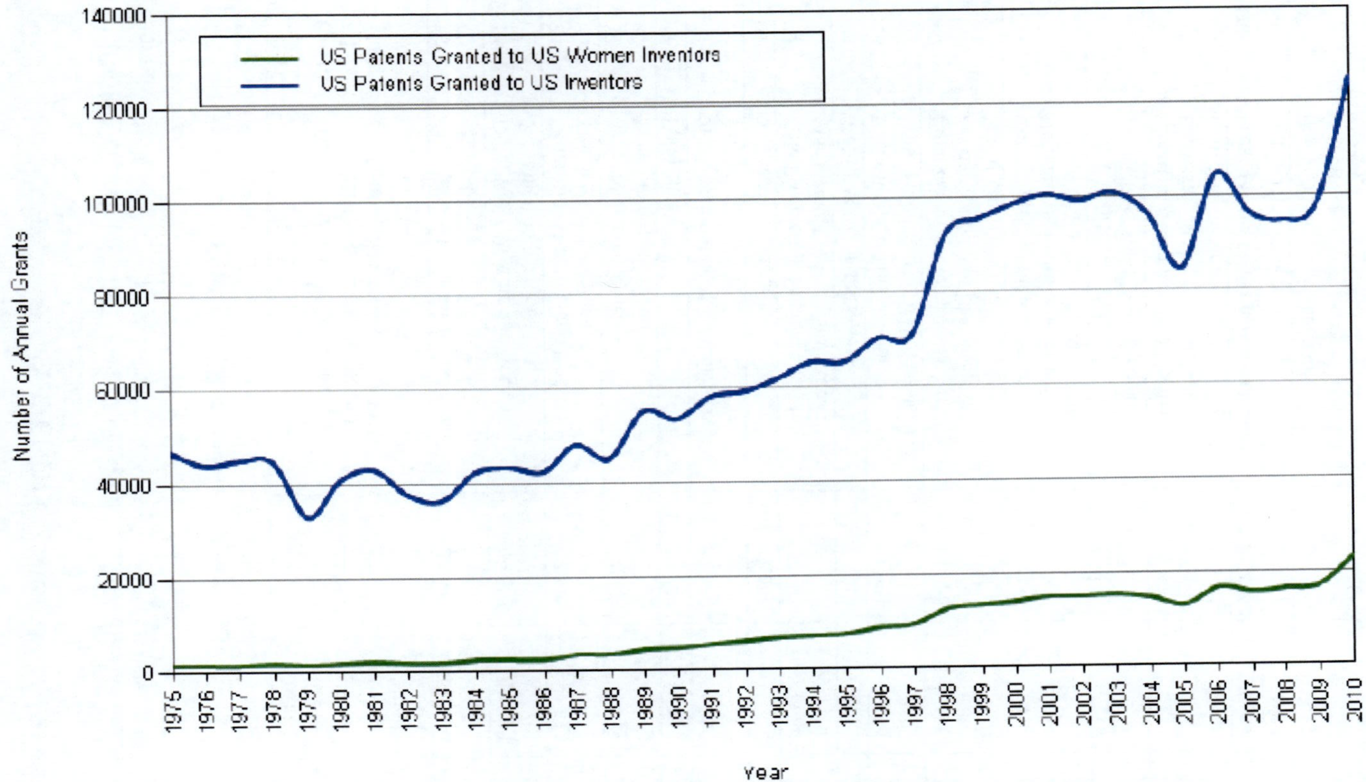

Annual Grants of U.S. Origin Woman-Inventor Patents compared with Annual Grants of All U.S. Patents, 1975-2010.

Figure 14. Patents Granted to Women vs. All Patents.

APPENDIX 2

Tables containing the data corresponding to charts are provided in Appendix 2.

Table A.1. Patents by Patent Class

Patent Class Code	Patent Class Title (according to the United States Patents and Trademarks Office (USPTO))	Total no. of Patents	No. of Patents with at least 1 Woman Inventor	% Women Patents
435	Chemistry: Molecular Biology and Microbiology	40,314	14,129	35.05
514	Drug, Bio-Affecting and Body Treating Compositions	49,801	13,434	26.98
424	Drug, Bio-Affecting and Body Treating Compositions	32,515	9,625	29.6
438	Semiconductor Device Manufacturing: Process	34,848	5,677	16.29
D06	Furnishings	26,707	5,297	19.83
428	Stock Material or Miscellaneous Articles	32,518	4,780	14.7
604	Surgery	22,666	3,838	16.93
707	Data Processing: Database and File Management or Data Structures	17,901	3,664	20.47
370	Multiplex Communications	28,613	3,615	12.63
D14	Recording, Communication, or Information Retrieval Equipment	17,071	3,602	21.1
D07	Equipment for Preparing or Serving Food or Drink Not Elsewhere Specified	14,138	3,496	24.73
530	Chemistry: Natural Resins or Derivatives; Peptides or Proteins; Lignins or Reaction Products Thereof	9,356	3,413	36.48
257	Active Solid-State Devices (e.g., Transistors, Solid-State Diodes)	26,534	3,412	12.86
709	Electrical Computers and Digital Processing Systems: Multicomputer Data Transferring	19,922	3,239	16.26
D09	Packages and Containers for Goods	13,414	3,174	23.66
D02	Apparel and Haberdashery	10,807	3,087	28.56
430	Radiation Imagery Chemistry: Process, Composition, or Product Thereof	14,736	2,987	20.27

Patent Class Code	Patent Class Title (according to the United States Patents and Trademarks Office (USPTO))	Total no. of Patents	No. of Patents with at least 1 Woman Inventor	% Women Patents
D21	Games, Toys, and Sports Goods	15,817	2,905	18.37
600	Surgery	23,491	2,812	11.97
426	Food or Edible Material: Processes, Compositions, and Products	12,503	2,719	21.75
D24	Medical and Laboratory Equipment	11,088	2,719	24.52
705	Data Processing: Financial, Business Practice, Management, or Cost/Price Determination	13,276	2,692	20.28
D03	Travel Goods and Personal Belongings	8,571	2,330	27.18
455	Telecommunications	20,520	2,322	11.32
536	Organic Compounds -- Part of the Class 532-570 Series	6,964	2,239	32.15
379	Telephonic Communications	14,613	2,224	15.22
D08	Tools and Hardware	16,757	2,191	13.08
D23	Environmental Heating and Cooling; Fluid Handling and Sanitary Equipment	13,423	2,140	15.94
2	Apparel	8,196	2,137	26.07
D12	Transportation	15,023	2,100	13.98
715	Data Processing: Presentation Processing of Document, Operator Interface Processing, and Screen Saver Display Processing	10,018	2,081	20.77
382	Image Analysis	14,614	2,076	14.21
606	Surgery	20,558	2,054	9.99
427	Coating Processes	13,777	1,928	13.99
524	Synthetic Resins or Natural Rubbers -- Part of the Class 520 Series	13,841	1,922	13.89
510	Cleaning Compositions for Solid Surfaces, Auxiliary Compositions Therefor, or Processes of Preparing the Compositions	6,619	1,877	28.36
714	Error Detection/Correction and Fault Detection/Recovery	15,879	1,853	11.67
800	Multicellular Living Organisms and Unmodified Parts Thereof and Related Processes	6,988	1,839	26.32
525	Synthetic Resins or Natural Rubbers -- Part of the Class 520 Series	12,027	1,795	14.92
385	Optical Waveguides	15,112	1,746	11.55

Table A.1. (Continued)

Patent Class Code	Patent Class Title (according to the United States Patents and Trademarks Office (USPTO))	Total no. of Patents	No. of Patents with at least 1 Woman Inventor	% Women Patents
D11	Jewelry, Symbolic Insignia, and Ornaments	6,380	1,746	27.37
206	Special Receptacle or Package	13,801	1,690	12.25
340	Communications: Electrical	22,264	1,640	7.37
345	Computer Graphics Processing and Selective Visual Display Systems	16,233	1,626	10.02
73	Measuring and Testing	27,183	1,618	5.95
711	Electrical Computers and Digital Processing Systems: Memory	14,422	1,618	11.22
210	Liquid Purification or Separation	20,186	1,596	7.91
436	Chemistry: Analytical and Immunological Testing	7,258	1,560	21.49
375	Pulse or Digital Communications	16,454	1,546	9.4
PLT	Plants	8,369	1,467	17.53
250	Radiant Energy	20,108	1,461	7.27
365	Static Information Storage and Retrieval	15,527	1,445	9.31
5	Beds	7,205	1,434	19.9
359	Optical: Systems and Elements	16,434	1,402	8.53
324	Electricity: Measuring and Testing	20,208	1,396	6.91
528	Synthetic Resins or Natural Rubbers -- Part of the Class 520 Series	9,479	1,389	14.65
702	Data Processing: Measuring, Calibrating, or Testing	12,051	1,360	11.29
252	Compositions	7,621	1,321	17.33
D28	Cosmetic Products and Toilet Articles	3,762	1,315	34.95
D10	Measuring, Testing, or Signalling Instruments	8,251	1,304	15.8
361	Electricity: Electrical Systems and Devices	19,122	1,290	6.75
D26	Lighting	8,724	1,282	14.7
607	Surgery: Light, Thermal, and Electrical Application	9,256	1,256	13.57
D19	Office Supplies; Artists' and Teachers' Materials	4,961	1,255	25.3
235	Registers	8,809	1,241	14.09
422	Chemical Apparatus and Process Disinfecting, Deodorizing, Preserving, or Sterilizing	10,462	1,240	11.85

Patent Class Code	Patent Class Title (according to the United States Patents and Trademarks Office (USPTO))	Total no. of Patents	No. of Patents with at least 1 Woman Inventor	% Women Patents
710	Electrical Computers and Digital Data Processing Systems: Input/Output	12,189	1,215	9.97
156	Adhesive Bonding and Miscellaneous Chemical Manufacture	15,332	1,206	7.87
713	Electrical Computers and Digital Processing Systems: Support	10,796	1,205	11.16
356	Optics: Measuring and Testing	14,657	1,200	8.19
502	Catalyst, Solid Sorbent, or Support Therefor: Product or Process of Making	7,964	1,174	14.74
29	Metal Working	20,223	1,172	5.8
280	Land Vehicles	17,839	1,168	6.55
360	Dynamic Magnetic Information Storage or Retrieval	12,690	1,164	9.17
264	Plastic and Nonmetallic Article Shaping or Treating: Processes	14,203	1,159	8.16
434	Education and Demonstration	4,837	1,159	23.96
423	Chemistry of Inorganic Compounds	10,076	1,147	11.38
119	Animal Husbandry	7,079	1,147	16.2
429	Chemistry: Electrical Current Producing Apparatus, Product, and Process	8,732	1,113	12.75
347	Incremental Printing of Symbolic Information	8,488	1,112	13.1
128	Surgery	8,521	1,098	12.89
526	Synthetic Resins or Natural Rubbers -- Part of the Class 520 Series	6,184	1,094	17.69
297	Chairs and Seats	7,753	1,068	13.78
439	Electrical Connectors	21,071	1,060	5.03
623	Prosthesis (i.e., Artificial Body Members), Parts Thereof, or Aids and Accessories Therefor	8,973	1,053	11.74
700	Data Processing: Generic Control Systems or Specific Applications	9,469	1,012	10.69
704	Data Processing: Speech Signal Processing, Linguistics, Language Translation, and Audio Compression/Decompression	6,154	1,012	16.44
717	Data Processing: Software Development, Installation, and Management	6,169	942	15.27
132	Toilet	2,911	938	32.22

Table A.1. (Continued)

Patent Class Code	Patent Class Title (according to the United States Patents and Trademarks Office (USPTO))	Total no. of Patents	No. of Patents with at least 1 Woman Inventor	% Women Patents
546	Organic Compounds -- Part of the Class 532-570 Series	4,588	935	20.38
106	Compositions: Coating or Plastic	6,354	927	14.59
204	Chemistry: Electrical and Wave Energy	8,696	907	10.43
362	Illumination	12,001	867	7.22
D30	Animal Husbandry	3,018	866	28.69
219	Electric Heating	12,640	852	6.74
D13	Equipment for Production, Distribution, or Transformation of Energy	6,898	848	12.29
248	Supports	12,242	840	6.86
273	Amusement Devices: Games	7,373	837	11.35
348	Television	11,915	836	7.02
548	Organic Compounds -- Part of the Class 532-570 Series	4,925	815	16.55
15	Brushing, Scrubbing, and General Cleaning	8,619	810	9.4
585	Chemistry of Hydrocarbon Compounds	5,559	805	14.48
716	Computer-Aided Design and Analysis of Circuits and Semiconductor Masks	5,702	796	13.96
701	Data Processing: Vehicles, Navigation, and Relative Location	8,541	788	9.23
D25	Building Units and Construction Elements	5,914	786	13.29
446	Amusement Devices: Toys	5,033	772	15.34
358	Facsimile and Static Presentation Processing	6,416	769	11.99
523	Synthetic Resins or Natural Rubbers -- Part of the Class 520 Series	4,861	761	15.66
62	Refrigeration	13,079	743	5.68
D32	Washing, Cleaning, or Drying Machine	4,003	733	18.31
123	Internal-Combustion Engines	15,037	721	4.79
205	Electrolysis: Processes, Compositions Used Therein, and Methods of Preparing the Compositions	6,185	709	11.46
4	Baths, Closets, Sinks, and Spittoons	5,719	696	12.17

Patent Class Code	Patent Class Title (according to the United States Patents and Trademarks Office (USPTO))	Total no. of Patents	No. of Patents with at least 1 Woman Inventor	% Women Patents
327	Miscellaneous Active Electrical Nonlinear Devices, Circuits, and Systems	12,393	695	5.61
549	Organic Compounds -- Part of the Class 532-570 Series	4,899	694	14.17
220	Receptacles	8,127	667	8.21
52	Static Structures (e.g., Buildings)	17,268	663	3.84
544	Organic Compounds -- Part of the Class 532-570 Series	4,016	658	16.38
208	Mineral Oils: Processes and Products	6,656	654	9.83
703	Data Processing: Structural Design, Modeling, Simulation, and Emulation	4,348	630	14.49
296	Land Vehicles: Bodies and Tops	8,308	627	7.55
372	Coherent Light Generators	7,017	621	8.85
712	Electrical Computers and Digital Processing Systems: Processing Architectures and Instruction Processing (e.g., Processors)	5,964	610	10.23
326	Electronic Digital Logic Circuitry	7,078	601	8.49
568	Organic Compounds -- Part of the Class 532-570 Series	5,925	600	10.13
222	Dispensing	10,256	598	5.83
134	Cleaning and Liquid Contact with Solids	6,059	598	9.87
166	Wells	13,752	597	4.34
224	Package and Article Carriers	4,989	595	11.93
174	Electricity: Conductors and Insulators	8,307	584	7.03
726	Information Security	4,255	571	13.42
378	X-Ray or Gamma Ray Systems or Devices	5,757	570	9.9
40	Card, Picture, or Sign Exhibiting	5,219	566	10.84
399	Electrophotography	5,690	559	9.82
482	Exercise Devices	7,765	541	6.97
521	Synthetic Resins or Natural Rubbers -- Part of the Class 520 Series	4,193	538	12.83
60	Power Plants	12,457	536	4.3
D34	Material or Article Handling Equipment	3,539	531	15
D15	Machines Not Elsewhere Specified	5,405	526	9.73
211	Supports: Racks	5,493	523	9.52

Table A.1. (Continued)

Patent Class Code	Patent Class Title (according to the United States Patents and Trademarks Office (USPTO))	Total no. of Patents	No. of Patents with at least 1 Woman Inventor	% Women Patents
442	Fabric (Woven, Knitted, or Nonwoven Textile or Cloth, Etc.)	3,255	523	16.07
706	Data Processing: Artificial Intelligence	3,095	518	16.74
508	Solid Anti-Friction Devices, Materials Therefor, Lubricant or Separant Compositions for Moving Solid Surfaces, and Miscellaneous Mineral Oil Compositions	3,774	509	13.49
602	Surgery: Splint, Brace, or Bandage	3,636	500	13.75
D20	Sales and Advertising Equipment	2,298	497	21.63
473	Games Using Tangible Projectile	11,934	494	4.14
8	Bleaching and Dyeing; Fluid Treatment and Chemical Modification of Textiles and Fibers	2,829	491	17.36
564	Organic Compounds -- Part of the Class 532-570 Series	3,478	486	13.97
D04	Brushware	2,121	485	22.87
216	Etching a Substrate: Processes	3,018	481	15.94
162	Paper Making and Fiber Liberation	3,864	476	12.32
451	Abrading	7,588	475	6.26
463	Amusement Devices: Games	3,994	474	11.87
341	Coded Data Generation or Conversion	7,147	463	6.48
137	Fluid Handling	14,647	460	3.14
560	Organic Compounds -- Part of the Class 532-570 Series	4,019	458	11.4
118	Coating Apparatus	5,171	457	8.84
239	Fluid Sprinkling, Spraying, and Diffusing	8,585	448	5.22
501	Compositions: Ceramic	2,973	446	15
433	Dentistry	5,832	444	7.61
D01	Edible Products	1,128	444	39.36
313	Electric Lamp and Discharge Devices	5,392	443	8.22
398	Optical Communications	4,084	441	10.8
342	Communications: Directive Radio Wave Systems and Devices (e.g., Radar, Radio Navigation)	8,432	440	5.22
504	Plant Protecting and Regulating Compositions	3,778	425	11.25

Patent Class Code	Patent Class Title (according to the United States Patents and Trademarks Office (USPTO))	Total no. of Patents	No. of Patents with at least 1 Woman Inventor	% Women Patents
351	Optics: Eye Examining, Vision Testing and Correcting	3,859	421	10.91
719	Electrical Computers and Digital Processing Systems: Interprogram Communication or Interprocess Communication (Ipc)	2,454	419	17.07
401	Coating Implements with Material Supply	2,365	415	17.55
148	Metal Treatment	4,586	412	8.98
562	Organic Compounds -- Part of the Class 532-570 Series	3,369	412	12.23
36	Boots, Shoes, and Leggings	3,655	403	11.03
33	Geometrical Instruments	7,144	397	5.56
D16	Photography and Optical Equipment	2,995	388	12.95
708	Electrical Computers: Arithmetic Processing and Calculating	4,971	385	7.74
450	Foundation Garments	598	384	64.21
725	Interactive Video Distribution Systems	3,164	382	12.07
310	Electrical Generator or Motor Structure	8,066	374	4.64
95	Gas Separation: Processes	3,793	373	9.83
24	Buckles, Buttons, Clasps, Etc.	4,349	371	8.53
312	Supports: Cabinet Structure	4,040	365	9.03
244	Aeronautics and Astronautics	7,646	359	4.7
540	Organic Compounds -- Part of the Class 532-570 Series	2,924	358	12.24
556	Organic Compounds -- Part of the Class 532-570 Series	2,739	357	13.03
718	Electrical Computers and Digital Processing Systems: Virtual Machine Task or Process Management or Task Management/Control	2,204	356	16.15
30	Cutlery	5,273	354	6.71
D05	Textile or Paper Yard Goods; Sheet Material	796	353	44.35
D18	Printing and Office Machinery	2,205	352	15.96
343	Communications: Radio Wave Antennas	6,939	350	5.04
47	Plant Husbandry	3,305	349	10.56
228	Metal Fusion Bonding	4,049	343	8.47

Table A.1. (Continued)

Patent Class Code	Patent Class Title (according to the United States Patents and Trademarks Office (USPTO))	Total no. of Patents	No. of Patents with at least 1 Woman Inventor	% Women Patents
558	Organic Compounds -- Part of the Class 532-570 Series	2,662	343	12.89
43	Fishing, Trapping, and Vermin Destroying	6,605	334	5.06
D22	Arms, Pyrotechnics, Hunting and Fishing Equipment	3,531	329	9.32
D29	Equipment for Safety, Protection, and Rescue	1,502	327	21.77
294	Handling: Hand and Hoist-Line Implements	4,233	320	7.56
333	Wave Transmission Lines and Networks	4,970	319	6.42
99	Foods and Beverages: Apparatus	4,220	317	7.51
229	Envelopes, Wrappers, and Paperboard Boxes	4,147	315	7.6
53	Package Making	6,499	311	4.79
330	Amplifiers	6,127	311	5.08
242	Winding, Tensioning, or Guiding	6,183	309	5
315	Electric Lamp and Discharge Devices: Systems	7,081	306	4.32
84	Music	5,248	303	5.77
349	Liquid Crystal Cells, Elements and Systems	2,201	302	13.72
135	Tent, Canopy, Umbrella, or Cane	1,913	285	14.9
396	Photography	4,325	281	6.5
380	Cryptography	3,281	281	8.56
160	Flexible or Portable Closure, Partition, or Panel	2,905	277	9.54
131	Tobacco	2,128	274	12.88
318	Electricity: Motive Power Systems	6,720	269	4
425	Plastic Article or Earthenware Shaping or Treating: Apparatus	6,592	264	4
221	Article Dispensing	2,725	264	9.69
75	Specialized Metallurgical Processes, Compositions for Use Therein, Consolidated Metal Powder Compositions, and Loose Metal Particulate Mixtures	3,360	263	7.83
180	Motor Vehicles	6,119	261	4.27

Patent Class Code	Patent Class Title (according to the United States Patents and Trademarks Office (USPTO))	Total no. of Patents	No. of Patents with at least 1 Woman Inventor	% Women Patents
D99	Miscellaneous	1,230	258	20.98
34	Drying and Gas or Vapor Contact with Solids	3,403	257	7.55
414	Material or Article Handling	9,392	256	2.73
522	Synthetic Resins or Natural Rubbers -- Part of the Class 520 Series	1,463	252	17.22
126	Stoves and Furnaces	5,992	251	4.19
65	Glass Manufacturing	3,801	249	6.55
215	Bottles and Jars	3,222	246	7.64
381	Electrical Audio Signal Processing Systems and Devices	4,796	244	5.09
506	Combinatorial Chemistry Technology: Method, Library, Apparatus	1,036	244	23.55
44	Fuel and Related Compositions	2,560	243	9.49
507	Earth Boring, Well Treating, and Oil Field Chemistry	1,935	241	12.45
405	Hydraulic and Earth Engineering	6,570	237	3.61
165	Heat Exchange	5,859	236	4.03
367	Communications, Electrical: Acoustic Wave Systems and Devices	4,868	234	4.81
601	Surgery: Kinesitherapy	1,973	234	11.86
417	Pumps	6,591	233	3.54
63	Jewelry	814	233	28.62
383	Flexible Bags	1,817	232	12.77
400	Typewriting Machines	3,091	224	7.25
320	Electricity: Battery or Capacitor Charging or Discharging	2,927	224	7.65
108	Horizontally Supported Planar Surfaces	2,777	224	8.07
141	Fluent Material Handling, with Receiver or Receiver Coacting Means	4,718	217	4.6
283	Printed Matter	1,529	206	13.47
331	Oscillators	3,941	205	5.2
223	Apparel Apparatus	1,219	205	16.82
363	Electric Power Conversion Systems	4,449	204	4.59
114	Ships	6,246	202	3.23
369	Dynamic Information Storage or Retrieval	3,198	202	6.32
117	Single-Crystal, Oriented-Crystal, and Epitaxy Growth Processes; Non-Coating Apparatus Therefor	2,045	202	9.88

Table A.1. (Continued)

Patent Class Code	Patent Class Title (according to the United States Patents and Trademarks Office (USPTO))	Total no. of Patents	No. of Patents with at least 1 Woman Inventor	% Women Patents
374	Thermal Measuring and Testing	2,624	200	7.62
175	Boring or Penetrating the Earth	5,169	199	3.85
55	Gas Separation	2,647	195	7.37
366	Agitating	3,481	193	5.54
503	Record Receiver Having Plural Interactive Leaves or a Colorless Color Former, Method of Use, or Developer Therefor	846	191	22.58
241	Solid Material Comminution or Disintegration	3,884	190	4.89
431	Combustion	3,348	190	5.68
416	Fluid Reaction Surfaces (i.e., Impellers)	3,638	189	5.2
200	Electricity: Circuit Makers and Breakers	5,802	186	3.21
D27	Tobacco and Smokers' Supplies	1,017	186	18.29
101	Printing	4,205	184	4.38
415	Rotary Kinetic Fluid Motors or Pumps	4,121	182	4.42
335	Electricity: Magnetically Operated Switches, Magnets, and Electromagnets	3,118	182	5.84
96	Gas Separation: Apparatus	2,519	177	7.03
323	Electricity: Power Supply or Regulation Systems	4,008	175	4.37
16	Miscellaneous Hardware (e.g., Bushing, Carpet Fastener, Caster, Door Closer, Panel Hanger, Attachable or Adjunct Handle, Hinge, Window Sash Balance, Etc.)	2,921	175	5.99
74	Machine Element or Mechanism	6,806	172	2.53
83	Cutting	5,197	171	3.29
307	Electrical Transmission or Interconnection Systems	4,065	167	4.11
368	Horology: Time Measuring Systems or Devices	1,878	166	8.84
164	Metal Founding	3,325	160	4.81
116	Signals and Indicators	1,726	160	9.27
56	Harvesters	4,475	159	3.55
70	Locks	4,289	158	3.68

Patent Class Code	Patent Class Title (according to the United States Patents and Trademarks Office (USPTO))	Total no. of Patents	No. of Patents with at least 1 Woman Inventor	% Women Patents
505	Superconductor Technology: Apparatus, Material, Process	1,110	158	14.23
198	Conveyors: Power-Driven	6,292	155	2.46
81	Tools	4,726	155	3.28
554	Organic Compounds -- Part of the Class 532-570 Series	1,344	154	11.46
271	Sheet Feeding or Delivering	3,313	152	4.59
209	Classifying, Separating, and Assorting Solids	3,817	149	3.9
281	Books, Strips, and Leaves	829	149	17.97
516	Colloid Systems and Wetting Agents; Subcombinations Thereof; Processes Of	1,057	148	14
102	Ammunition and Explosives	3,822	147	3.85
570	Organic Compounds -- Part of the Class 532-570 Series	1,168	147	12.59
112	Sewing	2,128	145	6.81
441	Buoys, Rafts, and Aquatic Devices	1,790	144	8.04
136	Batteries: Thermoelectric and Photoelectric	1,863	143	7.68
150	Purses, Wallets, and Protective Covers	485	143	29.48
251	Valves and Valve Actuation	4,778	142	2.97
292	Closure Fasteners	3,771	141	3.74
285	Pipe Joints or Couplings	5,512	140	2.54
182	Fire Escape, Ladder, or Scaffold	3,262	137	4.2
355	Photocopying	2,362	137	5.8
181	Acoustics	2,719	129	4.74
149	Explosive and Thermic Compositions or Charges	1,330	129	9.7
72	Metal Deforming	5,930	128	2.16
376	Induced Nuclear Reactions: Processes, Systems, and Elements	3,548	128	3.61
386	Motion Video Signal Processing for Recording or Reproducing	1,765	127	7.2
49	Movable or Removable Closures	3,203	123	3.84
54	Harness for Working Animal	505	122	24.16
227	Elongated-Member-Driving Apparatus	2,125	121	5.69
512	Perfume Compositions	485	121	24.95
403	Joints and Connections	3,588	117	3.26

Table A.1. (Continued)

Patent Class Code	Patent Class Title (according to the United States Patents and Trademarks Office (USPTO))	Total no. of Patents	No. of Patents with at least 1 Woman Inventor	% Women Patents
411	Expanded, Threaded, Driven, Headed, Tool-Deformed, or Locked-Threaded Fastener	3,337	117	3.51
353	Optics: Image Projectors	1,783	116	6.51
	Manufacturing Container or Tube From Paper; or Other Manufacturing From a			
493	Sheet or Web	2,482	114	4.59
277	Seal for a Joint or Juncture	3,695	113	3.06
190	Trunks and Hand-Carried Luggage	615	112	18.21
51	Abrasive Tool Making Process, Material, or Composition	1,088	110	10.11
404	Road Structure, Process, or Apparatus	2,910	108	3.71
419	Powder Metallurgy Processes	1,134	108	9.52
588	Hazardous or Toxic Waste Destruction or Containment	1,004	108	10.76
552	Organic Compounds -- Part of the Class 532-570 Series	777	106	13.64
D17	Musical Instruments	992	102	10.28
445	Electric Lamp or Space Discharge Component or Device Manufacturing	1,207	101	8.37
261	Gas and Liquid Contact Apparatus	2,309	98	4.24
472	Amusement Devices	979	97	9.91
38	Textiles: Ironing or Smoothing	483	97	20.08
192	Clutches and Power-Stop Control	3,459	96	2.78
338	Electrical Resistors	1,463	95	6.49
203	Distillation: Processes, Separatory	1,302	94	7.22
475	Planetary Gear Transmission Systems or Components	2,784	93	3.34
392	Electric Resistance Heating Devices	1,522	92	6.04
89	Ordnance	2,685	91	3.39
188	Brakes	3,881	90	2.32
66	Textiles: Knitting	836	90	10.77
138	Pipes and Tubular Conduits	2,569	89	3.46
187	Elevator, Industrial Lift Truck, or Stationary Lift for Vehicle	1,541	89	5.78
420	Alloys or Metallic Compositions	1,400	86	6.14
402	Binder Device Releasably Engaging Aperture or Notch of Sheet	610	85	13.93

Patent Class Code	Patent Class Title (according to the United States Patents and Trademarks Office (USPTO))	Total no. of Patents	No. of Patents with at least 1 Woman Inventor	% Women Patents
454	Ventilation	2,384	84	3.52
290	Prime-Mover Dynamo Plants	1,864	84	4.51
28	Textiles: Manufacturing	752	83	11.04
477	Interrelated Power Delivery Controls, Including Engine Control	1,168	81	6.93
534	Organic Compounds -- Part of the Class 532-570 Series	686	81	11.81
139	Textiles: Weaving	835	80	9.58
518	Chemistry: Fischer-Tropsch Processes; or Purification or Recovery of Products Thereof	671	79	11.77
336	Inductor Devices	1,465	78	5.32
232	Deposit and Collection Receptacles	776	75	9.66
42	Firearms	3,299	71	2.15
254	Implements or Apparatus for Applying Pushing or Pulling Force	2,791	70	2.51
452	Butchering	1,817	70	3.85
384	Bearings	3,136	69	2.2
440	Marine Propulsion	2,453	68	2.77
110	Furnaces	2,007	68	3.39
236	Automatic Temperature and Humidity Regulation	1,718	68	3.96
68	Textiles: Fluid Treating Apparatus	912	68	7.46
410	Freight Accommodation On Freight Carrier	1,652	65	3.93
48	Gas: Heating and Illuminating	1,069	63	5.89
432	Heating	1,663	62	3.73
144	Woodworking	2,177	61	2.8
152	Resilient Tires and Wheels	1,695	61	3.6
177	Weighing Scales	1,472	60	4.08
71	Chemistry: Fertilizers	923	59	6.39
100	Presses	1,968	58	2.95
127	Sugar, Starch, and Carbohydrates	445	57	12.81
301	Land Vehicles: Wheels and Axles	1,392	55	3.95
172	Earth Working	2,639	54	2.05
269	Work Holders	2,117	54	2.55
225	Severing by Tearing or Breaking	716	54	7.54
37	Excavating	2,163	53	2.45
267	Spring Devices	1,708	53	3.1

Table A.1. (Continued)

Patent Class Code	Patent Class Title (according to the United States Patents and Trademarks Office (USPTO))	Total no. of Patents	No. of Patents with at least 1 Woman Inventor	% Women Patents
337	Electricity: Electrothermally or Thermally Actuated Switches	1,524	52	3.41
27	Undertaking	458	52	11.35
303	Fluid-Pressure and Analogous Brake Systems	1,872	51	2.72
377	Electrical Pulse Counters, Pulse Dividers, or Shift Registers: Circuits and Systems	1,339	51	3.81
249	Static Molds	1,290	50	3.88
256	Fences	1,212	50	4.13
474	Endless Belt Power Transmission Systems or Components	1,905	48	2.52
122	Liquid Heaters and Vaporizers	1,561	47	3.01
418	Rotary Expansible Chamber Devices	1,906	45	2.36
408	Cutting by Use of Rotating Axially Moving Tool	2,068	44	2.13
293	Vehicle Fenders	727	44	6.05
494	Imperforate Bowl: Centrifugal Separators	815	43	5.28
105	Railway Rolling Stock	1,620	42	2.59
92	Expansible Chamber Devices	1,573	42	2.67
57	Textiles: Spinning, Twisting, and Twining	1,012	42	4.15
266	Metallurgical Apparatus	1,541	41	2.66
14	Bridges	642	41	6.39
169	Fire Extinguishers	1,221	40	3.28
7	Compound Tools	696	40	5.75
194	Check-Actuated Control Mechanisms	998	38	3.81
91	Motors: Expansible Chamber Type	1,638	36	2.2
720	Dynamic Optical Information Storage or Retrieval	348	35	10.06
124	Mechanical Guns and Projectors	2,413	34	1.41
104	Railways	1,357	33	2.43
111	Planting	1,134	33	2.91
850	Scanning-Probe Techniques or Apparatus; Applications of Scanning-Probe Techniques, e.g., Scanning Probe Microscopy [Spm]	331	32	9.67

Patent Class Code	Patent Class Title (according to the United States Patents and Trademarks Office (USPTO))	Total no. of Patents	No. of Patents with at least 1 Woman Inventor	% Women Patents
218	High-Voltage Switches with Arc Preventing or Extinguishing Devices	680	31	4.56
409	Gear Cutting, Milling, or Planing	1,346	29	2.15
173	Tool Driving or Impacting	1,242	29	2.33
332	Modulators	494	28	5.67
464	Rotary Shafts, Gudgeons, Housings, and Flexible Couplings for Rotary Shafts	1,346	27	2.01
202	Distillation: Apparatus	820	27	3.29
270	Sheet-Material Associating	783	27	3.45
346	Recorders	732	25	3.42
12	Boot and Shoe Making	305	25	8.2
406	Conveyors: Fluid Current	1,123	24	2.14
279	Chucks or Sockets	816	24	2.94
407	Cutters, for Shaping	783	24	3.07
186	Merchandising	197	23	11.68
412	Bookbinding: Process and Apparatus	302	21	6.95
168	Farriery	189	21	11.11
322	Electricity: Single Generator Systems	738	20	2.71
76	Metal Tools and Implements, Making	566	20	3.53
23	Chemistry: Physical Processes	192	19	9.9
299	Mining or In Situ Disintegration of Hard Material	1,494	18	1.2
184	Lubrication	991	18	1.82
462	Books, Strips, and Leaves for Manifolding	188	18	9.57
237	Heating Systems	532	17	3.2
19	Textiles: Fiber Preparation	489	17	3.48
289	Knots and Knot Tying	163	17	10.43
1	** Classification Undetermined **	96	17	17.71
140	Wireworking	649	16	2.47
352	Optics: Motion Pictures	614	16	2.61
305	Wheel Substitutes for Land Vehicles	598	16	2.68
87	Textiles: Braiding, Netting, and Lace Making	177	16	9.04
460	Crop Threshing or Separating	616	15	2.44
226	Advancing Material of Indeterminate Length	880	14	1.59

Table A.1. (Continued)

Patent Class Code	Patent Class Title (according to the United States Patents and Trademarks Office (USPTO))	Total no. of Patents	No. of Patents with at least 1 Woman Inventor	% Women Patents
373	Industrial Electric Heating Furnaces	604	14	2.32
492	Roll or Roller	288	14	4.86
527	Synthetic Resins or Natural Rubbers -- Part of the Class 520 Series	176	14	7.95
82	Turning	1,219	12	0.98
329	Demodulators	385	12	3.12
388	Electricity: Motor Control Systems	395	11	2.78
109	Safes, Bank Protection, or a Related Device	354	11	3.11
26	Textiles: Cloth Finishing	294	11	3.74
260	Chemistry of Carbon Compounds	51	11	21.57
246	Railway Switches and Signals	599	10	1.67
238	Railways: Surface Track	446	10	2.24
213	Railway Draft Appliances	425	10	2.35
86	Ammunition and Explosive-Charge Making	414	10	2.42
298	Land Vehicles: Dumping	446	9	2.02
159	Concentrating Evaporators	264	9	3.41
300	Brush, Broom, and Mop Making	128	9	7.03
178	Telegraphy	530	8	1.51
193	Conveyors, Chutes, Skids, Guides, and Ways	467	8	1.71
59	Chain, Staple, and Horseshoe Making	312	8	2.56
483	Tool Changing	242	8	3.31
212	Traversing Hoists	757	7	0.92
453	Coin Handling	288	7	2.43
201	Distillation: Processes, Thermolytic	274	7	2.55
191	Electricity: Transmission To Vehicles	248	7	2.82
449	Bee Culture	126	7	5.56
217	Wooden Receptacles	79	7	8.86
125	Stone Working	585	6	1.03
476	Friction Gear Transmission Systems or Components	196	5	2.55
231	Whips and Whip Apparatus	19	5	26.32
147	Coopering	9	5	55.56
157	Wheelwright Machines	307	4	1.3

Patent Class Code	Patent Class Title (according to the United States Patents and Trademarks Office (USPTO))	Total no. of Patents	No. of Patents with at least 1 Woman Inventor	% Women Patents
470	Threaded, Headed Fastener, or Washer Making: Process and Apparatus	258	4	1.55
171	Unearthing Plants or Buried Objects	167	4	2.4
413	Sheet Metal Container Making	208	2	0.96
196	Mineral Oils: Apparatus	94	2	2.13
291	Track Sanders	31	2	6.45
334	Tuners	70	1	1.43
69	Leather Manufactures	40	1	2.5
79	Button Making	9	1	11.11
163	Needle and Pin Making	5	1	20
D00	** Design Classification Undetermined **	2	1	50
185	Motors: Spring, Weight, or Animal Powered	71	0	0
142	Wood Turning	41	0	0
295	Railway Wheels and Axles	39	0	0
234	Selective Cutting (e.g., Punching)	31	0	0
245	Wire Fabrics and Structure	12	0	0
278	Land Vehicles: Animal Draft Appliances	3	0	0
199	Type Casting	2	0	0
258	Railway Mail Delivery	2	0	0
520	Synthetic Resins or Natural Rubbers -- Part of the Class 520 Series	2	0	0
314	Electric Lamp and Discharge Devices: Consumable Electrodes	1	0	0
276	Typesetting	0	0	0
	Total number of Patents (1975 - 2010)	**2,441,601**	**290,169**	**11.88**

Table A.2: Women Inventor Patents – Top 25 Patent Classes

Number of patents granted within patent class which have at least one woman inventor, 1975-1992

Patent Class	1975	1976	1977	1978	1979	1980	1981	1982	1983	1984	1985	1986	1987	1988	1989	1990	1991	1992
Food or Edible Material: Processes, Compositions, and Products (426)	45	24	14	24	29	30	49	22	42	45	57	68	47	68	100	88	100	103
Drug, Bio-Affecting and Body Treating Compositions (514)	29	40	48	55	37	61	67	46	70	91	91	77	133	168	190	178	222	266
Surgery (604)	25	22	20	18	6	14	13	23	24	24	37	35	82	44	82	82	92	98
Radiation Imagery Chemistry: Process, Composition, or Product Thereof (430)	22	10	15	15	13	16	34	33	24	28	30	30	21	30	58	71	75	72
Stock Material or Miscellaneous Articles (428)	19	23	12	29	16	22	38	23	38	36	71	74	68	86	104	113	103	138
Drug, Bio-Affecting and Body Treating Compositions (424)	17	14	19	17	26	31	36	25	23	42	45	52	86	93	148	155	181	205
Chemistry: Molecular Biology and Microbiology (435)	16	17	22	26	22	21	49	43	41	28	59	57	92	105	142	148	184	244
Organic Compounds -- Part of the Class 532-570 Series (536)	11	7	4	6	6	6	10	11	7	9	5	3	10	10	14	25	26	43
Semiconductor Device Manufacturing: Process (438)	8	8	2	11	12	6	13	12	12	20	20	18	36	34	34	43	67	58
Surgery (600)	7	2	4	9	2	4	5	6	9	14	13	21	21	21	40	38	41	46
Chemistry: Natural Resins or Derivatives; Peptides or Proteins; Lignins or Reaction Products Thereof (530)	5	4	2	10	2	7	8	7	11	19	15	12	19	24	41	26	50	65
Active Solid-State Devices (e.g., Transistors, Solid-State Diodes) (257)	4	1	9	4	4	2	6	5	3	7	9	14	14	10	25	36	46	45
Multiplex Communications (370)	2	0	1	3	1	3	2	1	1	8	6	4	11	12	11	15	14	13
Telecommunications (455)	1	2	3	3	6	2	4	4	1	2	3	1	2	4	8	10	5	13
Data Processing: Financial, Business Practice, Management, or Cost/Price Determination (705)	0	1	0	0	0	1	0	3	0	2	0	1	2	4	10	9	11	7
Furnishings (D06)	0	0	34	43	34	42	61	45	35	43	61	53	76	79	74	120	122	119

Patent Class	1975	1976	1977	1978	1979	1980	1981	1982	1983	1984	1985	1986	1987	1988	1989	1990	1991	1992
Equipment for Preparing or Serving Food or Drink Not Elsewhere Specified (D07)	0	0	27	19	32	26	26	35	17	13	38	42	35	27	38	49	39	71
Apparel and Haberdashery (D02)	0	0	18	14	10	19	21	14	21	20	39	31	46	45	64	63	79	83
Games, Toys, and Sports Goods (D21)	0	0	16	34	16	37	30	33	65	38	42	56	99	65	64	83	100	76
Travel Goods and Personal Belongings (D03)	0	0	13	21	17	15	13	22	17	14	18	21	35	21	25	51	56	61
Medical and Laboratory Equipment (D24)	0	0	6	7	6	14	12	22	21	28	17	18	29	32	41	34	45	73
Packages and Containers for Goods (D09)	0	0	5	10	16	17	22	15	13	16	24	11	23	14	18	26	34	40
Recording, Communication, or Information Retrieval Equipment (D14)	0	0	2	1	1	5	7	4	12	15	20	9	29	41	26	43	36	37
Data Processing: Database and File Management or Data Structures (707)	0	0	0	1	2	1	0	1	2	0	1	3	1	5	9	7	9	19
Electrical Computers and Digital Processing Systems: Multicomputer Data Transferring (709)	0	0	0	0	0	0	0	2	0	1	0	2	3	3	4	7	2	11

Number of patents granted within patent class which have at least one woman inventor, 1993-2010

Patent Class	1993	1994	1995	1996	1997	1998	1999	2000	2001	2002	2003	2004	2005	2006	2007	2008	2009	2010
Food or Edible Material: Processes, Compositions, and Products (426)	99	92	100	89	72	79	129	165	158	138	144	111	59	82	55	46	56	90
Drug, Bio-Affecting and Body Treating Compositions (514)	279	252	302	462	567	650	683	673	745	843	831	592	619	763	709	647	821	1127
Surgery (604)	93	140	148	158	178	220	174	167	208	194	283	194	145	133	122	110	148	282
Radiation Imagery Chemistry: Process, Composition, or Product Thereof (430)	96	113	101	129	111	146	139	177	183	171	150	159	104	146	122	98	108	137
Stock Material or Miscellaneous Articles (428)	132	133	125	175	186	239	247	220	240	257	310	262	258	210	180	158	184	251
Drug, Bio-Affecting and Body Treating Compositions (424)	218	245	234	281	486	551	686	552	630	692	644	434	358	451	424	409	440	675
Chemistry: Molecular Biology and Microbiology (435)	294	272	310	452	661	1005	1085	893	971	938	782	685	588	821	746	664	712	934
Organic Compounds -- Part of the Class 532-570 Series (536)	40	29	50	63	78	141	125	99	153	146	114	108	96	135	149	126	177	197

Number of patents granted within patent class which have at least one woman inventor, 1993-2010 (continued)

Semiconductor Device Manufacturing: Process (438)	63	78	82	62	88	130	192	304	450	508	449	442	406	413	364	334	396	502
Surgery (600)	55	75	76	76	87	136	152	158	156	186	206	185	121	169	125	117	160	269
Chemistry: Natural Resins or Derivatives; Peptides or Proteins; Lignins or Reaction Products Thereof (530)	74	42	58	81	137	172	173	165	174	141	123	130	149	210	373	348	249	287
Active Solid-State Devices (e.g., Transistors, Solid-State Diodes) (257)	38	65	49	68	75	119	118	98	159	194	270	277	261	287	232	231	269	358
Multiplex Communications (370)	31	42	45	71	54	66	85	128	103	145	159	198	206	321	252	369	504	728
Telecommunications (455)	7	19	21	33	33	65	101	102	109	108	95	141	135	230	246	214	246	343
Data Processing: Financial, Business Practice, Management, or Cost/Price Determination (705)	19	20	19	24	28	58	100	109	76	68	65	44	111	212	199	305	354	830
Furnishings (D06)	202	146	221	243	187	241	251	325	307	242	215	213	190	263	291	300	207	212
Equipment for Preparing or Serving Food or Drink Not Elsewhere Specified (D07)	121	82	82	96	74	136	125	171	191	128	181	197	161	215	305	257	175	265
Apparel and Haberdashery (D02)	129	122	97	92	112	158	115	110	89	120	160	122	104	181	185	219	180	205
Games, Toys, and Sports Goods (D21)	94	111	111	108	88	128	98	118	130	96	131	92	61	122	159	188	132	84
Travel Goods and Personal Belongings (D03)	79	65	84	74	74	104	132	120	103	105	92	104	93	142	140	115	127	157
Medical and Laboratory Equipment (D24)	84	88	95	94	101	134	137	150	180	146	189	107	75	95	154	187	122	176
Packages and Containers for Goods (D09)	72	56	75	72	75	105	114	169	234	108	177	127	149	198	276	337	224	302
Recording, Communication, or Information Retrieval Equipment (D14)	59	53	82	111	121	144	132	211	175	175	198	182	163	230	396	421	210	251
Data Processing: Database and File Management or Data Structures (707)	23	31	35	50	50	125	119	131	138	195	220	215	173	287	266	322	489	734
Electrical Computers and Digital Processing Systems: Multicomputer Data Transferring (709)	14	17	16	41	29	97	111	149	150	125	133	195	180	301	245	313	456	632

Share of patents granted within patent class which have at least one woman inventor, 1975-1992

Patent Class	1975	1976	1977	1978	1979	1980	1981	1982	1983	1984	1985	1986	1987	1988	1989	1990	1991	1992
Food or Edible Material: Processes, Compositions, and Products (426)	9.3%	5.4%	4.2%	9.0%	11.7%	9.9%	14.8%	8.5%	14.8%	17.5%	16.6%	25.1%	16.8%	21.4%	21.7%	19.9%	22.7%	25.2%
Drug, Bio-Affecting and Body Treating Compositions (514)	5.5%	6.1%	6.4%	7.3%	6.8%	8.1%	9.9%	7.8%	11.7%	12.3%	12.1%	10.9%	15.4%	19.5%	16.9%	17.1%	18.7%	23.4%
Surgery (604)	8.7%	7.6%	7.4%	9.6%	4.4%	5.4%	5.5%	8.1%	8.7%	7.9%	10.8%	8.1%	15.6%	8.9%	13.6%	13.0%	14.4%	12.7%
Radiation Imagery Chemistry: Process, Composition, or Product Thereof (430)	5.3%	2.9%	4.5%	5.2%	6.4%	6.2%	8.4%	11.0%	8.3%	10.3%	12.3%	12.0%	8.3%	12.3%	17.9%	21.9%	21.1%	23.0%
Stock Material or Miscellaneous Articles (428)	3.1%	3.9%	2.2%	5.1%	3.9%	3.9%	6.1%	3.9%	6.7%	5.9%	9.7%	9.9%	9.3%	11.6%	11.3%	12.4%	12.7%	14.5%
Drug, Bio-Affecting and Body Treating Compositions (424)	8.2%	5.7%	7.9%	7.7%	11.6%	14.6%	14.5%	9.9%	12.2%	14.0%	15.9%	15.9%	20.8%	21.4%	21.8%	23.1%	24.8%	27.9%
Chemistry: Molecular Biology and Microbiology (435)	7.9%	8.7%	11.6%	15.2%	17.9%	9.3%	16.3%	15.9%	17.6%	11.5%	23.4%	19.1%	19.8%	24.2%	24.3%	27.3%	30.9%	32.1%
Organic Compounds -- Part of the Class 532-570 Series (536)	10.3%	9.2%	4.8%	6.5%	10.2%	7.5%	12.8%	16.7%	12.3%	13.0%	11.4%	7.9%	25.6%	18.9%	18.4%	22.1%	24.3%	30.9%
Semiconductor Device Manufacturing: Process (438)	3.3%	4.6%	1.2%	6.7%	7.9%	3.4%	6.4%	5.9%	5.2%	8.1%	7.7%	6.3%	10.5%	11.1%	9.6%	13.8%	15.8%	12.0%
Surgery (600)	2.8%	0.9%	2.1%	5.0%	1.3%	1.5%	2.0%	2.6%	3.9%	5.6%	4.6%	6.2%	5.6%	5.8%	7.8%	7.8%	7.6%	8.7%
Chemistry: Natural Resins or Derivatives; Peptides or Proteins; Lignins or Reaction Products Thereof (530)	6.0%	7.1%	2.9%	9.7%	4.3%	8.0%	8.5%	9.3%	12.8%	16.7%	16.3%	13.3%	13.3%	17.5%	26.5%	20.8%	29.4%	28.3%
Active Solid-State Devices (e.g., Transistors, Solid-State Diodes) (257)	2.2%	0.5%	4.5%	2.9%	2.8%	1.2%	4.2%	4.6%	2.7%	5.3%	6.0%	6.8%	5.9%	4.7%	7.4%	9.0%	8.7%	10.3%
Multiplex Communications (370)	2.1%	0.0%	1.2%	3.9%	1.6%	3.6%	2.9%	1.3%	1.0%	6.6%	3.2%	2.7%	5.2%	6.6%	6.0%	7.2%	7.6%	6.4%
Telecommunications (455)	0.8%	1.4%	2.3%	2.8%	6.4%	1.8%	3.9%	3.8%	1.0%	1.9%	2.9%	1.1%	1.9%	3.5%	6.8%	8.5%	3.0%	6.6%
Data Processing: Financial, Business Practice, Management, or Cost/Price Determination (705)	0.0%	6.7%	0.0%	0.0%	0.0%	5.6%	0.0%	13.6%	0.0%	8.0%	0.0%	2.9%	3.8%	7.3%	11.2%	12.7%	15.1%	11.5%
Furnishings (D 06)	0.0%	0.0%	9.2%	10.2%	10.3%	11.3%	13.6%	10.1%	8.6%	9.8%	12.9%	11.3%	17.0%	16.1%	19.4%	23.7%	19.6%	17.9%
Equipment for Preparing or Serving Food or Drink Not Elsewhere Specified (D 07)	0.0%	0.0%	13.8%	9.6%	17.8%	11.0%	11.7%	16.6%	8.4%	7.5%	17.6%	15.4%	15.5%	15.9%	18.0%	19.3%	14.4%	23.6%
Apparel and Haberdashery (D 02)	0.0%	0.0%	31.6%	20.6%	20.8%	20.4%	20.6%	19.4%	26.3%	25.3%	28.5%	31.6%	33.1%	20.3%	33.7%	34.6%	36.2%	29.9%

Share of patents granted within patent class which have at least one woman inventor, 1975-1992 (Continued)

Games, Toys, and Sports Goods (D21)	0.0%	0.0%	7.4%	14.4%	7.7%	14.3%	9.6%	9.9%	21.7%	14.0%	12.8%	22.5%	30.4%	25.6%	18.1%	21.8%	18.8%	15.3%
Travel Goods and Personal Belongings (D03)	0.0%	0.0%	17.3%	19.3%	17.9%	15.6%	9.9%	16.7%	12.3%	13.9%	11.3%	17.6%	28.5%	16.7%	27.2%	23.7%	21.6%	27.0%
Medical and Laboratory Equipment (D24)	0.0%	0.0%	3.7%	5.1%	7.1%	11.0%	7.9%	10.2%	12.3%	11.6%	10.5%	7.6%	11.7%	15.9%	17.9%	16.2%	17.2%	24.4%
Packages and Containers for Goods (D09)	0.0%	0.0%	3.8%	5.8%	13.9%	8.2%	8.7%	8.0%	7.7%	9.2%	13.9%	5.9%	11.4%	9.0%	11.7%	9.5%	11.0%	15.2%
Recording, Communication, or Information Retrieval Equipment (D14)	0.0%	0.0%	1.4%	0.7%	1.1%	4.5%	4.2%	2.7%	9.0%	7.7%	8.0%	4.4%	11.0%	18.7%	11.7%	13.7%	10.8%	14.0%
Data Processing: Database and File Management or Data Structures (707)	0.0%	0.0%	0.0%	6.3%	33.3%	16.7%	0.0%	16.7%	28.6%	0.0%	7.7%	15.0%	5.6%	35.7%	23.1%	21.2%	27.3%	32.8%
Electrical Computers and Digital Processing Systems: Multicomputer Data Transferring (709)	0.0%	0.0%	0.0%	0.0%	0.0%	0.0%	0.0%	18.2%	0.0%	5.6%	0.0%	20.0%	17.6%	11.5%	19.0%	20.6%	5.4%	18.3%

Share of patents granted within patent class which have at least one woman inventor, 1993-2010

Patent Class	1993	1994	1995	1996	1997	1998	1999	2000	2001	2002	2003	2004	2005	2006	2007	2008	2009	2010
Food or Edible Material: Processes, Compositions, and Products (426)	25.1%	24.6%	25.8%	21.6%	21.1%	20.7%	23.9%	28.3%	29.0%	31.6%	34.8%	33.7%	31.4%	34.6%	27.6%	31.5%	32.6%	36.1%
Drug, Bio-Affecting and Body Treating Compositions (514)	21.9%	23.1%	23.2%	27.9%	26.1%	29.2%	29.2%	29.1%	31.0%	32.2%	34.6%	33.9%	37.0%	37.5%	38.1%	38.5%	40.2%	41.4%
Surgery (604)	11.7%	13.1%	15.4%	17.7%	20.5%	18.9%	16.8%	18.6%	21.8%	22.5%	22.9%	23.0%	23.1%	21.9%	24.4%	22.2%	23.1%	22.6%
Radiation Imagery Chemistry: Process, Composition, or Product Thereof (430)	18.9%	19.5%	19.8%	24.2%	22.8%	24.8%	21.6%	25.7%	27.0%	26.7%	24.9%	29.1%	26.9%	31.5%	32.6%	28.6%	33.2%	32.0%
Stock Material or Miscellaneous Articles (428)	14.2%	13.7%	12.7%	15.3%	15.3%	16.9%	16.3%	16.3%	17.6%	18.0%	21.2%	19.2%	24.0%	24.5%	21.6%	23.7%	26.8%	24.7%
Drug, Bio-Affecting and Body Treating Compositions (424)	26.8%	28.8%	26.6%	28.2%	29.9%	28.9%	33.6%	31.6%	32.3%	35.3%	34.3%	31.2%	32.8%	31.3%	34.4%	35.1%	38.5%	37.9%
Chemistry: Molecular Biology and Microbiology (435)	31.0%	30.5%	31.3%	31.6%	32.6%	36.5%	39.2%	37.9%	36.4%	39.2%	37.4%	37.8%	37.2%	40.4%	40.2%	39.8%	42.7%	40.7%
Organic Compounds -- Part of the Class 532-570 Series (536)	28.8%	24.2%	24.8%	25.5%	23.4%	32.2%	33.2%	31.9%	40.7%	37.9%	35.7%	36.4%	40.0%	39.2%	47.8%	40.4%	46.5%	43.3%

Patent Class	1993	1994	1995	1996	1997	1998	1999	2000	2001	2002	2003	2004	2005	2006	2007	2008	2009	2010
Semiconductor Device Manufacturing: Process (438)	11.5%	13.6%	12.3%	11.0%	11.3%	13.5%	12.6%	14.7%	17.9%	19.6%	18.7%	18.6%	19.5%	19.2%	17.6%	17.7%	20.5%	20.6%
Surgery (600)	8.4%	9.5%	9.8%	10.3%	11.9%	11.7%	13.3%	12.1%	12.5%	14.1%	14.9%	17.5%	15.2%	18.3%	15.4%	16.0%	18.2%	19.2%
Chemistry: Natural Resins or Derivatives; Peptides or Proteins; Lignins or Reaction Products Thereof (530)	31.2%	21.9%	29.7%	32.7%	35.9%	31.0%	34.8%	39.3%	42.2%	36.9%	34.3%	39.8%	47.3%	41.7%	56.9%	54.4%	49.0%	50.1%
Active Solid-State Devices (e.g., Transistors, Solid-State Diodes) (257)	10.9%	12.2%	9.5%	10.5%	12.0%	12.1%	11.1%	8.7%	12.6%	13.5%	15.2%	14.8%	14.9%	16.3%	14.4%	15.2%	17.7%	16.5%
Multiplex Communications (370)	12.0%	11.3%	9.9%	13.2%	10.8%	9.7%	10.3%	11.4%	8.9%	11.3%	11.1%	11.2%	12.4%	13.5%	13.2%	14.4%	16.2%	17.1%
Telecommunications (455)	3.2%	8.1%	7.1%	7.6%	9.1%	10.1%	12.5%	9.8%	11.5%	11.8%	10.2%	12.3%	12.0%	11.5%	13.9%	14.0%	14.2%	15.4%
Data Processing: Financial, Business Practice, Management, or Cost/Price Determination (705)	15.2%	15.9%	21.1%	20.7%	14.2%	14.4%	17.7%	17.6%	19.0%	18.0%	17.8%	16.7%	17.6%	20.5%	20.9%	23.0%	21.8%	24.3%
Furnishings (D 06)	21.4%	18.2%	21.1%	23.1%	21.7%	22.3%	23.0%	26.1%	24.6%	21.6%	19.6%	20.4%	24.5%	23.5%	20.4%	22.7%	18.5%	20.4%
Equipment for Preparing or Serving Food or Drink Not Elsewhere Specified (D 07)	28.5%	19.9%	21.5%	19.8%	20.2%	28.0%	26.9%	27.1%	31.4%	26.1%	29.8%	35.4%	33.3%	30.6%	33.6%	28.7%	23.6%	27.9%
Apparel and Haberdashery (D 02)	33.5%	32.3%	35.4%	32.5%	25.7%	25.8%	24.0%	26.6%	21.8%	33.6%	36.5%	28.2%	29.4%	28.4%	25.8%	28.8%	26.7%	29.2%
Games, Toys, and Sports Goods (D21)	19.4%	18.8%	18.2%	20.6%	17.9%	17.3%	15.9%	16.4%	21.8%	19.9%	22.5%	17.9%	14.5%	17.1%	21.5%	23.9%	20.5%	16.5%
Travel Goods and Personal Belongings (D03)	27.9%	23.4%	28.6%	25.7%	25.8%	31.0%	34.7%	33.6%	26.8%	30.0%	25.8%	30.4%	31.5%	30.9%	33.0%	29.5%	31.2%	34.1%
Medical and Laboratory Equipment (D24)	25.5%	23.1%	23.9%	25.5%	28.2%	32.9%	31.6%	29.7%	33.3%	32.1%	40.0%	30.2%	33.3%	30.9%	30.9%	32.2%	21.6%	22.7%
Packages and Containers for Goods (D09)	22.6%	16.1%	21.1%	22.0%	19.3%	23.5%	23.4%	27.6%	37.1%	22.4%	28.6%	27.5%	30.2%	27.5%	32.6%	38.1%	25.1%	31.1%
Recording, Communication, or Information Retrieval Equipment (D14)	13.4%	10.8%	14.0%	19.8%	21.1%	20.1%	19.7%	26.3%	25.6%	25.9%	26.2%	27.5%	31.9%	25.1%	35.0%	33.9%	16.1%	21.9%
Data Processing: Database and File Management or Data Structures (707)	20.4%	24.6%	20.7%	19.5%	16.5%	17.2%	15.1%	18.3%	18.8%	19.3%	20.7%	19.8%	18.7%	20.4%	21.2%	22.1%	22.7%	22.2%
Electrical Computers and Digital Processing Systems: Multicomputer Data Transferring (709)	18.2%	18.3%	13.9%	16.4%	13.0%	13.7%	14.3%	16.5%	16.8%	13.1%	14.2%	15.9%	15.2%	16.5%	14.2%	15.8%	18.8%	19.0%

79Table A.3: Women Primary Inventor Patents – Top 25 Patent Classes

Patents Granted within Patent Class which have a Woman as the Primary Inventor, 1975-1992

Patent Class	1975	1976	1977	1978	1979	1980	1981	1982	1983	1984	1985	1986	1987	1988	1989	1990	1991	1992
Food or Edible Material: Processes, Compositions, and Products (426)	22	16	8	10	16	22	24	11	14	12	28	22	22	29	43	41	43	41
Apparel (002)	19	22	20	23	14	20	25	19	26	36	26	31	62	28	45	40	63	62
Surgery (604)	17	13	15	13	5	11	10	15	17	18	26	29	51	40	51	57	53	55
Drug, Bio-Affecting and Body Treating Compositions (514)	15	15	17	28	15	27	27	18	37	45	42	32	50	64	67	67	89	93
Special Receptacle or Package (206)	14	12	7	11	10	12	19	15	14	16	16	21	17	23	39	38	42	24
Stock Material or Miscellaneous Articles (428)	12	17	8	12	7	11	17	17	22	19	43	38	31	37	51	62	42	77
Drug, Bio-Affecting and Body Treating Compositions (424)	9	8	12	6	13	12	18	13	15	23	22	25	40	42	65	63	85	85
Chemistry: Molecular Biology and Microbiology (435)	7	14	8	9	10	11	16	13	12	10	22	22	40	39	59	51	80	101
Semiconductor Device Manufacturing: Process (438)	5	8	2	6	5	2	5	7	1	8	11	4	15	14	13	17	24	21
Chemistry: Natural Resins or Derivatives; Peptides or Proteins; Lignins or Reaction Products Thereof (530)	4	0	1	4	1	4	1	2	5	14	4	8	4	10	16	11	13	16
Active Solid-State Devices (e.g., Transistors, Solid-State Diodes) (257)	3	1	7	3	1	2	3	2	1	3	2	8	4	6	10	17	10	16
Multiplex Communications (370)	2	0	0	2	1	1	1	1	0	3	3	2	6	3	4	3	5	4
Furnishings (D06)	0	0	29	40	30	35	53	37	31	37	52	47	69	62	54	91	88	106
Equipment for Preparing or Serving Food or Drink Not Elsewhere Specified (D07)	0	0	27	18	24	24	18	29	13	13	35	36	31	21	28	39	32	50
Tools and Hardware (D08)	0	0	25	6	20	9	15	4	11	20	8	14	7	11	27	26	28	34
Jewelry, Symbolic Insignia, and Ornaments (D11)	0	0	17	33	22	24	14	16	20	19	16	23	12	12	18	20	49	36
Apparel and Haberdashery (D02)	0	0	17	14	10	18	20	14	17	19	37	28	40	35	60	46	64	69

Patent Class	1975	1976	1977	1978	1979	1980	1981	1982	1983	1984	1985	1986	1987	1988	1989	1990	1991	1992
Travel Goods and Personal Belongings (D03)	0	0	13	20	14	13	10	19	14	13	15	20	33	15	21	48	51	53
Games, Toys, and Sports Goods (D21)	0	0	12	29	9	34	26	26	55	32	34	42	74	50	56	69	78	58
Transportation (D12)	0	0	7	5	11	5	12	4	4	13	9	18	19	10	13	21	17	30
Environmental Heating and Cooling; Fluid Handling and Sanitary Equipment (D23)	0	0	7	4	6	7	4	3	5	8	5	15	21	26	16	6	50	40
Medical and Laboratory Equipment (D24)	0	0	6	6	2	13	10	15	13	20	9	13	15	21	34	28	32	50
Packages and Containers for Goods (D09)	0	0	3	6	6	16	22	13	11	13	15	7	17	7	12	21	31	22
Recording, Communication, or Information Retrieval Equipment (D14)	0	0	1	1	1	3	4	4	4	10	15	8	19	33	10	17	21	20
Data Processing: Database and File Management or Data Structures (707)	0	0	0	0	2	0	0	0	0	0	0	2	0	3	5	2	5	10

Patents Granted within Patent Class which have a Woman as the Primary Inventor, 1993-2010

Patent Class	**1993**	**1994**	**1995**	**1996**	**1997**	**1998**	**1999**	**2000**	**2001**	**2002**	**2003**	**2004**	**2005**	**2006**	**2007**	**2008**	**2009**	**2010**
Food or Edible Material: Processes, Compositions, and Products (426)	50	45	43	31	39	31	53	75	77	52	61	48	22	42	20	16	17	41
Apparel (002)	38	32	41	65	65	89	108	94	109	97	44	53	44	59	42	40	26	73
Surgery (604)	46	84	75	77	75	111	67	85	94	90	133	74	63	60	60	45	57	95
Drug, Bio-Affecting and Body Treating Compositions (514)	104	82	107	161	192	195	240	218	255	224	205	155	160	200	176	169	253	292
Special Receptacle or Package (206)	43	33	37	39	47	53	55	55	55	58	44	40	49	38	32	46	36	51
Stock Material or Miscellaneous Articles (428)	55	60	45	79	66	98	97	93	88	94	113	105	89	70	65	65	64	114
Drug, Bio-Affecting and Body Treating Compositions (424)	82	87	96	104	189	209	275	205	248	282	268	175	136	163	153	166	170	266
Chemistry: Molecular Biology and Microbiology (435)	112	105	107	175	250	413	475	392	352	350	334	263	214	281	263	228	272	321
Semiconductor Device Manufacturing: Process (438)	24	28	21	20	27	44	75	110	149	188	153	167	134	113	116	114	130	167
Chemistry: Natural Resins or Derivatives; Peptides or Proteins; Lignins or Reaction Products Thereof (530)	33	22	24	30	53	57	61	76	58	48	43	45	46	61	222	182	100	118

Patents Granted within Patent Class which have a Woman as the Primary Inventor, 1993-2010 (Continued)

Active Solid-State Devices (e.g., Transistors, Solid-State Diodes) (257)	18	18	24	28	21	38	50	31	52	68	81	88	80	98	69	55	87	117
Multiplex Communications (370)	12	15	12	23	21	18	22	39	40	39	54	68	72	99	85	151	196	282
Furnishings (D06)	165	116	173	173	140	205	202	242	171	182	149	133	109	172	202	229	164	151
Equipment for Preparing or Serving Food or Drink Not Elsewhere Specified (D07)	61	53	55	64	45	95	91	119	142	86	114	114	108	135	222	191	105	166
Tools and Hardware (D08)	37	29	41	56	38	54	47	74	49	52	63	77	72	72	123	123	78	55
Jewelry, Symbolic Insignia, and Ornaments (D11)	56	53	52	40	50	57	65	61	55	65	70	80	49	86	75	103	60	69
Apparel and Haberdashery (D02)	104	107	86	66	90	128	100	92	76	98	122	95	92	160	154	192	155	167
Travel Goods and Personal Belongings (D03)	63	57	64	59	62	88	97	96	75	83	67	83	69	113	88	85	104	123
Games, Toys, and Sports Goods (D21)	80	95	89	88	71	89	72	67	89	63	86	65	51	77	101	86	63	38
Transportation (D12)	32	34	50	31	52	56	74	69	77	78	89	87	40	54	71	58	39	32
Environmental Heating and Cooling; Fluid Handling and Sanitary Equipment (D23)	34	42	27	27	34	54	60	65	65	81	71	59	62	104	63	119	76	84
Medical and Laboratory Equipment (D24)	56	64	72	60	57	78	92	101	101	88	92	60	46	52	104	103	75	101
Packages and Containers for Goods (D09)	52	32	47	56	51	73	64	103	125	71	105	84	68	123	154	184	107	165
Recording, Communication, or Information Retrieval Equipment (D14)	26	20	34	50	50	63	62	89	64	94	105	103	85	124	240	237	92	119
Data Processing: Database and File Management or Data Structures (707)	14	14	11	18	13	42	35	40	58	95	103	89	57	90	92	110	178	280

Share of Patents Granted within Patent Class which have a Woman as the Primary Inventor, 1975-1992

Patent Class	1975	1976	1977	1978	1979	1980	1981	1982	1983	1984	1985	1986	1987	1988	1989	1990	1991	1992
Food or Edible Material: Processes, Compositions, and Products (426)	4.6%	3.7%	2.4%	3.8%	6.5%	7.3%	7.3%	4.3%	4.9%	4.7%	8.2%	8.2%	8.0%	9.2%	9.5%	9.3%	9.8%	10.2%
Apparel (002)	14.0%	22.7%	14.2%	17.0%	16.3%	17.1%	19.1%	19.6%	26.0%	24.8%	16.7%	17.9%	27.2%	16.8%	19.1%	20.0%	19.8%	22.9%
Surgery (604)	5.9%	4.5%	5.6%	6.9%	3.7%	4.2%	4.3%	5.3%	6.2%	6.0%	7.6%	6.7%	9.8%	8.2%	8.5%	9.1%	8.3%	7.2%
Drug, Bio-Affecting and Body Treating Compositions (514)	2.9%	2.3%	2.3%	3.8%	2.8%	3.6%	4.0%	3.1%	6.3%	6.1%	5.7%	4.6%	6.0%	7.7%	6.1%	6.7%	7.7%	8.4%

Patent Class	1975	1976	1977	1978	1979	1980	1981	1982	1983	1984	1985	1986	1987	1988	1989	1990	1991	1992
Special Receptacle or Package (206)	3.8%	3.5%	2.4%	3.4%	3.9%	3.9%	6.8%	5.8%	4.9%	6.0%	5.4%	7.5%	4.8%	5.8%	7.8%	8.4%	9.7%	5.7%
Stock Material or Miscellaneous Articles (428)	2.0%	2.9%	1.5%	2.1%	1.7%	2.0%	2.7%	2.9%	3.9%	3.1%	5.9%	5.1%	4.3%	5.0%	5.6%	6.9%	5.2%	8.1%
Drug, Bio-Affecting and Body Treating Compositions (424)	4.4%	3.3%	5.0%	2.8%	5.9%	5.6%	7.3%	5.2%	8.0%	7.7%	7.9%	7.7%	9.8%	9.8%	9.7%	9.6%	11.8%	11.8%
Chemistry: Molecular Biology and Microbiology (435)	3.5%	7.3%	4.3%	5.3%	8.2%	4.9%	5.4%	4.9%	5.3%	4.1%	8.8%	7.4%	8.8%	9.1%	10.3%	9.6%	13.6%	13.5%
Semiconductor Device Manufacturing: Process (438)	2.1%	4.7%	1.2%	3.7%	3.3%	1.1%	2.5%	3.5%	0.4%	3.3%	4.2%	1.4%	4.4%	4.7%	3.7%	5.5%	5.7%	4.4%
Chemistry: Natural Resins or Derivatives; Peptides or Proteins; Lignins or Reaction Products Thereof (530)	4.9%	0.0%	1.4%	4.0%	2.2%	4.6%	1.1%	2.7%	5.9%	12.5%	4.3%	8.9%	2.9%	7.4%	10.5%	9.2%	7.9%	7.3%
Active Solid-State Devices (e.g., Transistors, Solid-State Diodes) (257)	1.7%	0.5%	3.6%	2.2%	0.7%	1.2%	2.1%	1.9%	0.9%	2.3%	1.3%	3.9%	1.7%	2.9%	3.0%	4.3%	1.9%	3.7%
Multiplex Communications (370)	2.1%	0.0%	0.0%	2.6%	1.6%	1.2%	1.5%	1.4%	0.0%	2.5%	1.6%	1.4%	2.9%	1.7%	2.2%	1.5%	2.8%	2.0%
Furnishings (D 06)	0.0%	0.0%	7.9%	9.5%	9.1%	9.4%	11.8%	8.3%	7.7%	8.4%	11.0%	10.0%	15.4%	12.7%	14.2%	18.1%	14.3%	15.9%
Equipment for Preparing or Serving Food or Drink Not Elsewhere Specified (D07)	0.0%	0.0%	13.8%	9.1%	13.4%	10.1%	8.1%	13.7%	6.4%	7.6%	16.6%	13.4%	14.1%	12.4%	13.3%	15.4%	11.9%	16.7%
Tools and Hardware (D08)	0.0%	0.0%	11.7%	3.3%	14.5%	4.8%	6.4%	1.8%	5.6%	7.9%	4.4%	6.3%	2.7%	4.0%	8.1%	7.1%	6.2%	6.9%
Apparel and Haberdashery (D02)	0.0%	0.0%	29.8%	20.6%	20.8%	19.4%	19.6%	19.4%	21.3%	24.1%	27.0%	28.9%	28.8%	16.1%	31.6%	25.3%	29.4%	24.8%
Jewelry, Symbolic Insignia, and Ornaments (D 11)	0.0%	0.0%	15.0%	20.9%	18.0%	16.7%	8.8%	10.8%	18.3%	27.9%	18.2%	21.3%	14.0%	18.8%	16.4%	20.6%	29.5%	22.5%
Travel Goods and Personal Belongings (D 03)	0.0%	0.0%	17.3%	18.3%	14.7%	13.5%	7.6%	14.5%	10.1%	12.9%	9.4%	16.8%	27.0%	11.9%	22.8%	22.3%	19.8%	23.5%
Games, Toys, and Sports Goods (D21)	0.0%	0.0%	5.5%	12.3%	4.3%	13.1%	8.3%	7.9%	18.3%	12.0%	10.5%	17.1%	22.8%	19.8%	16.0%	18.2%	14.7%	11.6%
Environmental Heating and Cooling; Fluid Handling and Sanitary Equipment (D23)	0.0%	0.0%	4.7%	3.1%	4.5%	5.0%	2.2%	1.5%	3.0%	4.4%	3.3%	8.8%	9.5%	13.3%	9.0%	2.3%	12.4%	11.0%
Transportation (D12)	0.0%	0.0%	3.5%	3.5%	8.7%	3.4%	6.7%	2.3%	2.2%	7.3%	5.4%	9.6%	8.2%	5.2%	5.4%	6.0%	4.5%	7.9%
Medical and Laboratory Equipment (D24)	0.0%	0.0%	3.7%	4.4%	2.4%	10.2%	6.6%	7.0%	7.6%	8.4%	5.6%	5.6%	6.0%	10.4%	14.8%	13.3%	12.3%	16.8%
Packages and Containers for Goods (D09)	0.0%	0.0%	2.3%	3.5%	5.2%	7.7%	8.7%	6.9%	6.5%	7.6%	8.9%	3.7%	8.5%	4.5%	7.8%	7.7%	10.1%	8.5%
Recording, Communication, or Information Retrieval Equipment (D 14)	0.0%	0.0%	0.7%	0.7%	1.1%	2.8%	2.4%	2.7%	3.0%	5.2%	6.0%	3.9%	7.3%	15.3%	4.6%	5.5%	6.4%	7.6%
Data Processing: Database and File Management or Data Structures (707)	0.0%	0.0%	0.0%	0.0%	33.3%	0.0%	0.0%	0.0%	0.0%	0.0%	0.0%	10.0%	0.0%	21.4%	13.2%	6.3%	15.2%	17.5%

Share of Patents Granted within Patent Class which have a Woman as the Primary Inventor, 1993-2010

Patent Class	1993	1994	1995	1996	1997	1998	1999	2000	2001	2002	2003	2004	2005	2006	2007	2008	2009	2010
Food or Edible Material: Processes, Compositions, and Products (426)	12.8%	12.1%	11.3%	7.7%	11.7%	8.4%	10.2%	13.3%	14.5%	12.3%	15.1%	15.1%	11.9%	18.1%	10.6%	11.6%	10.4%	17.2%
Apparel (002)	19.4%	14.8%	19.0%	20.2%	19.2%	22.0%	22.9%	21.1%	27.7%	25.9%	18.0%	17.8%	17.9%	20.0%	22.6%	25.5%	19.4%	25.3%
Surgery (604)	5.8%	8.0%	7.9%	8.7%	8.8%	9.7%	6.6%	9.6%	10.0%	10.7%	11.0%	9.1%	10.2%	10.0%	12.3%	9.4%	9.1%	7.8%
Drug, Bio-Affecting and Body Treating Compositions (514)	8.4%	7.8%	8.5%	10.1%	9.3%	9.2%	10.8%	9.9%	11.1%	9.0%	9.1%	9.4%	10.2%	10.4%	10.1%	10.7%	13.1%	11.5%
Special Receptacle or Package (206)	9.4%	6.7%	8.1%	8.4%	10.4%	8.7%	9.2%	10.3%	12.0%	14.4%	12.1%	12.5%	13.8%	12.1%	12.0%	12.9%	12.7%	12.9%
Stock Material or Miscellaneous Articles (428)	6.0%	6.3%	4.6%	7.0%	5.5%	7.0%	6.5%	7.0%	6.7%	6.8%	7.9%	7.9%	8.5%	8.4%	8.1%	10.1%	9.7%	11.7%
Drug, Bio-Affecting and Body Treating Compositions (424)	10.3%	10.4%	11.2%	10.7%	12.0%	11.4%	14.1%	12.3%	13.2%	15.0%	14.9%	13.1%	13.0%	11.9%	13.0%	15.1%	15.7%	15.8%
Chemistry: Molecular Biology and Microbiology (435)	12.3%	12.1%	11.0%	12.6%	12.8%	15.5%	17.7%	17.2%	13.8%	15.2%	16.6%	15.1%	14.0%	14.5%	14.8%	14.3%	16.9%	14.7%
Semiconductor Device Manufacturing: Process (438)	4.4%	5.0%	3.3%	3.6%	3.6%	4.6%	5.0%	5.5%	6.1%	7.5%	6.6%	7.2%	6.6%	5.4%	5.8%	6.2%	6.9%	7.1%
Chemistry: Natural Resins or Derivatives; Peptides or Proteins; Lignins or Reaction Products Thereof (530)	14.3%	12.0%	12.7%	12.3%	14.2%	10.7%	12.6%	18.7%	14.8%	13.2%	12.3%	14.3%	15.3%	12.6%	35.4%	29.9%	20.8%	21.9%
Active Solid-State Devices (e.g., Transistors, Solid-State Diodes) (257)	5.3%	3.4%	4.8%	4.5%	3.5%	4.0%	4.8%	2.8%	4.2%	4.9%	4.7%	4.8%	4.7%	5.7%	4.5%	3.7%	5.9%	5.6%
Multiplex Communications (370)	4.7%	4.2%	2.7%	4.4%	4.3%	2.7%	2.7%	3.6%	3.6%	3.1%	3.9%	4.0%	4.5%	4.3%	4.6%	6.1%	6.6%	7.0%
Furnishings (D 06)	17.5%	14.5%	16.6%	16.5%	16.3%	19.1%	18.6%	19.5%	13.9%	16.3%	13.7%	12.8%	14.1%	15.5%	14.3%	17.5%	14.9%	14.8%
Equipment for Preparing or Serving Food or Drink Not Elsewhere Specified (D07)	14.4%	12.9%	14.5%	13.3%	12.3%	19.6%	19.6%	19.1%	23.6%	18.0%	18.9%	20.8%	22.5%	19.3%	25.0%	21.8%	14.3%	17.7%
Tools and Hardware (D08)	6.8%	5.5%	7.1%	9.8%	7.3%	7.4%	7.0%	8.7%	8.4%	9.0%	9.2%	10.5%	14.1%	9.3%	12.9%	11.7%	9.5%	7.2%
Apparel and Haberdashery (D02)	27.0%	28.7%	31.4%	23.3%	20.7%	21.0%	21.1%	22.6%	18.7%	28.6%	28.9%	22.8%	28.0%	25.6%	23.2%	26.9%	23.7%	24.0%
Jewelry, Symbolic Insignia, and Ornaments (D 11)	25.0%	26.2%	17.2%	16.8%	18.4%	21.2%	29.1%	28.0%	20.8%	26.7%	32.9%	34.2%	25.3%	30.6%	26.8%	34.3%	25.8%	26.7%
Travel Goods and Personal Belongings (D 03)	22.3%	20.5%	21.9%	20.5%	21.6%	26.2%	25.6%	26.9%	19.5%	24.0%	18.8%	24.3%	23.6%	24.6%	21.0%	21.8%	25.6%	26.9%
Games, Toys, and Sports Goods (D21)	16.5%	16.0%	14.7%	16.8%	14.6%	12.1%	11.8%	9.3%	15.0%	13.1%	14.8%	12.8%	12.1%	11.0%	13.7%	11.0%	9.9%	7.5%

Patent Class	1993	1994	1995	1996	1997	1998	1999	2000	2001	2002	2003	2004	2005	2006	2007	2008	2009	2010
Environmental Heating and Cooling; Fluid Handling and Sanitary Equipment (D23)	11.6%	10.0%	7.4%	7.7%	9.6%	10.7%	11.0%	10.6%	11.7%	14.2%	12.5%	13.4%	11.8%	10.1%	8.3%	14.5%	11.9%	11.9%
Transportation (D12)	7.2%	7.5%	10.5%	6.2%	9.4%	8.1%	11.7%	8.7%	11.5%	12.5%	13.9%	11.6%	8.3%	7.7%	8.9%	7.8%	6.3%	4.5%
Medical and Laboratory Equipment (D24)	17.0%	16.9%	18.6%	16.3%	16.0%	19.4%	21.5%	20.1%	18.8%	19.6%	19.7%	17.1%	20.6%	17.2%	21.3%	18.1%	13.7%	13.4%
Packages and Containers for Goods (D09)	16.4%	9.3%	13.4%	17.1%	13.2%	16.4%	13.3%	17.0%	20.0%	14.8%	17.0%	18.2%	14.0%	17.4%	18.5%	21.1%	12.3%	17.3%
Recording, Communication, or Information Retrieval Equipment (D 14)	6.0%	4.1%	5.9%	9.1%	8.9%	8.9%	9.4%	11.3%	9.7%	14.7%	14.4%	16.2%	17.6%	14.2%	21.6%	19.8%	7.3%	10.8%
Data Processing: Database and File Management or Data Structures (707)	12.4%	11.1%	6.8%	7.2%	4.3%	5.9%	4.5%	5.6%	8.1%	9.6%	9.8%	8.4%	6.2%	6.6%	7.6%	7.8%	8.6%	8.8%

Table A.4: Women Non-Primary Inventor Patents – Top 25 Patent Classes

Number of Patents Granted within Patent Class which have a Woman as a Non-Primary Inventor, 1975-1992

Patent Class	1975	1976	1977	1978	1979	1980	1981	1982	1983	1984	1985	1986	1987	1988	1989	1990	1991	1992
Food or Edible Material: Processes, Compositions, and Products (426)	24	9	6	15	14	10	32	12	28	35	36	48	28	44	63	53	62	69
Drug, Bio-Affecting and Body Treating Compositions (514)	14	25	31	27	24	35	42	29	38	51	56	48	86	113	138	121	150	187
Radiation Imagery Chemistry: Process, Composition, or Product Thereof (430)	13	6	10	6	6	10	22	20	14	20	17	22	13	13	36	46	49	55
Chemistry: Molecular Biology and Microbiology (435)	10	4	15	17	14	12	34	31	30	20	39	38	66	75	98	113	120	175
Organic Compounds -- Part of the Class 532-570 Series (536)	8	5	2	6	2	3	9	11	6	6	3	2	6	8	7	17	22	34
Drug, Bio-Affecting and Body Treating Compositions (424)	8	6	8	11	13	19	19	12	9	21	27	34	50	59	96	104	109	143
Surgery (604)	8	10	6	5	1	4	4	10	7	6	11	11	43	10	36	28	43	50
Stock Material or Miscellaneous Articles (428)	7	8	5	17	9	12	21	6	16	18	30	36	40	52	58	58	61	69
Coating Processes (427)	4	7	5	9	5	8	12	8	8	11	10	15	20	19	32	27	24	34
Semiconductor Device Manufacturing: Process (438)	3	0	0	5	7	4	8	6	11	12	9	16	23	21	22	28	48	40

Number of Patents Granted within Patent Class which have a Woman as a Non-Primary Inventor, 1975-1992 (Continued)

Cleaning Compositions for Solid Surfaces, Auxiliary Compositions Therefor, or Processes of Preparing the Compositions (510)	2	2	2	2	6	4	7	3	11	7	17	12	15	17	22	21	26	39
Chemistry: Natural Resins or Derivatives; Peptides or Proteins; Lignins or Reaction Products Thereof (530)	1	4	1	6	1	3	7	5	6	6	13	5	15	17	27	18	41	52
Surgery (600)	1	1	1	4	0	2	2	2	3	9	2	9	14	13	26	19	26	25
Active Solid-State Devices (e.g., Transistors, Solid-State Diodes) (257)	1	0	2	1	3	0	3	3	2	4	7	6	10	4	15	20	37	31
Telecommunications (455)	1	1	1	1	4	2	1	3	0	0	1	0	1	0	5	4	3	4
Image Analysis (382)	0	2	1	0	0	0	0	0	1	0	0	3	3	5	10	12	11	10
Furnishings (D06)	0	0	5	5	5	8	10	10	5	9	10	7	14	21	22	39	43	16
Packages and Containers for Goods (D09)	0	0	2	5	10	2	2	3	2	4	10	4	7	7	6	6	5	18
Multiplex Communications (370)	0	0	1	2	0	2	1	0	1	5	3	2	6	10	7	13	10	9
Recording, Communication, or Information Retrieval Equipment (D14)	0	0	1	0	0	2	3	0	8	5	6	1	10	10	17	27	16	20
Data Processing: Presentation Processing of Document, Operator Interface Processing, and Screen Saver Display Processing (715)	0	0	1	0	0	0	0	0	2	6	3	2	8	4	7	5	8	11
Telephonic Communications (379)	0	0	1	2	2	1	2	2	2	6	5	12	5	14	10	22	12	16
Data Processing: Database and File Management or Data Structures (707)	0	0	0	1	0	1	0	1	2	0	1	1	1	3	4	5	6	9
Data Processing: Financial, Business Practice, Management, or Cost/Price Determination (705)	0	0	0	0	0	1	0	3	0	2	0	1	2	3	4	4	7	4
Electrical Computers and Digital Processing Systems: Multicomputer Data Transferring (709)	0	0	0	0	0	0	0	2	0	0	0	2	3	2	3	6	2	10

Number of Patents Granted within Patent Class which have a Woman as a Non-Primary Inventor, 1993-2010

Patent Class	1993	1994	1995	1996	1997	1998	1999	2000	2001	2002	2003	2004	2005	2006	2007	2008	2009	2010
Food or Edible Material: Processes, Compositions, and Products (426)	67	59	74	63	43	55	86	103	99	102	103	78	46	53	44	36	47	63
Drug, Bio-Affecting and Body Treating Compositions (514)	190	184	220	328	424	506	501	516	570	680	693	476	512	622	598	540	685	954
Radiation Imagery Chemistry: Process, Composition, or Product Thereof (430)	76	79	80	103	83	115	110	135	153	143	119	126	79	117	90	78	92	118
Chemistry: Molecular Biology and Microbiology (435)	212	197	221	323	505	728	824	662	741	734	575	529	463	649	572	516	548	736
Organic Compounds -- Part of the Class 532-570 Series (536)	34	24	35	49	63	104	82	83	129	115	93	91	67	98	114	102	143	168
Drug, Bio-Affecting and Body Treating Compositions (424)	146	174	159	194	335	386	482	406	450	489	437	306	260	333	317	307	348	516
Surgery (604)	54	68	86	93	115	129	117	100	136	132	193	143	100	91	72	78	107	214
Stock Material or Miscellaneous Articles (428)	89	86	87	107	135	161	168	145	169	189	220	182	187	157	127	106	140	173
Coating Processes (427)	24	46	42	53	51	67	80	62	74	83	85	71	66	32	46	43	69	104
Semiconductor Device Manufacturing: Process (438)	43	52	63	47	66	98	131	216	320	371	336	303	296	319	271	239	301	372
Cleaning Compositions for Solid Surfaces, Auxiliary Compositions Therefor, or Processes of Preparing the Compositions (510)	35	37	32	45	45	83	84	94	87	106	93	91	51	66	55	68	60	68
Chemistry: Natural Resins or Derivatives; Peptides or Proteins; Lignins or Reaction Products Thereof (530)	48	26	40	64	100	135	132	115	142	109	95	103	121	175	260	284	192	223
Surgery (600)	37	47	51	56	52	93	106	103	101	129	150	126	89	122	90	86	106	206
Active Solid-State Devices (e.g., Transistors, Solid-State Diodes) (257)	21	48	26	42	58	84	76	70	116	137	201	196	195	207	169	182	205	263
Telecommunications (455)	4	14	13	21	19	47	65	71	67	71	59	89	81	143	182	140	159	241
Image Analysis (382)	14	16	17	16	37	50	54	45	58	48	70	79	68	101	134	123	158	214
Furnishings (D06)	44	34	57	78	56	47	68	105	158	86	81	95	89	118	110	107	57	79
Packages and Containers for Goods (D09)	29	31	35	22	32	39	66	79	125	41	91	55	99	104	167	192	130	194

Number of Patents Granted within Patent Class which have a Woman as a Non-Primary Inventor, 1993-2010

Multiplex Communications (370)	19	29	35	53	36	49	66	91	64	110	109	134	140	235	175	234	338	499
Recording, Communication, or Information Retrieval Equipment (D14)	35	34	52	65	76	91	75	136	125	98	119	104	95	129	206	241	142	178
Data Processing: Presentation Processing of Document, Operator Interface Processing, and Screen Saver Display Processing (715)	9	16	25	28	47	64	55	91	85	54	85	58	75	120	121	171	197	195
Telephonic Communications (379)	22	44	55	64	50	78	78	69	66	94	81	123	88	114	97	94	92	138
Data Processing: Database and File Management or Data Structures (707)	11	19	26	34	40	94	96	102	87	119	147	146	127	215	192	235	355	525
Data Processing: Financial, Business Practice, Management, or Cost/Price Determination (705)	14	13	14	20	24	49	67	73	62	50	46	33	89	161	150	236	263	654
Electrical Computers and Digital Processing Systems: Multicomputer Data Transferring (709)	10	14	13	35	21	73	88	100	102	88	95	128	142	222	184	228	329	446

Share of Patents Granted within Patent Class which have a Woman as a Non-Primary Inventor, 1975-1992

Patent Class	1975	1976	1977	1978	1979	1980	1981	1982	1983	1984	1985	1986	1987	1988	1989	1990	1991	1992
Food or Edible Material: Processes, Compositions, and Products (426)	8.8%	3.7%	3.2%	10.6%	9.9%	6.1%	17.2%	8.7%	17.7%	21.5%	20.1%	30.8%	16.1%	21.4%	22.6%	19.6%	23.6%	26.3%
Drug, Bio-Affecting and Body Treating Compositions (514)	5.2%	7.8%	7.9%	6.5%	8.4%	8.6%	11.4%	9.2%	11.8%	13.4%	12.8%	11.9%	14.9%	19.0%	18.0%	16.6%	19.2%	22.6%
Radiation Imagery Chemistry: Process, Composition, or Product Thereof (430)	7.0%	3.9%	5.8%	4.1%	5.4%	7.1%	9.4%	11.6%	8.5%	11.9%	12.2%	15.1%	9.4%	7.8%	16.5%	20.2%	18.9%	24.2%
Chemistry: Molecular Biology and Microbiology (435)	9.2%	3.9%	14.2%	18.1%	19.4%	9.1%	17.5%	21.1%	21.7%	14.3%	24.4%	20.7%	24.7%	24.5%	24.8%	29.9%	28.2%	31.4%
Surgery (604)	9.8%	12.2%	7.8%	8.1%	2.6%	5.4%	5.2%	9.7%	6.7%	4.6%	8.1%	6.7%	18.8%	4.9%	14.6%	10.9%	13.9%	12.8%
Organic Compounds -- Part of the Class 532-570 Series (536)	11.0%	12.2%	4.5%	10.5%	7.1%	6.7%	19.1%	28.2%	18.8%	17.1%	13.0%	8.3%	23.1%	19.5%	13.0%	22.1%	31.0%	31.5%
Drug, Bio-Affecting and Body Treating Compositions (424)	8.5%	4.7%	5.8%	9.3%	10.6%	17.3%	15.1%	10.3%	10.2%	15.3%	17.1%	18.5%	21.4%	22.1%	23.1%	24.4%	22.1%	28.3%

Patent Class	1975	1976	1977	1978	1979	1980	1981	1982	1983	1984	1985	1986	1987	1988	1989	1990	1991	1992
Stock Material or Miscellaneous Articles (428)	2.7%	3.1%	2.0%	6.5%	4.6%	4.6%	7.5%	2.4%	6.1%	6.3%	8.6%	9.2%	10.6%	12.9%	11.8%	11.9%	13.8%	13.1%
Coating Processes (427)	2.5%	5.6%	3.7%	5.8%	5.2%	5.7%	8.3%	5.3%	6.9%	6.9%	6.0%	9.0%	12.1%	10.2%	16.7%	13.8%	11.1%	12.0%
Semiconductor Device Manufacturing: Process (438)	2.3%	0.0%	0.0%	5.4%	7.9%	4.2%	7.4%	5.6%	8.1%	8.9%	5.8%	9.6%	11.2%	12.4%	9.2%	14.4%	18.0%	13.1%
Cleaning Compositions for Solid Surfaces, Auxiliary Compositions Therefor, or Processes of Preparing the Compositions (510)	3.6%	2.7%	3.2%	3.1%	11.8%	7.7%	10.6%	7.7%	20.4%	12.1%	21.5%	22.6%	19.2%	23.3%	21.8%	23.1%	24.3%	35.1%
Chemistry: Natural Resins or Derivatives; Peptides or Proteins; Lignins or Reaction Products Thereof (530)	2.0%	18.2%	2.7%	12.2%	4.3%	7.7%	14.3%	10.9%	13.6%	9.0%	21.0%	8.2%	17.6%	17.2%	25.7%	19.8%	32.5%	30.8%
Surgery (600)	1.2%	1.4%	1.2%	5.5%	0.0%	1.8%	2.4%	2.3%	4.1%	10.1%	1.8%	6.0%	9.8%	8.3%	11.6%	7.9%	9.9%	8.9%
Telecommunications (455)	2.4%	2.2%	2.2%	3.8%	11.4%	4.0%	2.7%	8.1%	0.0%	0.0%	2.6%	0.0%	1.9%	0.0%	8.9%	6.1%	3.8%	4.0%
Active Solid-State Devices (e.g., Transistors, Solid-State Diodes) (257)	1.4%	0.0%	2.0%	1.7%	4.3%	0.0%	4.5%	4.6%	3.8%	5.6%	9.1%	5.1%	7.8%	3.4%	8.1%	8.3%	12.0%	11.5%
Image Analysis (382)	0.0%	8.3%	4.0%	0.0%	0.0%	0.0%	0.0%	0.0%	4.2%	0.0%	0.0%	6.7%	5.9%	9.4%	14.3%	16.4%	10.4%	8.2%
Furnishings (D06)	0.0%	0.0%	10.4%	7.2%	13.2%	11.3%	10.3%	10.0%	6.7%	9.4%	10.6%	8.6%	13.2%	19.3%	22.9%	26.9%	25.9%	11.3%
Packages and Containers for Goods (D 09)	0.0%	0.0%	7.1%	11.1%	37.0%	4.5%	3.4%	5.8%	6.7%	10.0%	17.5%	6.7%	10.8%	17.1%	13.6%	9.4%	6.0%	22.8%
Data Processing: Presentation Processing of Document, Operator Interface Processing, and Screen Saver Display Processing (715)	0.0%	0.0%	33.3%	0.0%	0.0%	0.0%	0.0%	0.0%	18.2%	22.2%	15.0%	14.3%	44.4%	18.2%	21.2%	19.2%	25.0%	20.4%
Recording, Communication, or Information Retrieval Equipment (D14)	0.0%	0.0%	1.8%	0.0%	0.0%	5.6%	5.2%	0.0%	12.5%	5.6%	5.2%	1.0%	7.5%	8.8%	14.8%	17.9%	9.9%	15.3%
Telephonic Communications (379)	0.0%	0.0%	1.3%	2.4%	4.5%	2.0%	2.9%	4.2%	3.9%	6.3%	6.5%	11.3%	4.2%	11.6%	8.6%	14.5%	9.8%	14.8%
Multiplex Communications (370)	0.0%	0.0%	2.6%	6.3%	0.0%	5.3%	2.9%	0.0%	2.0%	8.6%	3.0%	2.6%	4.8%	8.5%	7.1%	10.4%	9.1%	7.1%
Data Processing: Database and File Management or Data Structures (707)	0.0%	0.0%	0.0%	10.0%	0.0%	20.0%	0.0%	33.3%	40.0%	0.0%	11.1%	14.3%	16.7%	37.5%	18.2%	20.0%	26.1%	25.0%
Data Processing: Financial, Business Practice, Management, or Cost/Price Determination (705)	0.0%	0.0%	0.0%	0.0%	0.0%	9.1%	0.0%	30.0%	0.0%	15.4%	0.0%	7.1%	5.9%	9.4%	8.3%	10.0%	17.5%	11.4%
Electrical Computers an Digital Processing Systems: Multicomputer Data Transferring (709)	0.0%	0.0%	0.0%	0.0%	0.0%	0.0%	0.0%	28.6%	0.0%	0.0%	0.0%	20.0%	21.4%	13.3%	18.8%	23.1%	8.0%	22.7%

Share of Patents Granted within Patent Class which have a Woman as a Non-Primary Inventor, 1993-2010

Patent Class	1993	1994	1995	1996	1997	1998	1999	2000	2001	2002	2003	2004	2005	2006	2007	2008	2009	2010
Food or Edible Material: Processes, Compositions, and Products (426)	29.3%	26.6%	30.3%	25.2%	21.9%	22.8%	26.5%	27.7%	28.9%	33.7%	35.3%	35.6%	36.2%	32.3%	31.4%	31.3%	35.3%	33.9%
Drug, Bio-Affecting and Body Treating Compositions (514)	20.6%	23.1%	21.9%	25.6%	25.0%	29.5%	27.6%	28.9%	30.8%	33.0%	35.9%	33.3%	37.0%	36.5%	37.4%	37.2%	39.5%	41.8%
Radiation Imagery Chemistry: Process, Composition, or Product Thereof (430)	20.7%	18.2%	20.0%	24.5%	22.1%	24.1%	21.0%	23.8%	27.3%	27.1%	24.8%	29.0%	25.3%	30.5%	28.1%	28.2%	35.1%	34.8%
Chemistry: Molecular Biology and Microbiology (435)	30.9%	30.8%	29.9%	30.2%	32.2%	34.2%	37.9%	36.3%	35.2%	38.5%	35.1%	36.5%	37.2%	40.0%	37.9%	37.9%	40.1%	40.1%
Surgery (604)	14.6%	12.2%	16.9%	18.8%	23.8%	19.9%	19.0%	18.2%	23.1%	24.3%	24.1%	25.4%	25.5%	23.0%	23.0%	23.9%	25.1%	24.4%
Organic Compounds -- Part of the Class 532-570 Series (536)	32.4%	26.1%	22.6%	25.5%	23.8%	29.1%	26.5%	32.4%	40.6%	34.5%	34.4%	38.1%	32.7%	34.3%	43.0%	36.6%	43.7%	42.0%
Drug, Bio-Affecting and Body Treating Compositions (424)	26.1%	29.0%	26.2%	29.6%	28.8%	28.3%	32.9%	31.4%	32.0%	34.0%	32.3%	29.9%	32.2%	30.4%	34.1%	34.7%	39.1%	37.2%
Stock Material or Miscellaneous Articles (428)	16.2%	14.7%	15.3%	14.6%	17.7%	18.3%	16.9%	16.6%	17.9%	18.3%	21.5%	18.5%	23.8%	25.5%	20.4%	21.8%	26.9%	23.0%
Coating Processes (427)	10.0%	14.2%	15.1%	17.4%	14.7%	17.9%	20.2%	14.5%	20.4%	21.4%	21.0%	21.2%	24.4%	16.9%	20.2%	18.9%	24.0%	24.2%
Semiconductor Device Manufacturing: Process (438)	11.4%	13.4%	13.8%	12.2%	12.4%	14.2%	12.1%	14.1%	17.5%	19.9%	19.4%	17.1%	19.0%	19.5%	17.4%	16.4%	20.0%	19.6%
Cleaning Compositions for Solid Surfaces, Auxiliary Compositions Therefor, or Processes of Preparing the Compositions (510)	28.5%	32.5%	20.4%	28.1%	29.2%	32.2%	32.2%	36.6%	34.7%	38.3%	37.8%	45.0%	39.5%	40.5%	40.7%	47.2%	40.8%	38.9%
Chemistry: Natural Resins or Derivatives; Peptides or Proteins; Lignins or Reaction Products Thereof (530)	26.2%	19.5%	27.8%	32.3%	33.3%	31.0%	33.4%	34.2%	42.0%	35.7%	32.9%	38.1%	47.5%	41.6%	46.0%	51.8%	43.1%	45.6%
Surgery (600)	10.9%	10.7%	11.9%	13.6%	12.4%	13.9%	15.2%	12.3%	12.2%	15.4%	16.2%	17.5%	17.6%	19.2%	16.8%	16.8%	17.5%	20.8%
Telecommunications (455)	3.2%	9.7%	7.2%	7.7%	8.6%	11.1%	12.5%	10.6%	11.4%	12.1%	9.8%	12.2%	11.6%	11.6%	15.6%	14.4%	14.2%	16.8%
Active Solid-State Devices (e.g., Transistors, Solid-State Diodes) (257)	9.9%	14.2%	7.9%	10.3%	14.3%	13.0%	10.4%	9.4%	13.3%	13.8%	16.0%	15.1%	15.8%	16.5%	14.7%	16.8%	18.7%	16.2%
Image Analysis (382)	11.7%	11.3%	14.0%	10.4%	16.6%	12.5%	13.5%	11.7%	11.6%	12.4%	13.4%	13.4%	15.3%	14.0%	18.1%	16.0%	17.5%	19.9%
Furnishings (D06)	20.7%	19.7%	20.6%	24.1%	25.0%	16.0%	19.8%	24.3%	34.4%	25.4%	25.7%	27.0%	31.7%	30.4%	24.4%	24.4%	15.6%	23.0%
Packages and Containers for Goods (D 09)	22.7%	25.4%	29.4%	16.7%	19.6%	19.8%	29.2%	29.9%	39.8%	18.2%	28.1%	25.5%	33.2%	25.9%	34.5%	39.6%	26.9%	33.6%

Patent Class	1993	1994	1995	1996	1997	1998	1999	2000	2001	2002	2003	2004	2005	2006	2007	2008	2009	2010
Data Processing: Presentation Processing of Document, Operator Interface Processing, and Screen Saver Display Processing (715)	14.3%	16.7%	18.7%	13.9%	21.1%	18.4%	16.0%	23.5%	22.9%	15.4%	24.8%	19.3%	19.9%	21.5%	23.0%	30.3%	26.9%	23.0%
Recording, Communication, or Information Retrieval Equipment (D14)	15.9%	13.3%	18.0%	21.3%	21.7%	22.2%	21.2%	29.7%	28.0%	24.8%	26.1%	27.0%	30.6%	24.3%	29.3%	30.0%	17.8%	23.0%
Telephonic Communications (379)	17.1%	21.7%	21.2%	21.6%	20.2%	18.1%	17.5%	17.9%	15.5%	20.3%	16.6%	20.5%	20.9%	18.0%	20.9%	24.7%	23.2%	26.9%
Multiplex Communications (370)	11.4%	12.3%	11.7%	14.2%	10.5%	10.4%	12.1%	11.4%	8.3%	12.6%	10.9%	10.8%	12.1%	14.1%	13.0%	12.2%	14.8%	15.8%
Data Processing: Database and File Management or Data Structures (707)	13.1%	24.1%	23.4%	17.4%	19.8%	20.6%	17.9%	20.5%	16.4%	16.9%	19.7%	19.2%	19.3%	21.1%	20.8%	21.2%	21.3%	20.9%
Data Processing: Financial, Business Practice, Management, or Cost/Price Determination (705)	18.2%	18.3%	26.9%	29.4%	20.9%	20.5%	21.1%	19.1%	25.8%	21.5%	20.7%	21.0%	22.0%	24.1%	23.5%	26.8%	23.6%	28.0%
Electrical Computers an Digital Processing Systems: Multicomputer Data Transferring (709)	19.2%	19.7%	15.1%	18.2%	14.2%	14.8%	16.0%	15.6%	15.8%	13.1%	14.6%	15.3%	16.7%	16.7%	14.6%	15.5%	18.5%	17.8%

Table A.5. Patents filed versus patents granted to women-1975-2010

Year	No. of Patents Filed	No. of Patents Granted
1975	1395	1328
1976	1672	1284
1977	1770	1523
1978	1706	1600
1979	1829	1294
1980	1901	1643
1981	1900	1884
1982	2172	1637
1983	2276	1750
1984	2642	2206
1985	3102	2445
1986	3507	2503
1987	3950	3229
1988	4716	3341
1989	5143	4496
1990	6053	4712
1991	6473	5490
1992	6893	6103
1993	7830	6735
1994	9758	7006
1995	12814	7463
1996	11583	8766
1997	14299	9390
1998	14658	12577
1999	16351	13424
2000	17893	14039
2001	18565	14974
2002	19178	15087
2003	18288	15414
2004	17031	14738
2005	15978	13211
2006	13851	16637
2007	11059	15874
2008	6213	16321
2009	2948	17061
2010	552	22984
Total	**287949**	**290169**

Table A.6. Patents filed versus patents granted to men – 1975-2010

Year	No. of Patents Filed	No. of Patents Granted
1975	43619	46148
1976	44959	43737
1977	44454	44366
1978	42960	44098
1979	42211	32394
1980	42298	40015
1981	39870	42493
1982	40018	37055
1983	37989	35913
1984	39753	41557
1985	41697	42696
1986	42625	41469
1987	46531	47088
1988	51236	43910
1989	54514	53718
1990	58331	51840
1991	59411	56529
1992	62792	57505
1993	66747	59878
1994	75203	63160
1995	89274	63247
1996	85577	68032
1997	100062	68710
1998	99628	89050
1999	105395	92372
2000	112144	95364
2001	113427	97425
2002	114169	95988
2003	109649	97768
2004	102169	93361
2005	93908	81986
2006	79446	101523
2007	60406	92871
2008	34249	91342
2009	14976	94850
2010	2598	121257
Total	**2294295**	**2370715**

Table A.7. % Successful Women Patent Applicants/% Successful Men Patent Applicants, 1975-2002

Year	Ratio of Successful Applicants
1975	0.90
1976	0.79
1977	0.86
1978	0.91
1979	0.92
1980	0.91
1981	0.93
1982	0.81
1983	0.81
1984	0.80
1985	0.77
1986	0.73
1987	0.81
1988	0.83
1989	0.89
1990	0.88
1991	0.89
1992	0.97
1993	0.96
1994	0.85
1995	0.82
1996	0.95
1997	0.96
1998	0.96
1999	0.94
2000	0.92
2001	0.94
2002	0.94

Table A.8. Patents filed versus patents granted to women-1975-2002

Year	No. of Patents Filed	No. of Patents Granted
1975	1395	1328
1976	1672	1284
1977	1770	1523
1978	1706	1600
1979	1829	1294
1980	1901	1643

Year	No. of Patents Filed	No. of Patents Granted
1981	1900	1884
1982	2172	1637
1983	2276	1750
1984	2642	2206
1985	3102	2445
1986	3507	2503
1987	3950	3229
1988	4716	3341
1989	5143	4496
1990	6053	4712
1991	6473	5490
1992	6893	6103
1993	7830	6735
1994	9758	7006
1995	12814	7463
1996	11583	8766
1997	14299	9390
1998	14658	12577
1999	16351	13424
2000	17893	14039
2001	18565	14974
2002	19178	15087
Total	**202029**	**157929**

Table A.9. Patents filed versus patents granted to men-1975-2002

Year	No. of Patents Filed	No. of Patents Granted
1975	43619	46148
1976	44959	43737
1977	44454	44366
1978	42960	44098
1979	42211	32394
1980	42298	40015
1981	39870	42493
1982	40018	37055
1983	37989	35913
1984	39753	41557
1985	41697	42696
1986	42625	41469
1987	46531	47088

Table A.9. (Continued)

Year	No. of Patents Filed	No. of Patents Granted
1988	51236	43910
1989	54514	53718
1990	58331	51840
1991	59411	56529
1992	62792	57505
1993	66747	59878
1994	75203	63160
1995	89274	63247
1996	85577	68032
1997	100062	68710
1998	99628	89050
1999	105395	92372
2000	112144	95364
2001	113427	97425
2002	114169	95988
Total	**1796894**	**1595757**

Table A.10. Trademark applications filed by year

Year	No. of Trademark Applications Filed
1980	2139
1981	2561
1982	5027
1983	3596
1984	4232
1985	4506
1986	4712
1987	5192
1988	5709
1989	6930
1990	11016
1991	11216
1992	10890
1993	14470
1994	14285
1995	16597
1996	18763

Year	No. of Trademark Applications Filed
1997	19736
1998	21032
1999	33655
2000	33009
2001	25718
2002	29957
2003	33226
2004	38080
2005	42071
2006	44385
2007	49256
2008	46026
2009	42950
2010	44533
Total	**645475**

Table A.11. Trademark applications filed by women by year

Year	No. of Trademark Applications Filed
1980	396
1981	521
1982	1076
1983	723
1984	972
1985	1220
1986	1162
1987	1349
1988	1450
1989	1716
1990	2596
1991	2685
1992	2461
1993	3466
1994	3467
1995	3787
1996	4433
1997	4775
1998	5135
1999	7683

Table A.11. (Continued)

Year	No. of Trademark Applications Filed
2000	7974
2001	6615
2002	8135
2003	8830
2004	10163
2005	11357
2006	11934
2007	14353
2008	13741
2009	12604
2010	13171
Total	**169950**

Table A.12. Trademark applications filed by men by year

Year	No. of Trademark Applications Filed
1980	1780
1981	2100
1982	4038
1983	2940
1984	3359
1985	3460
1986	3716
1987	4028
1988	4467
1989	5457
1990	8767
1991	8850
1992	8657
1993	11386
1994	11070
1995	13155
1996	14728
1997	15399
1998	16287
1999	26505
2000	25430

Year	No. of Trademark Applications Filed
2001	19493
2002	22514
2003	24621
2004	27073
2005	29585
2006	31153
2007	34063
2008	31835
2009	29807
2010	31104
Total	**476827**

Table A.13. Total trademarks granted by year

Year	No. of Trademarks Granted
1980	1133
1981	2720
1982	2671
1983	2855
1984	3243
1985	4268
1986	3114
1987	3349
1988	3388
1989	4147
1990	4361
1991	3250
1992	6323
1993	5913
1994	5041
1995	6738
1996	7501
1997	9209
1998	8213
1999	8266
2000	10913
2001	10946
2002	14499
2003	13080

Table A.13. (Continued)

Year	No. of Trademarks Granted
2004	11807
2005	13637
2006	17724
2007	20537
2008	23709
2009	21398
2010	20547
Total	**274500**

Table A.14. Trademarks granted to women by year

Year	No. of Trademarks Granted
1980	189
1981	480
1982	529
1983	643
1984	704
1985	1077
1986	828
1987	878
1988	918
1989	1103
1990	1120
1991	841
1992	1656
1993	1492
1994	1262
1995	1746
1996	1941
1997	2290
1998	2180
1999	2208
2000	2975
2001	2905
2002	3786
2003	3750
2004	3367

Year	No. of Trademarks Granted
2005	3821
2006	5045
2007	5811
2008	7274
2009	6617
2010	6533
Total	**75969**

Table A.15. Trademarks granted to men by year

Year	No. of Trademarks Granted
1980	959
1981	2295
1982	2192
1983	2296
1984	2619
1985	3328
1986	2396
1987	2597
1988	2600
1989	3216
1990	3393
1991	2535
1992	4895
1993	4585
1994	3904
1995	5174
1996	5703
1997	7069
1998	6197
1999	6243
2000	8149
2001	8264
2002	10937
2003	9566
2004	8686
2005	9803
2006	12452
2007	14241

Table A.15. (Continued)

Year	No. of Trademarks Granted
2008	16074
2009	14618
2010	13881
Total	**200867**

Table A.16. Trademarks granted to women – Share of total trademarks granted to individuals

Year	Share of Trademarks Granted to Individuals (%)
1980	16.70
1981	17.65
1982	19.81
1983	22.52
1984	21.71
1985	25.25
1986	26.62
1987	26.23
1988	27.10
1989	26.62
1990	25.78
1991	26.12
1992	26.45
1993	25.69
1994	25.56
1995	26.47
1996	26.41
1997	25.39
1998	27.05
1999	27.28
2000	27.88
2001	27.06
2002	26.61
2003	29.17
2004	28.99
2005	29.11
2006	30.14

Year	Share of Trademarks Granted to Individuals (%)
2007	30.15
2008	32.42
2009	32.44
2010	33.31

Table A.17. Trademarks granted to men – Share of total trademarks granted to individuals

Year	Share of Trademarks Granted to Individuals (%)
1980	84.72
1981	84.41
1982	82.07
1983	80.42
1984	80.76
1985	78.03
1986	77.02
1987	77.59
1988	76.76
1989	77.61
1990	78.11
1991	78.73
1992	78.18
1993	78.94
1994	79.06
1995	78.43
1996	77.59
1997	78.37
1998	76.90
1999	77.12
2000	76.38
2001	76.97
2002	76.87
2003	74.41
2004	74.79
2005	74.67
2006	74.38
2007	73.89

Table A.17. (Continued)

Year	Share of Trademarks Granted to Individuals (%)
2008	71.64
2009	71.66
2010	70.78

Table A.18. Successful women trademark applications %/Successful men trademark applications %

Year	Ratio of Successful Women to Men Applicants
1980	0.89
1981	0.84
1982	0.91
1983	1.14
1984	0.93
1985	0.92
1986	1.11
1987	1.01
1988	1.09
1989	1.09
1990	1.11
1991	1.09
1992	1.19
1993	1.07
1994	1.03
1995	1.17
1996	1.13
1997	1.04
1998	1.12
1999	1.22
2000	1.16
2001	1.04
2002	0.96
2003	1.09
2004	1.03
2005	1.02
2006	1.06

Year	Ratio of Successful Women to Men Applicants
2007	0.97
2008	1.05
2009	1.07
2010	1.11

Table A.19. Trademarks granted to women – Share of applications filed by women

Year	Share of Trademark Applications Filed by Women (%)
1980	47.73
1981	92.13
1982	49.16
1983	88.93
1984	72.43
1985	88.28
1986	71.26
1987	65.09
1988	63.31
1989	64.28
1990	43.14
1991	31.32
1992	67.29
1993	43.05
1994	36.40
1995	46.11
1996	43.79
1997	47.96
1998	42.45
1999	28.74
2000	37.31
2001	43.92
2002	46.54
2003	42.47
2004	33.13
2005	33.64
2006	42.27
2007	40.49

Table A.19. (Continued)

Year	Share of Trademark Applications Filed by Women (%)
2008	52.94
2009	52.50
2010	49.60

Table A.20. Trademarks granted to men – Share of applications filed by men

Year	Share of Trademark Applications Filed by Men (%)
1980	53.88
1981	109.29
1982	54.28
1983	78.10
1984	77.97
1985	96.18
1986	64.48
1987	64.47
1988	58.20
1989	58.93
1990	38.70
1991	28.64
1992	56.54
1993	40.27
1994	35.27
1995	39.33
1996	38.72
1997	45.91
1998	38.05
1999	23.55
2000	32.04
2001	42.39
2002	48.58
2003	38.85
2004	32.08
2005	33.14
2006	39.97

Year	Share of Trademark Applications Filed by Men (%)
2007	41.81
2008	50.49
2009	49.04
2010	44.63

Table A.21. Trademarks granted to women – Share of trademarks granted to men

Year	Share of Trademarks Granted to Men (%)
1980	19.71
1981	20.92
1982	24.13
1983	28.01
1984	26.88
1985	32.36
1986	34.56
1987	33.81
1988	35.31
1989	34.30
1990	33.01
1991	33.18
1992	33.83
1993	32.54
1994	32.33
1995	33.75
1996	34.03
1997	32.39
1998	35.18
1999	35.37
2000	36.51
2001	35.15
2002	34.62
2003	39.20
2004	38.76
2005	38.98
2006	40.52
2007	40.80
2008	45.25

Table A.21. (Continued)

Year	Share of Trademarks Granted to Men (%)
2009	45.27
2010	47.06

Table A.22. Trademarks granted to women by industry (top 5 industries)

Year	Advertising and Business	Clothing	Education and Entertainment	Miscellaneous Services; Scientific and technological services, and research and design relating thereto; Industrial analysis and research services; Design and development of computer hardware and software; Legal services	Paper Goods and Printed Matter
1980	5	18	19	16	40
1981	18	48	73	74	79
1982	22	56	61	70	81
1983	21	72	85	85	131
1984	22	88	104	90	103
1985	28	155	126	134	147
1986	18	103	79	102	170
1987	30	98	95	119	148
1988	43	128	81	136	124
1989	35	130	123	177	154
1990	45	154	118	193	161
1991	21	106	110	138	121
1992	70	170	244	278	246
1993	50	181	232	214	225
1994	54	149	166	174	196
1995	73	199	265	263	275
1996	89	246	283	281	324
1997	140	293	350	355	332
1998	173	254	390	258	383
1999	201	225	366	316	336
2000	357	307	526	443	403
2001	337	300	504	438	410
2002	439	430	691	518	494
2003	385	424	758	314	534
2004	347	411	710	176	453
2005	367	548	745	137	509
2006	524	717	981	143	587

Year	Advertising and Business	Clothing	Education and Entertainment	Miscellaneous Services; Scientific and technological services, and research and design relating thereto; Industrial analysis and research services; Design and development of computer hardware and software; Legal services	Paper Goods and Printed Matter
2007	645	882	1188	163	698
2008	858	1132	1579	205	825
2009	731	1077	1380	184	728
2010	810	1080	1396	165	639

Table A.23. Trademarks granted annually – individuals vs. businesses

Year	No. of Trademarks Granted to Individuals	No. of Trademarks Granted to Businesses
1980	1132	1
1981	2719	1
1985	4265	3
1986	3111	3
1987	3347	2
1988	3387	1
1989	4144	3
1990	4344	17
1991	3220	30
1992	6261	62
1993	5808	105
1994	4938	103
1995	6597	141
1996	7350	151
1997	9020	189
1998	8059	154
1999	8095	171
2000	10669	244
2001	10737	209
2002	14228	271
2003	12856	224
2004	11614	193
2005	13128	509
2006	16740	984

Table A.23. (Continued)

Year	No. of Trademarks Granted to Individuals	No. of Trademarks Granted to Businesses
2007	19274	1263
2008	22436	1273
2009	20400	998
2010	19611	936
Total	**257490**	**8241**

In: Patent and Trademark Activity …
Editor: Dianna M. Ogden
ISBN: 978-1-63117-740-8

Chapter 2

INTELLECTUAL PROPERTY AND WOMEN ENTREPRENEURS: QUALITATIVE ANALYSIS*

National Women's Business Council

EXECUTIVE SUMMARY

In September 2011, the NWBC commissioned a broad study to analyze the relationship between women entrepreneurs and intellectual property. It consisted of two parts:

- Quantitative Research
- Qualitative Research

The quantitative research was completed in February 2012. A report, *Intellectual Property and Women Entrepreneurs, Quantitative Analysis,* was released by the NWBC on February 27, 2012 and presented at a featured meeting on March 1, 2012 in Washington, DC.

The current report covers the qualitative research whose stated goal was to conduct focus groups with women entrepreneurs, businesswomen and professionals, probe the questions that were raised in the quantitative study as well as additional ones of interest to the NWBC. Six focus groups were conducted in different parts of the US. Two of these focus groups were with

* This is an edited, reformatted and augmented version of a study conducted for the National Women's Business Council by Delixus, Inc., dated September 10, 2012.

women who had successfully obtained a patent or trademark, two were with women who had applied for but did not receive a patent or trademark and two were with women who had never applied for a patent or trademark. In addition to specific issues raised by the quantitative analysis, the following questions were also addressed by the focus groups:

- What are the perceived barriers facing women entrepreneurs surrounding protecting their IP?
- What are the actual barriers?
- How do we address these barriers?
- What are the long term effects on businesses that receive patents and successfully market their IP?

Accordingly, six focus groups were held, four in northern California and two in the Washington, DC metropolitan area. These locations were chosen based on the concentration of women patent and trademark holders in these regions. Data from the USPTO was used to recruit a random sample of women entrepreneurs. The assistance of the local chambers of commerce was also solicited in recruiting women who had never applied for a patent or trademark. Appropriate incentives were offered to the participants to cover costs.

The focus groups were conducted in accordance with OMB Regulations. The OMB control number was 3245-0380. The Paper Reductions Act of 1995 requires that Federal agency information collections employ effective methodologies appropriate to the purpose for which the information is to be collected (5 CFR 1320). This study meets the OMB requirements.

The study yielded significant insights into the IP processes as they affect women and women entrepreneurs. While major strides have been made in facilitating access to patent and trademark services, there remain significant opportunities for further improvement. The perceptions of the participants, the realities, the suggested fix as well as answers to questions raised in the quantitative study are summarized below.

Questions Raised by the Quantitative Analysis

What factors motivate women entrepreneurs in their successful pursuit of a patent or trademark?

Perceptions of risk and reward, increasing the value of the company, adding credibility to one's business, gaining recognition and increasing revenues are some of the principal factors that motivate women to successfully pursue their patent and trademark applications.

Why do women entrepreneurs abandon their patent or trademark application?

A host of factors, perceived and real, influence this issue. Some of the most important factors are: Fear and awe of the process, the absence of clear, easy to understand documentation, lack of financial resources to obtain professional help, discouragement from family, friends and advisors, and the demands of multiple roles as an entrepreneur, mother and caregiver.

Why do some women entrepreneurs never apply for a patent or trademark?

Perceptions of the patent and trademark process as complex, expensive and drawn out play a large part in the decisions of women entrepreneurs not to file for IP protection. Other reasons include: lack of a support system, websites that are not user friendly and mired in legal language, obscurity of the process and a perception that a cost-benefit analysis of IP protection does not justify the investment in time and money.

What are the barriers to reducing gender inequality?

Women entrepreneurs who strive in a business world dominated by men face an uphill battle in getting acceptance as intellectual peers. Women are still expected to be mothers and caregivers in the traditional sense while they struggle to build up their businesses. They perceive that they are not taken seriously in the work place. Lack of finance is a persistent opinion.

Is there a gender gap in financing?

There appear to be demographic differences between women who were successful in obtaining finance and those who did not. Women who were experienced and more business savvy took the time to prepare credible business plans as backup to their credit applications and were successful whereas less experienced women used an ad hoc approach to obtaining finance and were less successful.

What accounts for the increasing participation of women in hi tech industries?

Changing perceptions of gender roles in American society, the entry of more women into science and engineering, increasing access to higher education, legislation and law suits have all contributed to the successful entry of women into hi tech sectors.

Why is there a gender gap in the assignment of patents and trademarks?

Most women tend to be small businesspersons as compared to men who may have jobs with large corporations. Employees of large corporations assign their patents and trademarks to their employers while self employed entrepreneurs do not.

How has the recession impacted women entrepreneurs?

The prolonged recession since 2007 has had a profound impact in the workplace. Women entrepreneurs, by and large, look upon the recession as a challenge and an opportunity. The recession appears to have increased entrepreneurship among women. This aspect needs further study.

There is ambivalence about the benefits of holding a patent

Women entrepreneurs were more positive about the benefits of a trademark than of a patent. The expense, perceived complexity and the long wait for a patent has created ambivalence about the value of owning a patent.

Questions of Interest to the NWBC

Perceptions

- The patent and trademark processes are too complex, drawn out and expensive.
- Intellectual property can be stolen easily. It costs a great deal of money to defend IP.
- The patent and trademark processes are not well known or well understood by women entrepreneurs.
- The USPTO website is not user friendly.
- Women are discouraged from going into science and technology.
- Women prefer to hear a female voice at the other end of the phone when they call the USPTO.
- The current patent and trademark processes are archaic and hearken back to a bygone era.
- Women are harassed by salesmen and attorneys once a patent or trademark application is made public.

- There is scant assistance and guidance after the first rejection from the patent and trademark office.
- The patent and trademark processes are more focused on "legalese" than on fostering entrepreneurship.
- The patent and trademark processes have not kept up with emerging technologies.
- International protection is absent.
- The patent and trademark processes favor large business.
- There persists a gender gap in IP generation and protection.

The Reality

- There are no support systems for women, especially working single mothers.
- The patent and trademark processes are indeed too complex, drawn out and expensive.
- The USPTO website can be made more user friendly.
- Funding for marketing and business development is scarce.
- The current IP processes favor big business.
- Protecting a patent or a trademark can be very expensive. Most women cannot afford it.

The Remedies

- Simplify the process.
- Improve the website.
- Hold regional seminars and webinars.
- Increase visibility of existing federal programs.
- Consider a two-tier process to help micro-business and entrepreneurs.
- Use emerging technologies to improve service to small business.
- Add a "hot line" to help entrepreneurs.
- Use customer satisfaction surveys and other feedback to provide two-way training to service providers and consumers.
- Advice to entrepreneurs: "Read and follow the instructions".

Does IP protection help entrepreneurship?

More research is required to determine if there is a correlation between IP protection and entrepreneurship. The complexity and cost of obtaining a patent or trademark, and the difficulty of protecting the IP from infringement, act as deterrents to many a small businesswoman. On the other hand, there are also cases where a patent or trademark has clearly helped a business grow and become a success story.

Each major finding is addressed in the body of the report with quotes from the participants. Wherever possible, the contrast between perception and reality is brought out. Suggested improvements to the IP protection processes are highlighted.

Although the focus groups included only women, many of the insights gathered herein have general applicability and would be of benefit to businesses owned by men as well.

The information in these focus groups must be taken as a point source reflecting the opinions of a small, albeit a select and influential group of women entrepreneurs who live in different parts of the United States. There is no attempt here to generalize these findings to a national audience or to draw statistical inference from them. Despite these limitations, the opinions offered and the insights gathered serve as useful guidelines for further research.

LOCATIONS AND LOGISTICS

Two regions were identified for the focus group studies:

- Northern California/San Francisco Bay Area/Silicon Valley
- Washington DC Metropolitan Area

These regions were selected based on an evaluation of USPTO data on patents and trademarks to ensure that an adequate number of participants were available for the focus groups. For each region, a centralized location was chosen for the proposed focus group considering the availability of transportation, parking, facilities, cost and convenience of the participants. A cluster of towns and cities within a commuting radius of the proposed location was identified for the recruitment. The names of the selected towns and cities for each selected region are provided below:

Region 1: Northern California/Silicon Valley

Walnut Creek, CA
Pleasant Hill, CA
Lafayette, CA
Moraga, CA

Oakland, CA
Berkeley, CA
Concord, CA
Clayton, CA
Orinda, CA
Martinez, CA
Pittsburg, CA
Alamo, CA
Danville, CA
Pleasanton, CA
Fremont, CA
Dublin, CA

Region 2: Washington DC

Washington, DC
Arlington, VA
Falls Church, VA
Bethesda, MD

RECRUITMENT

The USPTO Database as Well as Contacts with Local Chambers of Comerce Were Used to Recruit the Participants

Recruitment Process

Women entrepreneurs who have applied for a patent or trademark represent a special and select group in the US population. As such, the recruitment of a random sample of qualified women entrepreneurs and women professionals within a commuting radius of a specific location presented a challenge. The following process was used for the recruitment:

- For each region, select the towns that are within a commuting distance from a preferred location for a focus group meeting.
- Start with the USPTO database for patents and trademarks for the selected towns and cities.

- Apply successive filters to the USPTO database:
  - Filter 1: Sort by first name to locate only patents and trademarks filed by women.
  - Filter 2: Identify and tag patents and trademarks as abandoned/dead or alive.
  - Filter 3: Locate women with their addresses or by the names of companies.
    Note: This was a challenge as companies were not always willing to provide information about their employees. Furthermore, a significant number of women had moved from the documented address.
  - Filter 4: Locate the telephone numbers of women innovators from commercial sources.
  - Filter 5: Since a large number of addresses did not match the telephone numbers, the Realquest software supplied by CoreLogic was procured and used to trace addresses.
    Realquest is the website for standardized nationwide real estate data and information which includes more than 145 million properties. It is a property and ownership search engine. This search engine enabled us to track and confirm the addresses of patent and trademark applicants and holders when phone numbers were not easily accessible. Also, when a woman's maiden name was used, we were able to locate her by her address on the USPTO application. And then, using her husband's name at the same address, we were able to find phone numbers listed only in the husband's name.

The support of local Chambers of Commerce was extremely helpful for recruitment. Social media using Facebook and Craig's lists were also used.

These efforts and the successive filters yielded enough women entrepreneurs/ professionals to recruit a focus group of 8 to 12 persons for each region. The overall yield was 3 percent or less.

Telephone Calls

Telephone calls were made to the identified potential participants using a standardized script which explained the purpose of the call and the importance of the study. A trial run was made with 5 calls and the script was modified for maximum response. An average of three calls was required per telephone address to complete a yes/no response from a person.

Objectives and Approach

The Objectives

The goal of the focus groups is to probe in-depth the issues raised by the NWBC as well as throw additional light on insights gathered from the quantitative analysis in phase 1 of the study. Specifically, the focus groups probed the following issues:

- What are the long term effects on businesses that receive patents and trademarks and successfully market their IP?
- What are the perceived barriers facing women entrepreneurs surrounding the protection of their IP?
- What are the actual barriers?
- How do we address these barriers?
- Is there a gender gap in the patent and trademark process?
- Are women showing increasing leadership in innovation?

The Approach

To meet these objectives, Delixus adopted a comprehensive, detailed and responsive approach:

1. The focus groups were conducted in accordance with OMB guidelines 5 C.F.R. § 1320.3(c): which were incorporated into the plan by reference. The OMB control number was 3245-0380.
2. Six focus groups were held:
    - Two with women who have obtained patent or trademark protection
    - Two with women who applied for but did not obtain a patent or a trademark
    - Two with women who never applied for a patent or a trademark.
3. Locations and dates: As outlined below.
4. Focus group participants were selected at random from a regional sample.
5. Each focus group session started with introductions, a statement of purpose and assurance of confidentiality in accordance with OMB requirements. The disclosure form read and signed by each participant is shown in Appendix 1.
6. The proceedings of the focus groups were recorded, transcribed, analyzed and a narrative was developed to capture the perceptions, the

realities, the suggested improvements as well as success stories and failures.

Questions and Themes

The questions to be asked and theses to be presented before the focus groups were grouped around the issues that were of interest to the NWBC and the ones highlighted by the quantitative study. A common set of questions, summarized in the protocols listed below, were used for all focus groups:

Protocols Section 1: Issues Raised by the Quantitative Study

Observations from the Quantitative Analysis	Lead-in Question	Follow-on Questions
Our quantitative analysis shows that "there is no statistically measurable difference in the proportion of successful women Trademark applicants and successful men Trademark applicants. The analysis shows no bias in the processing of trademark applications."	Is this conclusion in synch with your perception? If it is not, why is that so?	• Are there differences in the employment patterns of men and women? • Are there differences between men and women in R&D opportunities? • Are there differences in the way men and women perceive risk and reward?
"U.S. based women demonstrate increasing leadership in patent and trademark activities."	Do you agree with this observation? Why?	• What accounts for this trend? • Do women have more opportunities to take the lead in research and development?
"There is a surge of innovation by women in some of the emerging high-tech industries."	Do you agree with this statement? If not, why?	• What accounts for the greater participation by women in the high-tech sector?
"The number of patents granted to women is increasing at an accelerating pace."	Why is there a noticeable jump in patent activity in the midst of a continuing, prolonged recession?	• Is it a reflection of more women becoming entrepreneurs? • Does it reflect increasing investment by U.S. companies in R&D? • Does it reflect an increasing awareness by women of the benefits of patent protection?

Observations from the Quantitative Analysis	Lead-in Question	Follow-on Questions
		• Does it show increasing participation in patent activity by recent immigrants? • Are the standards for granting of patents more lenient now as compared to those thirty years ago?
Our quantitative analysis shows that "19.77% of all patents by men were unassigned as compared to 29.41% for women."	Why do you think this is so?	• Is there a difference between men and women in independent entrepreneurship? • Are women more likely to be independent entrepreneurs and keep their patents unassigned while men are more likely to be leading the research in businesses and corporations?
"The ratio of successful women patent applicants to successful men patent applicants varies from a low of 73.36% in 1986 to a high of 93.57% in 2002."	What factors influence this trend?	• Opportunity? • Education? • Social factors? • Legislation?

Protocols Section 2: Questions of interest to the NWBC

Questions raised in the RFQ	Lead-in Question	Follow-on Questions
Introductions		
What are the perceived barriers facing women entrepreneurs	Have you ever applied for a patent or trademark? If so,	• How complex was the process? • How drawn out was the process? How expensive was it?
surrounding protecting their IP?	what are your perceptions of the process?	• Were you concerned that your ideas would get stolen once they were disclosed? • What is your perception of the USPTO web site? Is it user friendly? • Were you familiar with the patent and trademark process before you applied for IP protection? • How responsive are the current patent and trademark processes to modern technological needs? • entrepreneur?

(Continued)

Questions raised in the RFQ	Lead-in Question	Follow-on Questions
		• Do you perceive that there is a gender gap in patents and trademarks? Why do you think so? What specific difficulties did you face in pursuing IP protection as a woman • If your first application was rejected, what did you do? Where did you get help from? Do you perceive that as a woman entrepreneur you experienced specific hurdles in getting follow-on help? • Do you perceive that the participation of women in patent and trademark activity is increasing? Why do you think so? What do you think accounts for this increase/ decrease? Are there economic or cultural factors at work here? • What is your perception about IP protection in the international marketplace? What is your experience in this matter? Do you perceive a gender bias in the international marketplace? Why do you think so?
What are the actual barriers?	Please describe your actual experience with the IP process.	• Are there specific difficulties that you experienced as a small business? • Are there specific difficulties that women owned business experience? • Are there specific difficulties that single mothers (entrepreneurs) experience? • Is financing available to women entrepreneurs? Is there a gender bias in obtaining finance for business? • Are there cultural barriers that women entrepreneurs face?

Questions raised in the RFQ	Lead-in Question	Follow-on Questions
		• How familiar are you with the help that is available from the USPTO? • How familiar are you with the assistance offered by SBA programs to women entrepreneurs?
How do we address these barriers?	What suggestions would you offer to improve the process for women entrepreneurs?	• How would you make the process simpler? • Do you have specific recommendations that would help small business? • Do you have specific recommendations that would help women owned businesses? • What can the SBA do to help women entrepreneurs? • What can the USPTO do to help women entrepreneurs? • How can technology help?
What are the long term effects on businesses that receive patents and successfully market their IP?	Do you know of specific case histories of women entrepreneurs who received a patent or trademark and built a business upon it?	• What accounted for their success/failure?
Closing comments		

TRANSCRIPTIONS AND NARRATIVE

The focus groups were conducted as planned, in Northern California and the Washington, DC metro area in the time period August 25, 2012 to August 30, 2012. Audio recordings were made and transcribed and a narrative was developed from the transcripts.

There was convergence on several issues among the disparate focus groups. These issues were captured and highlighted in each of the major areas of interest, namely, perceptions, reality, fix and the benefits of IP protection. These are stated in the participant's own words.

1. Focus group 1 in Walnut Creek, CA, Women who successfully applied for and received IP protection.
2. Focus group 2 in Walnut Creek, CA, Women who applied for but did not receive a patent or trademark.
3. Focus Group 3 in Walnut Creek, CA, Women who have never applied for a patent or trademark.
4. Focus group 4 in Walnut Creek, CA. Women who have never applied for a patent or trademark.
5. Focus group 5 in Arlington, VA. Women who successfully applied for and received IP protection.
6. Focus group 6 in Arlington, VA. Women who applied for but did not receive a patent or trademark.

QUESTIONS RAISED BY THE QUANTITATIVE ANALYSIS

What Are the Factors That Motivate Women Entrepreneurs in Their Successful Pursuit of a Patent or Trademark?

As with other questions in this study, the motivations for applying for and successfully pursuing a patent or trademark are complex. Perceptions of risk and reward, increasing the value of the company, adding credibility to one's business, gaining recognition and increasing revenues all enter into the equation. Financial ability to hire professional help in pursuing IP protection appears to be a major differentiator between those who successfully pursue a patent or trademark application and those who abandon the pursuit. We reproduce below some of the comments from the participants in the focus groups to illustrate this observation.

"I applied for patents to increase the value of my company. Down the line I wanted to sell it as an entity. I had no trouble getting a patent but I did go through a patent attorney. It cost me a little money. But it made it a little easier. I thought it was worth it."

"I have a positive experience with trademarks. I know someone who works in the patent office (who helped me). I found different groups in the USPTO system. I read up on everything. I tried every group. But then I have three years' experience in the health field. I applied in the fall. I heard next May."

"We have an expression in nursing that if it's not documented, then it didn't happen. That's the advantage of a patent or a trademark because it forces you to document and this country runs on documentation."

"The reason I applied (for a trademark) is that it adds credibility and it adds value to a business. You get protection and in addition when people see these names…they take you seriously."

"I thought it was important to get the name recognition."

"It generates more revenue."

"I think it was definitely worth dealing with that company that specialized in handling trademark applications."

Why Do Women Entrepreneurs Abandon Their Patent or Trademark Applications?

A host of perceived and real factors, influence this issue. Some of the most important factors are: Fear and awe of the process, the absence of clear, easy to understand documentation, lack of financial resources to obtain professional help, discouragement from family, friends and advisors, and the demands of multiple roles as an entrepreneur, mother and caregiver. Here are a few representative comments:

"The discouragement from society, from parents or friends rather than any rejection from the USPTO is what accounts for a patent or trademark application abandonment. People say…"Oh, girl! Why don't you play with your dolls? Why do you want to do something in hi tech".

"I came up with the idea. I made the drawings, and I got some of the people at CalPoly in the manufacturing business. So I started creating it. And then I just stopped because of the discouragement (from peers)."

"I was married once and I don't think my husband would have supported me in what I am doing and I would not have realized what I have realized. For a man it is different. If a man is trying something, the woman would support him. If there are more patents and trademarks for men, that might be a reason."

"Fear of the process, not knowing and understanding it. I delayed eight years from the time I knew I needed to do it (file for a trademark)."

"In most women's situations, they are a little entity and that's why they are abandoning them because they are footing the bill."

"Not understanding the process because it is not laid out. So that you can print it off and say, step 1 on January 1, step 2 on January 2 and so on."

"It is a lot more work to do for a patent than it is for a trademark. It is a lot more involved."

"Once you have a patent or once it is pending, you have deep enough pockets, if it is a good enough product to defend it."

"Women have multiple roles.

"I still think there is some gender differentiation especially with the older generation. maybe not so much with the younger generation."

"I had to reapply for my trademark. I did not know I had to renew it. Somehow I found it I couldn't use it any more. A friend of mine works in the patent office. I had lunch with her. I asked her, "My trademark has expired. What do I do?" I had to reply for it all over again. Very irritating!"

Why Do Some Women Entrepreneurs Never Apply for a Patent or Trademark?

Perceptions of the patent and trademark process as complex, expensive and drawn out play a large part in the decisions of women entrepreneurs not to file for IP protection. Other reasons include: lack of a support system, web sites that are not user friendly and mired in legal language, obscurity of the process and a perception that a cost-benefit analysis of IP protection does not justify the investment in time and money. A few comments from the participants are reproduced below:

"To me, the reason I did not apply for a patent or trademark is that I don't understand how the process works. I don't know how to go about it. I have asked different people. Not everyone has a patent or trademark for their product. I am not sure it will help me."

"There is nobody out there to help me. The process is so obscure. I am getting along fine without a patent or trademark. I didn't even know I could get one. It does not bother me one bit."

"I am not familiar with the process. What does it take to get a trademark?"

"I looked up the internet once. It was all so complex, I just gave up."

"I have heard it takes anywhere from two to seven years. By the time I get a patent, probably what I am doing will have changed, anyway."

"Awe of the process…In my mind it was not something a little person would do."

"It is very expensive. I am told it can cost up to ten thousand dollars to get a patent."

"I am doing very well in business. I don't see any advantage to getting a patent or trademark."

Barriers to Reducing Gender Inequality

The question was asked: What barriers do women entrepreneurs face in reducing gender inequality in patents and trademarks?

Traditional cultural paradigms do not breakdown easily; they only wither away. Women entrepreneurs who strive in a business world dominated by men face an uphill battle in getting acceptance as intellectual peers. Women are still expected to be mothers and caregivers in the traditional sense. The pressures of modern life wherein a large number of women are single mothers struggling to support a family and at the same time pursuing entrepreneurship add to the stresses on women. Further research needs to be done to understand quantitatively and qualitatively the influence of various social and business factors on the success or failure of women entrepreneurs. Some comments from the focus groups are offered below:

"As a woman, they do not listen to you. I am the CEO of a company. Once I answered a call from a customer. He said, "Could I speak to some man who knows the business?"

"I think it is societal values. People do not take a woman seriously as they do with a man. They ask you, "How do you know you are going to be successful?" Who asks a man that question?"

"A large number of women are single mothers. Women are single, with or without children. And they have to support themselves. They are pretty much on their own. They have to be pretty inventive."

"They expect you to do things for free. I mean it's constant. I was just asked to take on a production for a very, very major author. "Well, I can do all of this but I'm not going to do it for free." Well, it was like everybody was flabbergasted. And I say, "Well, why don't you give it to…" and I named some male colleagues. (laughter) I mean it's really blatant. It's not in my imagination at all. Male chauvinism? I lost a client over the same thing because they weren't even paying as much as everybody else. And they tried to talk me down. They tried to do other things. They tried to take my intellectual property. And my contract they had signed for 6 years and turned it completely around. And this is a man's world."

"I was working at a university when they started promoting men in nursing, in the late 1990s. They (the men) jumped the gun and said, "I'm male. I'm good. I can lead."

"Men's workday ends at 5. Women's ends when they go to bed. And that's a fact."

"Yes. Women have several jobs every day and only one of them is in the work place. The other jobs, well, they do not get paid for them---traditional roles that women perform. So, yes, it is exhausting."

My own experience is…when I first started to apply for a patent I was told by an ex-patent examiner, "Get your husband on it and you will have a better chance."

"I think that what is happening to women even in all of our evolution, is that we're still expected to be June Cleavers (TV show character).

"Even with us doing what we do in the work force, is that when we come home we take off our cool Brooks Brothers/Ann Taylor suit and put on our June Cleaver dress and the apron: "Hi honey. Dinner's ready… And she cooked in high heels."

"I still think it is a man's world. I think a woman has to struggle to get accepted especially when you present your product and you try to sell it. They are always all men. Everywhere there are men. There are very few women."

"Yes, I think there is still some discrimination. It makes a difference if you are a man or a woman."

"There's another layer of complexity to your question. From my own experience, the first years that I made significant money, and by significant I mean I earned a six figure income, I really was very happy but inside myself I really looked at whether this impacts my femininity.

"Now I was doing a man's role. I was supposed to be at home cooking dinner and taking care of kids. And I had a hard time because when I was working for (Fortune 100) corporation in my day, working with all men. Your personality changes; you become harder. You feminine side is gone because you have to make sure you're staying up with the guys…you're running with the bulls."

Increasing Participation of Women in Hi Tech Industries

The quantitative analysis showed that 12.95% of the patents in Photography and Optical Equipment had at least 1 U.S. woman inventor. For Optical Waveguides, 11.55% of the patents had at least 1 woman inventor.

Optics, Eye Examining, Vision Testing and Correcting came in third at 10.91%. This is a noteworthy trend as hi tech industries tend to generate high paying jobs and have a substantial effect on the output of the nation's goods and services. Several factors influence this trend. Changing perceptions of gender roles in American society, the entry of more women into science and engineering, increasing access to higher education, legislation and law suits have all contributed to the successful entry of women into hi-tech sectors. However, there persists a wide gender gap that needs to be addressed. These observations are illustrated by a few selected comments from the focus group participants reproduced below:

"There are several other factors here. People do not talk about women's lib any more. Back in the 1960s we were breaking through a lot of stereotypes ---of a women being a secretary to a man, being the support system at home and not going out in the work place. So, all of that has changed and that is what-- forty, fifty years or more. It is changing attitudes about what women can do. It is women getting into different fields of education and also getting more advanced degrees."

"Society is more accepting of what women do. But there is still a lot of drag. They get pulled down."

"It's money."

"And there are no barriers."

"And it's the future."

"There's more opportunity, more education."

"I think more women are going into the sciences than in the past."

"I think women are becoming more independent because their roles in the workplace are changing. Although the U.S. has achieved some equality between men and women, in the board rooms women are under-represented. There was a study done in a Fortune 500 company. It showed that 27.4 percent of Fortune 500 companies have no women executive officers. For that reason, women feel that they need to be more empowered."

"Now, over the years, there has been an evolution so that there is more equality in the work place.

"There have been a lot of law suits too."

Why Is There a Gender Gap in the Assignment of Patents and Trademarks?

The question was asked: The quantitative analysis showed that more men assign their patents and trademarks to companies as compared to women. Why do you think it is so?

This question relates to the relative participation of men and women in entrepreneurship. Most startups are small businesses headed up by individuals or a small group. The answers from the participants confirmed that indeed most women tend to be small businesspersons as compared to men who may have jobs with large corporations.

"More men work for large corporations than do women. Women tend to be small entrepreneurs. I think there are more resources when you work for large organizations so that they can go for their patents or the support that you would have within an organization. Small entrepreneurs do not have such resources."

The Impact of Recession

The question was asked: "How has the recession impacted women entrepreneurs?"

The prolonged recession since 2007 has had a profound impact in the work place. While many women have lost their jobs, the perception is that the recession has hit men harder than women.

Women entrepreneurs, by and large, look upon the recession as a challenge and an opportunity. They show a remarkable resilience in not just sustaining their business but in innovation as well. This aspect of intellectual property protection, namely, the impact of recession on patents and trademarks needs to be investigated further.

"What I find that in the recession, women's jobs are safer than men's jobs."

"It has leveled the playing field for one thing. And everybody has had to step back and rethink."

"The recession affected my pet sitting business because people were no longer traveling and my niche market was doing overnights. Two sides of the coin: really bad for pet sitting so I said, "Well, like she said there's money out there…let me recreate myself."

"The recession has caused me from licensing my patent to selling them outright. Because companies that had before saw an opportunity to licensing and making big bucks are very hesitant because of the market."

"Recession has also forced us to work harder."

"It's just increased their game. Their hustle level just got more intense. They just started to draw on everything within them and it just made them up their game."

The Role of Finance

The question was asked: How difficult is it for women entrepreneurs to pursue IP protection because they do not have access to financing? Is there a gender gap in financing?

There was unanimity on the importance of finance in business but there was a difference of opinion among the women entrepreneurs as to what factors influenced a successful loan application or a grant. There appear to be demographic differences in the success rate. Women who were experienced and more business savvy took the time to prepare credible business plans as backup to their credit applications and were successful. Younger and less experienced women were not as careful in their applications. They had less of a track record and were less successful in obtaining loans. The demographic aspect of finance for women entrepreneurs needs to be investigated further. Here are a few excerpts from the focus groups:

"I've had pretty good luck getting a loan."

"I have too and I think it was a demographic. I was a woman. I was middle aged. I think I hit the nail."

"I created a serious business plan but the bottom line was that I didn't get any sales yet. At that point he had to bet on me. He (the investor) is betting on a demand, on sales. My feeling is that before you get to that point, you're at a disadvantage if you're a woman."

"In terms of getting an answer to your question about whether there is a gender gap, I think that gender gap happens in the beginning when they're just betting on you as a person."

"Well you have to show what are yours returns, what are your distributions. What is the take away from this? How are you going to benefit as a patron? You have to have everything spelled out."

"The basic driver in Silicon Valley is education. If you happen to have a PhD from Stanford or MIT or something like that, that makes a difference, whether or not you are a man or a woman. That's number one. Number two, your team."

"Then there are specific programs that are available to minorities, to women, etc. There was a very successful case that was pointed out to us using Cloud Funding in Oakland, California."

"I think there is more than one track. I think there is intellectual property and there is product. A product may be easier to sell although you do not know if he is backing you or the product."

"Everyone knows about the Shark Tank. There is a national group and the district group is based here in Georgetown University called the Dolphin Tank. I think to some extent they help you with investments but mostly they help you with your pitch."

"If you already have a patent or trademark, does it make it easier to procure a loan, or it doesn't matter? I think it doesn't matter. The patent does not help you."

"I would like to have a website which would tell me where the funds are, where women have an opportunity to start, hopefully (to obtain loans) at a discounted interest rate."

There Is Ambivalence among Women Entrepreneurs about the Benefits of Holding a Patent

Most women entrepreneurs are ambivalent about the benefit of a patent. The expenses are high and the waiting period is long. Unless it is a product that has a large market potential, the perception is that a patent is not worth it. There are also concerns about patent encroachment, especially in the international market.

Women entrepreneurs are more positive about the benefits of a trademark. The process is easier, waiting periods are short and the benefits of name recognition are widely appreciated.

"If I had to do it over again, I would put the product in the marketplace. If it does well, it doesn't take any time to do a provisional patent."

"And I just think that you've spent so much money and energy for the patent but you don't get much back. That's my really big issue. Right now I should be starting to make money but then because of so much legal fees I can't start making money. And I have so many legal bills. It's just not worth it."

"I think we should differentiate between patents and trademarks. Trademarks are a good idea, even if you are a small business. You want to get your name out there and protect it with a trademark. You want people to remember your product so that you get business, whereas with a patent, unless you are a big corporation, they can walk all over you. You see that patents are being disregarded in other countries. How are you going to go to China to sue somebody? Or, a European patent that is infringing on yours?"

"If I had a friend who was going for a patent, I would say, good luck to you, it is going to cost you a lot of money and it may well be that a big corporation is going to steal your idea, tweak it a little bit. You are just not going to be able to sue a big corporation. You hear of some such stories but that is one in a million. Basically it is not going to be very successful."

PERCEPTIONS

The Patent and Trademark Processes Are Too Complex, Drawn out and Expensive

This is the most common perception of women entrepreneurs. Indeed, this perception is so widespread that it becomes a hard core belief. It cuts across industries, regions or the degree of success with the patent and trademark process. Those who have never applied for a patent or a trademark express this opinion most often. Those who did apply but were not successful in obtaining a patent or trademark did surmount the perceived difficulties of filing an application but were frustrated when they got their first rejection, objection or request for further explanations. Those who have successfully obtained IP protection seem to have used legal counsel or to have carefully and meticulously followed the instructions given by the USPTO.

As we explore this issue deeper, we find that it is a systemic issue that is tied in with a large number of issues - the paperwork, the legal requirements, the time it takes to understand the processes, the cost of obtaining IP protection and the long timelines, From the perspective of the entrepreneur, there is a disconnect between the business needs of entrepreneurs and the legal requirements of IP protection. Entrepreneurs who are often pressed to be the first on the market with their products or services are torn between spending their time pursuing patent and trademark protection and the demands of marketing and sales. Very often, technology or market conditions have changed so much in the time needed to obtain IP protection that the patent or trademark may have lost its relevance in the marketplace.

If perceptions are reality, they modulate business strategies and business decisions. Most women entrepreneurs approach the IP protection process with a combination of enthusiasm and bewilderment. Those who have not obtained a patent or trademark in the past are most likely to feel frustrated by the seemingly complex processes.

Submitted below are some quotes from the focus group participants about this issue.

"I looked into patents but after looking into it, it was so convoluted with nothing for me. I couldn't just grab anything. I couldn't hold onto the information. Last week, I even looked into the internet and it was just too much of nothing."

"...The reason why it never worked for me is the complexity of the process. In a legal system that I don't want to have anything to do with, the legal system is not friendly to women.

"I think there is a perceived cost that doubles with the lack of information."

"My own personal perception is it is expensive. The process time is lengthy to do it. And then once, even if it is done, the investment to acquire an attorney to pay for the initial cost, to even present it to the patent office, is almost like you wait X number of months and then somebody has already done it. You invested all this money and now there is no return."

"What is the benefit of it all? As you were saying, I have come up with this idea, why bother? And I told my friend I have this idea where you can button your pants (laughter) and I was excited. My friend said: "Excuse me honey but that is already out there". So I felt good. I didn't waste much time developing this thing to find out that it is already out there."

"...So I ended up getting a patent attorney. It cost me a fortune. I wouldn't change it. But it will take me years to pay to recover the funds. I am glad I got him because he wrote all the patents as one patent. I don't think I could have done it on my own."

"I want it to be very easy...1, 2, 3 steps - makes it very easy to apply. But when they give you an official rejection, then it's go through the appeal process which is very-- you have to be an attorney. I have a master's degree in finance. I started to do a joint JD. I started to read that and you know, you needed to have an attorney."

"And he says, "Why didn't you pursue this (patent)?" I said, "Well, I am a single parent with two kids. I work at (a Fortune 500 company) all day long. Where is my time?"

"When I did feel like I had all my market research done and I was ready to actually apply for it, oh my gosh, it was just doing the paperwork itself and the diagrams, and how it works, getting all that information where I thought that even one of my clients who has special needs could understand this. And sending it in and having them come back to me saying, "No, we do not understand this. You need to make this a little clearer. This looks like…this process looks similar to this one here, how is yours different?"

"I question, having the patent for a while now, whether it is really worth the effort. I think on future things that we will probably go ahead and do a provisional and just see if there is a market out there for it and go ahead and manufacture it, license it, whatever, and put it out there. If it looks like something that is going to take off and really needs the protection of a patent, then maybe go ahead and proceed with the patent process."

"I think it (the process) is intentionally intimidating…. I think they don't want to fix it because they don't perceive it as broken."

"If somebody infringes on your right, you have to go after them and I do think to myself sometimes that if somebody was infringing, to what extent would I go after them? I guess I could write them a nasty letter but would I go to court, probably not. It's expensive."

"So I said, "….What should I do? I have this idea, I even have a name." He said, "Well, I would definitely trademark that." So, I did go online. I didn't find it difficult….Since I had applied in July of 2010, I got a letter in September saying that they were reviewing it. And by the following March, I had my certificate."

"They have these multiple filing dates. You file one and then after two years you have to file again and after 10 years – I think I'm on the 12 year mark this year on one."

"Mine expired and I didn't even know it. On the back of the certificate it says, in the 7th year you have to reapply. And I don't know about the 2 year thing. I never had -. But mine went out and I didn't even realize it and I couldn't reapply."

Fears About IP Theft Are Widespread

Fear is a strong deterrent to innovation. To successfully patent or trademark an innovation one must not only meet legal requirements but must have the capability to defend the idea from poachers. Deep pockets are often a requirement for legal defense. This fact acts as a filter on innovation ideas. Most vulnerable are small and micro-businesses that do not have the financial means to defend their IP in a competitive economy dominated by big businesses.

The widespread fear of theft was a surprise factor that popped up as we probed deeper into why women do or do not file for IP protection. Case after case of IP theft was narrated by the participants. While some of this perception may be attributed to the fact that the entrepreneur failed to do adequate research into the existing art, many of the cases were genuine and were an expression of the frustrations felt by women who had an original idea but as soon as they shared it with someone, it was stolen. The theft may come from colleagues, competitors, friends as well as bosses. What is surprising is that the fear of theft was rampant among those who had never applied for a patent or trademark as well as with women who had applied for and either obtained IP protection or had abandoned the application after it was filed.

While the contributions made by large businesses in innovation are recognized, documented and protected, the contributions of small and micro businesses are underrepresented in the research because so much of it is lost before it surfaces at the reportable levels. Further research needs to be done to quantify the extent to which small and micro businesses contribute to innovation.

While the number of patents and trademarks are one measure of the innovative vibrancy of the economy, it does not adequately represent the innovative ideas that are abandoned because they were stolen or not pursued because the innovator felt that it did not make economic sense to invest time and energy pursuing an idea that would be stolen anyway.

"You know, I want to make enough money to enjoy life, to help my family, to do some things with the youth. And I wrote a poem and …then I heard $$$$ (person) sing my poem on TV. And even now my mind goes: 'What?' It was word for word. That's what got me…"

"At a yoga teacher conference I shared my idea about the type of yoga that I was working on with the owner. The next thing I knew he had it on his website: $$$$ (name of a product), which is what I had come up with."

"Yes, he owns half of the patent now because the gentleman went behind my back, filed it, sold it to $$$$ (person) to get the funds because he had the money."

"…it has been really frustrating. We did everything that we should have done. I followed everything that my patent attorney said to do. "Okay, file provisional first". Then we also filed a utility (application) but we are still waiting for it to be approved. But while you are waiting for your patent to be approved, it is a long process, and people are just taking advantage of that and they just come up with the (copied products)…"

"We've had a lot of copycats since we introduced our product. These big companies, they take our name - it is almost the same. And the next problem with trademarks is how do you defend them? And now we have stuff constantly coming from Asia. They are so bold. They will send you an email with a picture of your product."

"..They cross engineered it and it's still not as good. But they are a big company. They market in a totally different way.

"They are going to steal the idea. They are going to do everything they can so you really have no protection. So you have a piece of paper that says you have a patent."

"I would like to have that patented, trademarked or copyrighted but after the experience that I had after a year…I don't even know if it is worth going through it …."

"What I know of it is that it is a very expensive process to patent. The concern is, you spend all that money, I mean thousands of dollars, and somebody can copy it anyway. All they have to do is change that one little thing. Sometimes you wonder if it is worth it. And you also need a big legal team behind it so that you can even fight it. So if they copy your product, unless you go after them with a huge amount of money at the cost of tens of thousands, it doesn't make sense."

"And I had my intellectual property stolen by one of the largest non-profits in the country."

"There is a group in Europe using my domain name. When they started using it, they put a little letter before it."

"I presented it at an international leadership conference in Prague and I am seeing things that are verbatim all over the place…close enough to home that I am suspicious. Good ideas can happen to different people at the same time but why it's the exact same words, I am not sure."

"And it is interesting to note that people in the business are sometimes the worst offenders for intellectual property."

"...A lot of investors say, if you file for a patent, you have to publish it, all the details, publicly. Everybody can look at it and know what you are doing there.

Moderator: You mean copy it?

Participant: Learn something from it. Eventually, it doesn't really protect your work.

Moderator: Do you all agree that you feel that if you were to get a patent it does not necessarily protect you?

Participants (in unison): Absolutely.

Moderator: There appears to be a consensus around the table, more or less?

Participants: (in unison) "Yes."

There Is Lack of Knowledge About the Patent and Trademark Process

While the available information about the patent and trademark process is comprehensive and complete, it is not easily available to potential users or is not easily understood by them. To the first time user, the patent and trademark process is often a mystery. She approaches the process with a degree of awe, often with preconceived notions gathered from friends and colleagues. She is looking for a support system that would explain in simple, easy to understand terms the requirements, the process, the methodology and the steps that need to be followed in the application process. The issue is one of both simplicity and ease of use. Of particular concern is the need of a support system to sustain an innovator after that first rejection from the patent office. While considerable strides have been made in the direction of providing simple, easy to follow instructions, there remains considerable room for improvement, especially as the process applies to small and micro businesses.

"When you work for an employer, even though I worked for so long, I never knew that I could do a patent while you are working for an employer because you think that your ideas are a part of the project though I am the one who is researching - but I am researching on their time."

"Over the years I came up with ideas all the time, and I thought, "Wow, I should go for a utility patent or a design patent. It is a great idea". And then I let it fall through. So I am here because I know I am ignorant about the process and I think it is time for ideas to work for me."

"The reasons many women do not apply for IP protection are: lack of knowledge."

"…It points back to the barriers that I was thinking of. I am not sure if they are real or perceived. Not understanding the value of the business and how having these things of IP will create value, not understanding the importance of creating a brand, not having a basic understanding of intellectual property."

"For me, the actual barriers are the time lines. You're not sure what you're doing. Like what I said, is it a trademark or a service mark? By the time you probably figure out what you probably should have been doing, you're already too late."

"…..When you talk about lack of information, well, that is the very first barrier that they are preventing (you from patents and trademarks)."

The USPTO Website Is Not User Friendly

One of the themes that surfaces again and again in the focus group discussions is that the patent and trademark process is not sufficiently responsive to small and micro business or to individual entrepreneurs. The perception that the USPTO website is not user friendly should be understood in that context. Summarily, the existing website is comprehensive and user friendly but the perception is that it requires a great deal of patience and perspicacity to wade through it. It is not so much a question of a lack of information; the information is all there. It is rather a question of how it is presented and how user friendly it is for someone who is totally unfamiliar with the IP protection process. This reinforces our observation that a two step process for IP protection would go a long way towards addressing this issue and helping the individual entrepreneurs or micro businesses. Innovation by individual entrepreneurs and micro businesses is one fountainhead of creativity that is perhaps not tapped as efficiently as it can be. A first step may be taken in this direction by implementing a website geared specifically to small entrepreneurs. The institution of a two tier IP protection schema would require higher level authorization or perhaps even a legislative remedy.

Here are some quotes from the focus groups:

"I didn't do the patent drawings although my office used to do that. We specialized in …, and I had a very good firm for that and that was doable except that figuring out how to do it from the government's website is a chore. And there's a fair amount of wrong information on it. When you call their little help desk and it seems you always get some old guys who "really want to help you honey" and they said, "No no. Don't send in this form. Do this. Here's the list of what you need" but it's not described in plain terms on the government website. It's awful."

"I would say that my experience with the trademark back in the old days when you didn't have the computer was much easier. Because things were on paper and they were much more simplified. Now that they use the computer everything is so wordy, so complicated and impossible to find. So it has gotten much more complicated."

"Because right now, when I look at it... it's just too much "legalese". I don't get it. And I'm an educated person."

Women Are Discouraged from Going into Science and Technology

As observed in the quantitative study that preceded the qualitative work, the contribution of women in the scientific and technical disciplines, as measured by the number of patents and trademarks granted, has shown a sustained and noteworthy increase over the last twenty years. Nonetheless the perception persists that women are discouraged from pursuing careers in science and technology. Cultural paradigms die hard. The American culture, like the culture of so much of the world, is a prisoner of long held notions about the role of women in society, the differences between men and women based on "the right side of the brain" versus "the left side of the brain", childcare, family responsibilities and a host of other set ideas. Certainly, the gender gap, as measured by patents and trademarks filed and granted, is decreasing. But it is also true that the gap persists. Cultural norms in America are varied; one shoe does not fit all. Whether the gender gap relates to how boys and girls are brought up in families or if indeed the gap can be closed and how are subject matters for further research.

These observations are illustrated by a few select comments from the focus group participants:

"I think that we as women are often not encouraged to do science, not encouraged to think about technical things and that is where I want to excel."

"When we are on our own, then there is so much cultural stigma, ancestral background of limitations and roles."

"But there are women who would let the traditional barriers stop them. There are some of us who are saying: "With the support of my sisters I know we can do this together". But some of us are saying: "I can't wait. I could die where I live right now, not making it to eighteen. And so I got to step out now, hell or high water. So I got to do it right now. So there are two ideas running in parallel."

"I always thought that mothers taught men or fathers taught men to be aggressive and positive about themselves. It is a natural thing for them to be positive about what they want and where they want to go and what they want to receive from it."

"...Even with all the advancements that women have made - the female are still looked upon - "well honey, well sweetie, why don't you..."

"...My personal belief is just that men are different from the day they are born."

"I was the only African American female in this company and the thing in medical device sales is that it is male dominated. And I have always feared that I would bring up an idea, it would be taken from me because I was perceived to be young and maybe I did not know what I was doing."

"I came here (to the US) thinking there is no gender (gap), no difference, discrimination. And I am shocked that there is really a lot here that I did not think it existed."

"It is the subculture. I mean like the Indians. They want you to be more mathematical. So you head towards the engineering field or something related but there are other cultures that are, for instance the Filipino, I mean they are saturated in nursing."

"I was raised bi-internationally... all of the males have been raised with the understanding that they will go into that career side (engineering) while the women are trained in education, academics, literature, the fine arts, dancing."

"...It is different depending upon financially where you are growing up, sociologically who are the people that you are surrounded by, culturally, in the global perspective, do you believe you are one with people who are in India or do you believe that in China?"

"You know it is different. There are outside relationships. What women have with their superiors is just working, and have coffee talk conversations but there is always the sports talk, and that kind of leads to other things. They learn about patents and copyrights and that leads to other conversations."

"The networking is so important. After work, I see that the guys go to the bar and talk. I was not a part of that group."

A Female Voice at the Other End of the Phone?

The USPTO has made enormous strides in hiring and training women patent examiners. A majority of patent examiners, perhaps as many as sixty percent, are women. Nonetheless, the perception persists among women entrepreneurs that there are an insufficient number of women patent examiners. The perception arises not so much from who answers a call for help but how it is handled. Most women who call the USPTO for help or visit their regional offices for help are entrepreneurs or individual innovators who do not have the financial means to hire an attorney. They require detailed answers and pointers towards information that may be available somewhere on the website. Sensitivity training for the USPTO help desk is perhaps the answer.

Here are a few quotes:

"My experience when I called or went to the office in San Francisco, I always spoke to men. I didn't see women. I didn't have the opportunity to talk to a woman."

"I do remember when you were talking about the attorney that there was actually a woman who really helped me because I had some problems in terms of trying to get the service mark....We had to go back and forth. I was impressed with how she really was working hard to make sure that I got this."

An Archaic Process?

Calls for a strategic rethinking of the patent and trademark process were made by some of the participants. The current process labors under the burden of history, the rapidity of technological obsolescence and the pressures that it creates to bring a product or service rapidly to market. Progress has been made in accommodating these challenges but it is perceived to lag behind the needs of the times. The reference to an archaic patent and trademark process comes up in multiple contexts while probing the issues of process complexity, inordinate timelines, costs and gender bias. The voice of small business and of women innovators who are suggesting a strategic rethinking and simplification of the IP protection process deserves to be heard. It could be one of the major benefits of this important study.

A few select quotes are reproduced below:

"I feel that the process itself is so archaic."

"They have not made any changes in the process itself since inception. It is outdated. At one time all patents, copyrights and trademarks were done by men because women were raising kids. We were doing the woman thing. It (the process) was geared to what they were doing. I do not know, if it is (male) ego or something, it has not changed. And now that more and more women are offering their ideas, and they are coming into their own right of supplying good ideas and products - that verbiage is still the same. It has not changed."

Women Are Harassed by Salesmen and Attorneys Once the Application for a Patent or Trademark Is Disclosed

A patent or trademark disclosure is perceived by many women to be self defeating. Not only does it reveal to potential competitors the details of the product, process or service that the disclosure is supposed to protect, it attracts poachers and invites an avalanche of solicitations from attorneys and others who aggressively try to entice the businesswoman into buying their services. The entrepreneur who is struggling to keep a business alive under enormous financial stress is burdened further with the task of fending off the solicitors. This is a "downer" and acts as a dampener on innovation. A simplified IP protection process that provides temporary protection for, say two years, to an innovator would go a long way towards helping small businesses focus their energies on the marketing and sales of their innovation. If the innovation is accepted by the market, a second tier process with more stringent requirements can perhaps take over. It would also help if there are laws against undue solicitation and aggressive poaching during this initial period of gestation.

A few voices are articulated here:

"It's like the ambulance chaser. It felt very much like the attorneys chasing you as if you just got hit by a car. It was really a turnoff."

"I got a lot of mail with bills, like the same amount as the trademark and patent application was a lot of mail…the one company that looks like the US patent office. There are a few of those."

"I guess that is one comment I can make about the patent office is that of course your information is publicly available but then that means you have all these ambulance chasers who send you mail and they try and make it look like it is from the government and you have to use them and then you see they are charging lots of money and I just had this little freelance business."

There Is Scant Assistance and Guidance Following the First Rejection from the Patent and Trademark Office

While most women entrepreneurs approach the initial filing of a patent or trademark application with some awe and trepidation, they do manage to overcome that first hurdle with perspicacity and assistance from the patent office as well as their own support systems. However, it is that first rejection letter from the patent office that is the biggest hurdle in the successful pursuit of a patent or trademark. Most women just do not know where to turn for help at this stage because the rejection letter from the patent examiner is often stated in legal language not understood by laymen. Individual entrepreneurs and inventors do not always have the financial means to consult attorneys. So, frustration sets in.

This frustration is articulated in select quotes submitted below:

"It has been an interesting scene; the process…The paperwork is crazy. The initial application is easy. You just go online, you fill everything out. Once that stuff comes back it is so completely overwhelming…I have a Masters degree too and I did not even understand what they are asking me."

"I think the biggest thing in the whole process is: "Hurry up and stop and wait." It feels like a stalling process. You don't really know where to go to get the answers unless you have all the money to pay someone to help you. And the amount of time to do the research is exhausting and frustrating and takes you away from doing the actual work to get this product that you want to put out and you want to share with others."

The Patent and Trademark Processes Are Too Focused on "Legalese" Rather Than on Fostering Entrepreneurship

Inventors and entrepreneurs tend to be highly individualistic, well versed in their disciplines but typically short on training in legal matters. Often they tend to be visionaries, passionate about their work and their innovative ideas but lack an understanding of the legal and commercial aspects of their products and services. A highly competitive economic environment that changes so rapidly with evolving technology puts enormous pressure on the entrepreneur to get her ideas out in the marketplace as fast as possible. These requirements run into the perceived slow pace with which patent and trademark applications are processed. These processes are governed by strict statues and commercial law. The requirements for protection are at odds with the requirements of the fast moving modern commercial marketplace. If fostering entrepreneurship is the goal, not just the granting of a patent or a trademark, then there needs to be a strategic rethinking of the goals as well as the process of IP protection.

The inherent tensions between legal requirements and the pressing demands of the commercial world are articulated by a focus group participant in her own words.

"I felt there was a lot of "legalese" that I didn't understand when I was reading them. So I come from, I'm actually adopted. My father is a physics professor and my mother is a botanist, biologist and I had them look at it, and they were confused."

The Patent and Trademark Processes Have Not Kept up with Emerging Technologies

The perception is that the patent and trademark processes take too long. The average estimated time for obtaining a patent is approximately 3.6 years. Not only do most applicants not understand what goes on once their application is submitted, they do not even know what stage of the process their application is. To them, the process is a "black box". The focus groups showed an overwhelming desire for improved communications. At the minimum, the applicants would like to know where their application is in the process and the estimated time for the completion of the process.

"If you go on UPS or FedEx to track your package, you can see exactly the process and where your package is and the estimated time of delivery. Why can't they put that kind of knowledge to this so that anybody who has applied for one (patent or trademark) can log on and see at what stage your application is?"

International Protection Is Absent

Notwithstanding international treaties that govern IP protection, the perception is widespread that there is scant protection for patents and trademarks in the international marketplace. Specifically, the perception has set in that Asia does not honor patents and trademarks. This perception is particularly strong among small businesswomen and individual entrepreneurs who lack the means to defend their IP should there be an infringement of their patents or trademarks. Large businesses have the financial means to defend their IP and the news and social chatter reflect the arm wrestling between big players for ownership of IP. However, it is in the small business arena where much of the perceived infringement takes place. The frustrations of the individual entrepreneur and the small businesswomen are underrepresented.

Here are a few representative comments:

"And you do all this work and then a company in Southeast Asia - and they are doing it anyway. I have been hearing stories about how big companies are…. Is it even worthwhile?"

"I just want to say for other countries the patent is not respected. In Russia, for example, they can do anything. They can copy the name."

"One of my ex co-workers used to work for the company where I worked. She has this business also. She builds software. Someone from China copied it and was making money. So my co-worker wrote to him and also wrote to the Chinese embassy. It turns out that person was caught. He was willing to do free advertising for my co-worker. It turned out all right. But she is still sore it was stolen."

The Patent and Trademark Process Favors Large Business

Whether it is the front end or the back end, the patent and trademark process is perceived to favor large business. The successful pursuit of IP protection often requires legal help which is expensive. The entrepreneur or the small businesswomen who struggles between the competing requirements of establishing a business, meeting payroll, responding to local, state and federal government regulations, answering volumes of official and non-official paperwork, and marketing and sales cannot afford high quality legal counsel. By contrast, big business has in house legal departments which specialize in patents and trademarks and are able to wade through the fine technicalities of a successful patent or trademark. A simplified initial process with interim protection for a year or two and minimal accompanying fees would go a long way towards addressing this issue.

"So, I chose to abandon that service mark. However, I found it interesting that two years later, the exact same name was given a registered service mark and it provides the exact same pill bottles, a receptacle for medication. So that was approved with the exact med minders versus med e-minders. I was a dotcom (.com) - that was a voice telephone communications - denied - but somebody else a year later gets the same patent with the same name, and is giving out the exact same product. That's clearly for me. So the inconsistent application of approval and rejection..."

Is There a Gender Gap?

Perceptions on this issue are split. Despite the quantitative evidence that the gender gap is decreasing, the perception persists that the gender gap exists and prevents women from achieving their innovative potential. Long held perceptions die hard. On the other hand, it is also true that women face a glass ceiling in corporations and encounter a gender bias in the commercial world. On balance, it may be stated that the legislative initiatives taken over the last thirty years and the social transformations taking place in a technology driven workplace are hammering away at the gender gap. It is incontrovertible that in most fields the gender gap is shrinking. But the process must continue.

Here are a few observations from the focus group participants:

"But it is still a man's world. Businesswise ... you know, it is all men. Who are the CEOs? Very, very few women."

"And you know the saying about women, you are talking about CEOs. What are people saying about women's rights? Aggressive go getters, we just become the big Bs."

"Certainly, the financial industry is very much a man's world when it comes to ownership and leadership. Women do a lot of the work in the field. But they don't own and lead. So you see the glass ceiling, whether they are there intentionally. And some of that just becomes a boys club mentality."

"The glass ceiling is still there. Unless there is a big lawsuit going on in the corporation, all of a sudden you see the glass ceiling going away."

"I think that there's a bigger problem. I think that women, when they get to a higher level position, are not really good at mentoring younger women. I think it's almost like that girl high school mentality."

"What I feel is that in the big corporations, I feel that a woman can't be a soft woman. You have to be aggressive. You have to be half man. I used to sit in the conference room and have meetings. I was the only woman sitting there in a round table like this one, and all men in blue suits. And, you know, they would say, "you get the coffee." And one day I said, "No, I'm not doing it."

"Men more easily fraternize with men. You may just pick up information at a bar or just a casual conversation: "I'm thinking of trademarking this or that" Some of your buddies (may have the information). That might happen less if there's a larger share of women who are patent attorneys."

"I think women have made a lot of strides but there is still a gap because men wrote the rules and there's still this boys club which is very active and that's because they had a running start and so it's still an unlevel playing field."

"Women don't network enough (agreement from others saying umm) and I think men network more and we may not network for a different reason because it comes across as we're bragging or we're doing something and to me that is a gender barrier and cultural barrier."

"I think because I came from Russia and I grew up in that type of society and I got used to being very strong and being a fighter so I came here and to me it's much easier for me in the United States. I don't see the barriers. If you put something in front of me I'll just go for it and if I see somebody stand in my way I just go around (Laughter) so maybe it helps that I'm from a different country." (More laughter)

Dissenting and Ambivalent Voices

"I don't think it makes a difference whether you are a man or a woman."

"I think that it is (decreasing)."

"I guess if you put six other people in this room who were of a different culture, economic or a minority or perhaps grew up in Iowa rather than New York or whatever, I think there would be different answers."

"We all divided up and there was the silent generation, the baby boomers, the Generation X, the Generation Y and the Millennium. It was so fascinating how everybody had a different take on that story and it was just so interesting how, for example, the women in Gen X and Gen Y had a far different view than the baby boomers and the silent generation."

"The very modern liberated women, once you're married and you have children, they do a disproportionate share of housework no matter how modern their husbands are, no matter whether they're from the young generation or old." (Laughter)

"If we can educate women and men because I believe collaboratively we're better together if men and women can learn to work together rather than separately."

"My boss has been working with $$$$ (company) for 11 years. She is the only woman in that whole team….I was surprised (and I thought) there must be so many women now in hi tech. She said: "Are you kidding, I have been with $$$$ (company) for 11 years. I am in the sales department and they are all men. I am the only one."

"I worked with a small company. I was the only woman engineer; all the others were men. It was a factory. That is where I did my thermal engineering. And there was a difference. I could see the difference. People, men who got employed after me, they became ahead of me."

"I think from where we were twenty years ago, it is decreasing but I wouldn't say significantly. I think that for every one female CEO that there may be thousands of males."

"The reality is my life stops when my family says: "Stop your life" and that is necessary. I don't see that with the men in my family. They never have to stop their life. As a matter of fact, when it came time for the annual hunting thing, the men went off no matter what was happening. The women still had to do what they had to do and that is a gender barrier that isn't disappearing."

"Women for the past however many years, really have had to fight to have equality with men and you do get that: "This is what I need to do to get what I need."

"I think in seminar presentations there definitely is (a gender gap). If a guy was doing the same kind of things I was doing, nobody would be arguing with him including at the university level. They would never ask them to do anything for free and I get asked to do things for free all the time."

"I haven't had any really negative experiences. I got very lucky with the interior plantscaping business because at the time maybe it was the Small Business Administration. But they would have these seminars where they invited Fortune 500 companies to attend and you were allowed to present yourselves to any of these companies who wanted to do business with women. It was fantastic. So I was hired because I was a woman. What could be better?"

"Men in general seem more open to helping. But with women it is a more competitive environment and they aren't necessarily open to helping another woman or maybe choosing another women when they give a grant or something, I don't know. But in general my experience has been that women haven't been as helpful even though they are also women."

"It depends on the individual. There are plenty of women who will nurture a woman. Hopefully most of them do. There may be a few who do not."

"From personal experience I think they are closing. A lot of younger people, especially too in the financial sector, around technology, there are a lot more young females coming out of college applying for those positions."

"In some people's minds they still think that women can only do certain things, certain types of work even if it's in the high tech world."

What are the Real Barriers?

Lack of Support Systems for Women, Especially for Single Parents

Child-bearing and child rearing impose responsibilities on women that are different from those on men. These responsibilities are accentuated in a society wherein single motherhood is not uncommon. Although reliable statistics are not available, if the divorce rate is accepted as a metric of single parenthood, then about half the women entrepreneurs in the state of California would be single women. Women, especially single women, face the perennial challenge of balancing the tensions between family and career. The requirements of supporting a family act a brake on innovative pursuits. Support systems for single parents are either scarce or totally absent. It is a long term societal issue. It is real. It is here. It requires continuous attention and innovative solutions.

Here is a voice speaking up on this issue:

"With a single parent, or any parent, it is an issue if you have to stop work at 3 o'clock to go to the school. Guess what? If I am working at a certain place, I can't leave at 3 o'clock, if you have to leave at six. But if you have your own business, it is kind of like, well, I am going to stop, so I am going to stop taking appointments or you are going to stop designing shoes because you got to go somewhere. So those were real barriers, having the support that you need, whether you are a single parent or not, having to stop at a certain time to go somewhere."

The Patent and Trademark Processes Are Too Complex, Drawn out and Expensive

The entire IP protection process requires a critical and strategic re-examination. What is the goal of IP protection? Is it an end in itself or is it geared towards encouraging innovation and entrepreneurship, and ultimately the economic well being of the country? If it is the latter, then, are there alternate ways to provide IP protection to entrepreneurs, small and micro businesses, even if it be in an interim, limited period, so that the entrepreneur can focus on growing her business? The current study shows that there is a conviction, shared across the entire spectrum of women entrepreneurs, from those who have never applied for IP protection to those who have successfully done so, that the current processes are too complex, drawn out, expensive, and perhaps not in synch with the requirements of a fast moving, technologically-driven age.

Here are a few voices articulating this view:

"I have looked into trademarking and it was a lot of work and very costly and so I decided not to."

"It is just frustrating. I feel like I am of normal intelligence and able to read and I have a pretty good vocabulary. I was very thrown and I was very frustrated… It was the trademark process. I was trying to get my name trademarked."

Funding Not Available

Entrepreneurship requires money. This is a truism that is often overlooked. It requires funds to start a business, finance the marketing and sales efforts, meet payroll and pay for the overhead, pay taxes and fees and at the same time keep the engine of innovation churning. The startup costs can be quite high. Most women entrepreneurs, especially those who are single parents, struggle to balance the financial needs to grow a business with the needs to support a family. Credit is scarce and grants are few and far between. Additionally, the information for such grants in often buried in layers of obscure official disclosures and announcements. A single clearinghouse that would assist women seeking financial help would be of enormous benefit to aspiring innovators and small businesswomen.

"You always hear about women in business. "Oh you get grants." You know I have been on the internet hours and hours, looking for this grant. Where are they? Where is the funding for women in business?"

"As a woman we do not have a lot of access to financial resources. Those are always my biggest challenges."

"I have looked for those grants, like SBIR. But I really do not know which one is applicable to my business. I really need some help. I approached a government contracting officer. She referred me to one of her friends who was working on the SBIR programs. But I didn't get a response from her."

The question is: "Where do we find the resources? Is there a website, a government agency that we can tap into? Where do we find it?"

IP Processes Favor Big Business

A consequence of the long, drawn out patent and trademark process is that they favor large businesses. It costs money to file and pursue IP protection. And it requires a minimal knowledge of the legal requirements. Entrepreneurs, small and micro businesses do not have the resources to stay the course and to see through an application to success. This is an inherent flaw of a single process that applies to all applicants. A suggestion that has often come up in the focus groups is this: Is it possible to have a simplified process for small business that requires minimal investment and provides IP protection for an interim period of, say two years, so that the small businessperson can focus on marketing and sales rather than be concerned with looking over her shoulder for IP infringement?

Here are a few voices from the focus groups:

"Well, there are deep pockets. Just like a service mark or a trademark, whether it's registered or it's not. It's really about marketing. But if somebody has deep pockets, they can stop you. The money talks. I'm not going to be able to stop somebody who steals my idea. I don't have enough money to fight the big guys if they take the idea."

"I think the better way to do it is to put a place mark here and say, "I have registered this idea, I have a provisional patent on it" and then we'll go out and see if there's actually a market there and see if it makes sense to go ahead and get that kind of protection."

"It is difficult for small business people to go after the big ones (in case of patent violation) but it is easy for the big people to go after you."

Protecting a Patent or Trademark Can Be Very Expensive

Even after a patent or trademark has been obtained, there remains the burden of defending it against legal challengers and infringement. Legal costs are high. While a large business may spend $10 million defending a patent, a small businessperson cannot even think in terms of $10,000. So the legitimate question that comes up is this: Of what benefit is IP protection that cannot be defended? This is a real barrier for which there are no easy solutions.

Here are some observations from the focus group participants:

"But I asked the patent attorney, "So if I've found somebody infringing on the patent, how much would it cost me to pursue it?" Well to send a letter, it could cost me $2,000. So, then otherwise, $9,000" (Exaggerated laughter)

"The burden to protect that patent falls back on us. Is the government going to step up and say: "We are going to bat for you. We are going to go after these people" "No."

"We had to pay an attorney $1,200 just for a couple of letters."

WHAT CAN BE DONE TO OVERCOME THE BARRIERS?

Increase Visibililty of Existing Federal Programs

The importance of marketing and advertising the current services offered by the USPTO and other agencies cannot be overemphasized. Many of the perceptions about the patent and trademark process are simply a reflection of the fact that potential users are unfamiliar with what is already out there. An example would illustrate this observation. In March 2012, the SBA along with the NWBC and the USPTO offered a seminar highlighting a quantitative analysis of patents and trademarks covering a period of thirty years. Several women in the focus groups expressed their appreciation for what they learned at the conference. Indeed, it inspired them to revisit their decisions to seek IP protection. More such conferences and seminars would help along with a user friendly website that explains the process in layman's terms, a simplified process and woman-friendly online and/or phone help.

Here are a few comments that illustrate this observation:

"In March I came here because I got an email saying they were having the public meeting at the patent and trademark office. I drove down 200 miles, because I said, "You know what? They are opening the door. They are letting me in"…I register, I come. They introduce a report about the gap how women are not getting as many patents and trademarks. I hear this in person. I made this decision before I left home, "I am going to make this trip count. I am filing something before I leave."

"And it was just a miracle that I got this notice that this new report that reviewed 35 years of information was going to be introduced. It is a free program and all you have to do is register and come… What I saw was a gold mine. So some of the perceived barriers can be removed based on education, awareness, some type of training program and even more open houses, something similar to that because we got a chance to hear the people who run the patent office, under secretary and different folks. I would never have had the opportunity to hear these people and when they said how valuable a patent or trademark was, that was just unbelievable."

"And I was surprised to read that they said that they have given examiners more time to communicate with the applicants to review the merits well before they make their decision, place a greater emphasis on the examiners interaction with the patent applicants early in the process to clarify claims and enhance thoroughness… they also mentioned something called an ombudsman program to help resolve questions about applications as people were going through the patent process."

"The Women's Initiative is one organization but the IDA is a Federal program. So there are resources out there. It is just how do you hear about it?"

"It (the course offered by the IDA) is three months and it is a very comprehensive course. If you go in there with an idea with very little self esteem and not know what to do, you leave there with a very good business plan, a lot of support, consultants. They help you go from your business idea and win awards from the National Women's Business Council. And they are for low income women."

"What I do find is that the way information like this is marketed, that you need to have a real marketing entity to get it (the information) out."

"So here is this resource, the Small Business Development Center who can help."

"If they have this ombudsman program, it should be advertised. It should be put on the website that this program is here to help you, assist you and maybe have something you can click on for more information and mention ombudsman so that most people understand that here is someone who can walk you through the process, if they do have all these different things this person says they have implemented them. Why am I reading about it here and not seeing it on the website?"

"And if they really intend to have women earn more trademarks, maybe they should have outreach for women. I didn't see anything like that on their website."

"The USPTO could align itself with the Chambers of Commerce or whatever it is in different states and counties. So people who are opening up new businesses know right away that, "Do you have something that needs to be trademarked?" before you're out in the market."

"Maybe if the USPTO would have a campaign about what a trademark is, put it out there and let people know."

"I went to the SBA and they assigned someone to me. Most of them are retired business owners and he spent a year with me working on everything, financial, marketing, all for free."

"Actually, they have an electronic filing system for patents. I personally tried that. I think that it's a good system for filing a patent. I thought that since it's going to cost me that much, why don't I try it since they have this filing system. I can just get all the details and do it myself. So I tried it. To me I think that it's pretty easy to use."

Simplify the Process

The current process is perceived by women entrepreneurs to be complex, long and expensive. It should be possible to make it easy for an innovator to file for IP protection. A two-tier process, explained in greater detail in an earlier section, would be one way of achieving this. A process which can be followed in easily understood 1.2.3 steps would go a long way towards encouraging entrepreneurs, small and micro businesses to seek IP protection. It would be a boost to innovation. The economy would benefit.

"I think they just need to break it down a little more in layman's terms. I think the material that was this thick could have been this thin and said the same thing. It is just an awful lot… of paperwork that is unnecessary."

"The first thing, I would get rid of all the legalese. Just say it…. The timeline should be shorter. What? 3 to 5 years, it is ridiculous. 6 months to a year, because you will be doing other things with your business, your products, 6 months to a year - you are trying to get into your business -I am going to give it my best shot for a year…"

"What I would like to know is: 'What is the process that they go through?' I have no clue. I am just sitting here (asking) who is looking at it, how many stages are there in the process? Why is the cost so high? Why can't you have a simple 1, 2, 3 kind of process…"

"I think the application has to be simplified and the language has to be simplified but there has to be a first step and you can just write a basic description of the idea and you are able to submit that to the Office. Or there could be a different branch of the Office which could issue you your documents."

"If you don't put it out there (put your product on the market) and you're waiting for the patent to be done, it could be five or six years. And then there's something else and it could be old." (3)

"I think the notification of the 7th year (for trademarks) has to be redone as opposed to just having it on the back of the certificate."

Improve the Website

The USPTO website is comprehensive and it contains just about any information that a potential user may seek. But the perception is that it is too complex. A user friendly website with a section that is specifically directed to small business and entrepreneurs would be extremely helpful. Usability tests may be conducted after redesign to measure its effectiveness. Website modification is a dynamic process. It requires periodic updating to keep up with user demand and changing technologies.

Here are a few observations from the focus groups:

"Just simplify the website. It's too complicated."

"I would agree, *a la* the Copyright Office, because that's a pretty recent changeover that they made."

"There should be a website with 1–2–3 (easily understood steps to get your patent or trademark application completed). A designated website and make it very basic. You know, when someone says its 1 - 2 - 3, to me that says it's easy."

Hold Regional Seminars and Webinars

Periodic seminars held in different regional centers would increase the exposure of current services available to women entrepreneurs. A shift from the center to the regional centers appears to be what is required here. Webinars, conducted in conjunction with a simplified patent and trademark process and user friendly websites would be of tremendous benefit to aspiring innovators.

"One of the things is, like the patent office to say to women: "Do you have an idea where you need help trademarking or patenting? We are here to help you and have a representative come maybe three or four times a year to, not just Walnut Creek (California), but come to an Oakland (California), come to a Compton (California), come to each area and (listen to) this woman talk about being a part of the women's initiative."

A Two-Tier Process to Help Micro Business?

Time and again, the discussions in the focus groups gravitated towards the complexity and cost of the current patent and trademark process. A recurrent suggestion was that the process can be separated into two distinct phases. The first phase would be an interim phase, perhaps registering a claim and giving IP protection for a period of two years during which time an entrepreneur would introduce her product or services into the market and test its sales potential.

The second phase would be more comprehensive involving detailed investigations and providing IP protection for a long period.

It would be worthwhile to look into the feasibility of such a two-tier approach, especially as it may apply to small and micro business and individual entrepreneurs.

"The fee I can afford, a little bit high for the chance of it being rejected. It should be something like: 'Apply, then pay more if you are approved', is something I would like to suggest."

"I think the application has to be simplified and the language has to be simplified but there has to be a first step and you can just write a basic description of the idea and you are able to submit that to the Office. Or there could be a different branch of the Office which could issue you your documents."

"I think the better way to do it is to put a place mark here and say, 'I have registered this idea, I have a provisional patent on it', and then we'll go out and see if there's actually a market there and see if it makes sense to go ahead and get that kind of protection."

Technology to the Rescue

While there are no limits to how technology can be applied to reshape the patent and trademark process, the suggestion here is limited to the tracking and status reporting of applications. There was a broad consensus in the focus groups for the implementation of a tracking mechanism that would give an entrepreneur visibility about the status of her application. The example of Federal Express and UPS was often cited. This recommendation deserves consideration.

"I actually think that the patent office is going to have to change. It's not going to be paperwork. They're going to have to ping me back with clarification. And so that may reduce any gender bias."

"Now that we are in the age of the internet, maybe (they will send us a notice). When it was all paper based, things were different."

Add a Hotline to Help Women Entrepreneurs

Women entrepreneurs and businesswomen have special needs over and beyond those of other entrepreneurs and businesspeople. Some of these needs have been articulated in earlier sections- a supporting system for working mothers, need for capital, the desire for talking to another woman and so on. A helpdesk, especially tailored to address the needs of women entrepreneurs, preferably staffed by women advisors would certainly be a step in this direction.

"I would add in a hotline, have someone available (to answer) if I am going in the right direction, what else can I do. So they should attach a hotline to help small business. At least someone you can interact with and can help you. Not just materials online but an actual person who you can call on or have a meeting with who can explain things and you can ask questions rather than just maybe a pamphlet or on a computer screen."

Better Feedback and Training

The recommendation here is to take periodic surveys and learn the real needs of women entrepreneurs. The information gathered can be used to evolve effective strategies and implement continual improvement of patent and trademark services.

"I think the director or the CEO of that business needs to screen and put out a survey: 'How did you like the customer service? How were you treated today?', and let people give their honest opinion or what happened to them."

"More feedback. And if need be, bring in somebody else who can do the job…Or job training."

"What would be nice is if there was a place where you could go and say, 'Could you tell me if I should go ahead with my idea without applying and spending all that money?"

Follow the Instructions

Many of the frustrations of those who have never applied for IP protection or those who abandon a patent or trademark application after filing for one result from failure to follow instructions. A simplified guidebook with easy to follow instructions and a user friendly website would increase the success rate of women who obtain patents and/or trademarks.

"It was an appeal (on a trademark). Because they said, in the letter it told you exactly, you have to read everything that they sent–online and everything that they send you. And read it more than one time. I was a little emotional about it. I had to read it over and over. And it said exactly what to do. And whatever it was that's what I did. And I couldn't believe it worked."

RELATIONSHIP BETWEEN ENTREPRENEURSHIP AND IP PROTECTION

More Research Is Needed to Determine if There Is a Correlation between IP Protection and Entrepreneurship

Many a participant in the focus group expressed the opinion that a patent or trademark is not a pre-requisite to entrepreneurship. This issue also requires a deeper study. The issues are subtle and require a segmentation of perceived benefits from a patent or trademark measured against associated costs. For instance, a legitimate question would be: What is the marginal increased revenue associated with the perception that a client is buying a product or service because it is patented or is trademarked? In other words, do customers buy a product or a service because it is patented or trademarked? The focus groups were split on this issue.

"I personally don't think that having a patent is that important anymore".

"It is a perceived notion that you have to have this protection before you move forward or God forbid somebody else should come in and lay claim to what you are doing. That is not true. Not in my experience. I don't know where the preconceived notion comes from. Maybe it is of our own making."

"It is very frustrating. It is very costly. It is not for the weak of heart or pocketbook. And that is unfortunate because it eliminates a lot of many worthy ideas from coming to the market because there are these barriers."

"I don't see where there is a value to it. I really don't. The idea initially was to bring our ideas to market, go through the patent process first, receive a patent on it and therefore it would automatically have value in the marketplace. That is very naïve, very naïve. But again because you have never been through it, you have this perception that if you have patent, or patent pending or whatever, on your packaging that somehow it is going to motivate that buyer to make (the decision) to buy. That is not true."

"Everyone is working on their logo. You haven't sold a widget. (Laughter) You don't have a widget. But they're spending money on logos."

"But I'm not sure whether giving it a patent or a trademark would have really made that much difference."

"It's probably better to figure out where your customers are coming from rather than spending too much time applying for (a patent or trademark)."

"I'm saying I'm not going to spend too much time applying for the logo because I had to go through - do I need a trademark, do I need a service mark. And I'm thinking I need 7 things. But maybe I just need one thing to get started – from the USPTO, some protection and then I can expand it. Does it need to be blue? No, it can be black and white for now. So, all of that were becoming barriers for me."

"It takes a while to get a trademark and that would lead me to think they're more credible and in my business, that's what I'm all about – is trust and accountability. It's hard sometimes to find that. You know in a lot of industries now there's a lot of fraud."

"To the extent that it (the IP process) has (helped entrepreneurs), women are empowered by it…To me, there's a benefit there whether it's real or perceived."

Is There a Correlation between IP and Business Growth?

This is also an issue that needs to be investigated further. The focus group discussions highlight some cases where an individual entrepreneur built up a successful business based upon her patent or trademark. But there is a growing opinion among women entrepreneurs that a patent or trademark does not necessarily help a business grow. Indeed, the perception is that the risk of divulging a trade secret through a patent or trademark disclosure and the cost of obtaining and protecting a patent or trademark are not worth the trouble unless it is an idea that has a huge market potential. It is difficult to assess how many women have given up seeking IP protection because of these perceptions. A flip side of the question is how many women build up their businesses without applying for or receiving a patent or trademark. The issue warrants further research.

"Well, look at QVC. There are a couple of inventors that have many patents. There's one that does the storage thing, jewelry storage. And she started out small and she does a lot of storage things for travel jewelry boxes and she's got many patents. She just started out with one. She was just an ordinary person who designed this product, went to QVC and now she says, 'Well, that was easy.' She got the exposure of television and she started selling it. So she started doing another one, similar to that but a little bit different. And she kept on patenting them. But what I think she did was go to China, looked at what they had that wasn't patented over here and she just patented it over here. Because her concepts are pretty…"

"I worked for a woman as a pattern maker for a maternity wear manufacturer. And she didn't get a patent because she had her product out for just a year. She didn't have the money. Back then, it was going to cost her $10,000 that she didn't have. So she was running her company. And at that time I was the only employee so I was the only person getting paid. She's still in business. She started in 1981. She didn't get a patent and now I see her products everywhere."

A Concluding Comment

The focus groups provided a powerful testimonial to the courage, determination and perspicacity of women entrepreneurs who struggle against heavy odds to innovate and succeed. We conclude by offering the following testimonial of a homeless woman in San Francisco who found her way to dignity and respect through entrepreneurship:

"…I have been on my own since I was 12. I was given up at the age of 4 … I am from Canada. I have basically - I hate to even say this - I have been homeless all my life except for the last ten years. So when I say I have been blessed, I sincerely mean it. I have done the whole thing, the drinking - I don't know if that is a Native American thing or not. For the last eight years I have not touched liquor and I do not even want to look at a liquor bottle. So where I'm at, I still have that low self esteem. I remember walking around with just a bag with a blanket and a cosmetics system. To me when I go to a place now and I would leave the house with one bag and I come back with two. I feel like, I wonder if they still think I am still homeless. I am that and it will always be with me. But I am very grateful. I don't care. I don't go to church on a regular basis. I go past Saint Barnabas which is at the 101 and take two seconds to just go in there and say a quick prayer and say I am thankful. I think I will always have that. I was very nervous about coming here and talking to you guys. Oh shoot, excuse me (holding back tears) excuse me (encouragement from other participants), you know, that is how I felt. I don't fit in there. When I have my stand one day a week in the Civic Center, even though it is a couple of blocks, you are dealing with people on different levels, some are very intelligent, some are CEOs, and I could interact with them on that because my comfort zone is that little tent and my little hundred hats or whatever hanging up. And my other half is there all the time. He supports me a hundred percent. He is my model. I was going to wear a hat today. Well, I can't wear that on me. O God, I think I have said enough."

Moderator: "Thank you… thank you so much."

APPENDIX 1

Disclaimer Read and Signed by All Focus Group Participants

Purpose of the focus group:

The purpose of this focus group is to explore in-depth issues surrounding intellectual property protection for women entrepreneurs.

Sponsoring Agency:

This study is sponsored by the National Women's Business Council (NWBC), Washington, DC.

How the information gathered in the focus groups will be used:

The proceedings of the focus groups will be recorded, transcribed and descriptively analyzed to capture patterns and categories of themes and perspectives and gain further insights into the issues which have been quantitatively analyzed.

The NWBC will use the information gathered in the focus groups to make recommendations to Congress and the White House on issues relating to intellectual property protection for women entrepreneurs.

The results of the focus groups will only be reported to the sponsoring agency in the aggregate. The last names of the participants or other identifiable microdata will not be used in the final reports.

Who is conducting the focus group study:

Delixus, a corporation registered in the State of California, is conducting this focus group study under contract with the NWBC. Dr. Nazeer Ahmed, CEO, Delixus will serve as the moderator.

Duration of each session:

Each session will last approximately 1 hour.

Participation is voluntary:

Participation in the focus group study is entirely voluntary. Any participant can walk out of the focus group at any time.

OMB Approval:

One does not have to participate unless the Office of Management and Budget (OMB) has approved the session. The OMB has approved this session. The control number is 3245-0380.

Signature of the focus group participant

INDEX

A

B

C

N

O

P

Q

R

S